THE DAMNED

"THREE DAYS DEAD"

THE DAM

"THREE DAYS DEAD"

NEO

SCRIPT/STORY – CULLEN BUNN
ART/STORY – BRIAN HURTT

BOOK DESIGN BY
STEVEN BIRCH AT SERVO

EDITED BY
RANDAL C. JARRELL

Published by Oni Press, Inc.
Joe Nozemack, publisher
James Lucas Jones, editor in chief
Randal C. Jarrell, managing editor
Doug Sherwood, editorial assistant
Jill Beaton, editorial intern

This collects issues 1-5 of the Oni Press
comics series *The Damned.*

ONI PRESS, INC.
1305 SE Martin Luther King Jr. Blvd.
Suite A
Portland, OR 97214
USA

www.onipress.com
www.thedamnedcomic.com

First edition: May 2007
ISBN-13: 978-1932664-63-8
ISBN-10: 1-932664-63-7

1 3 5 7 9 10 8 6 4 2
PRINTED IN CANADA.

Lemme guess. You're one of those guys thinks
he's got it all figured. You run your little grifts, call in a
few ill-earned favors, and never make a promise unless
there's something bigger and better in it for you.
  Well, I'm gonna help you out and let you in on a little
secret—not the real secret, mind you ... this is just the
tip of the tombstone. You see, you think you've got an
edge over everybody else in the smarts department ...
and the families love guys like you. You're pretty sure
you know every trick in the book and can weasel your
way out of any problem. But what you don't know is
you're dealing with the oldest tricksters to ever put on a
pinstripe, and they always collect on their bargains.
  I should know. I was just like you.

Maybe you're thinking if I tried to pull a few fast ones
and lived to tell about it, you might get lucky, too.
Make no mistake, there's nothing lucky about my situation.
I got one thing and one thing only pulling for me.

Sometimes, the only person you can trust is a dead man.

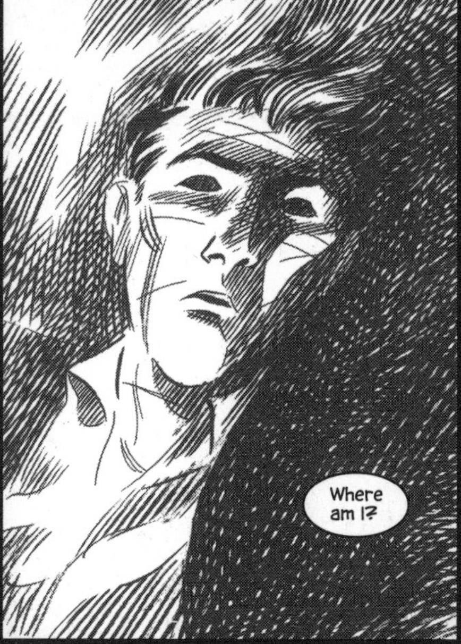
Where am I?

CHAPTER 1

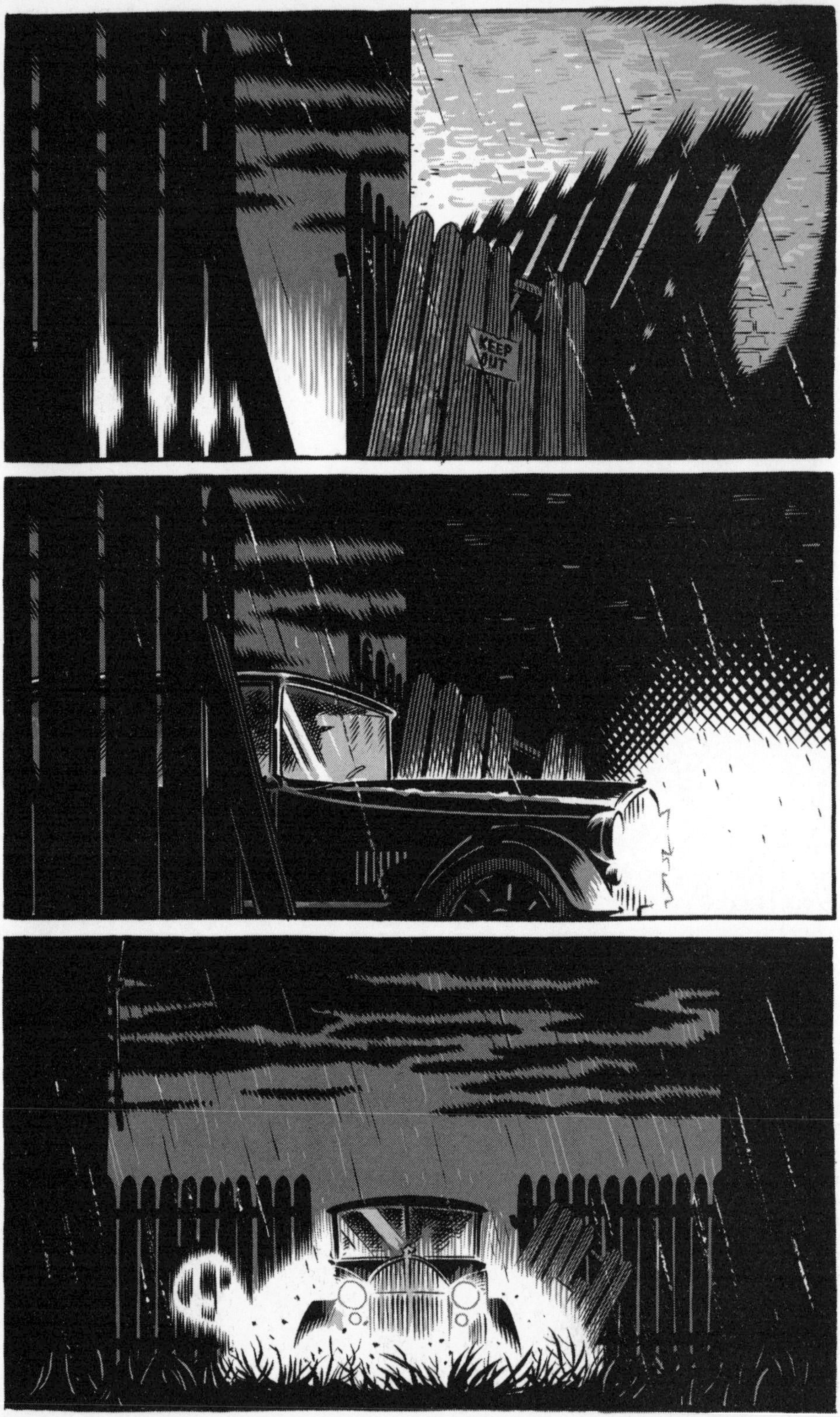
KEEP OUT

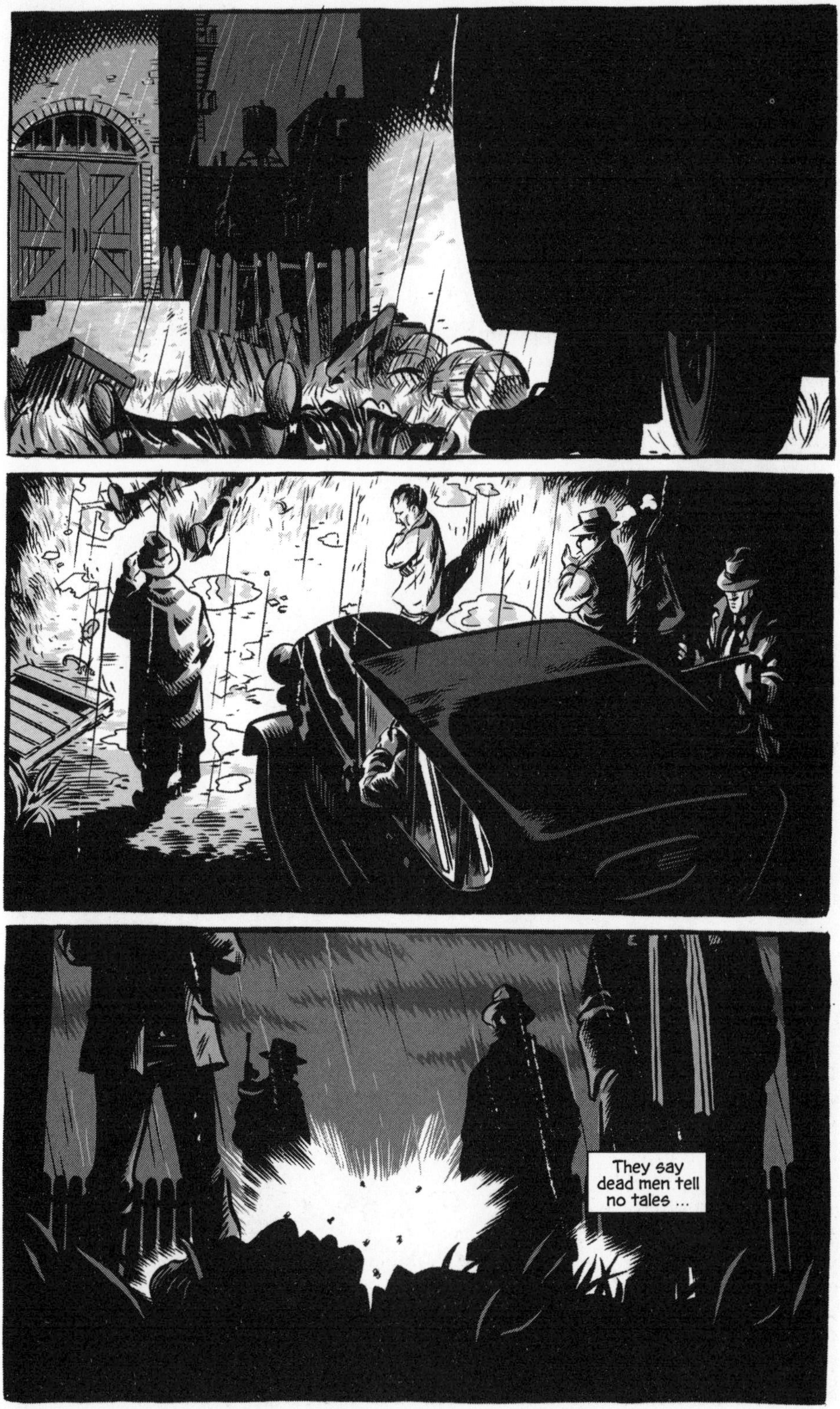
They say dead men tell no tales ...

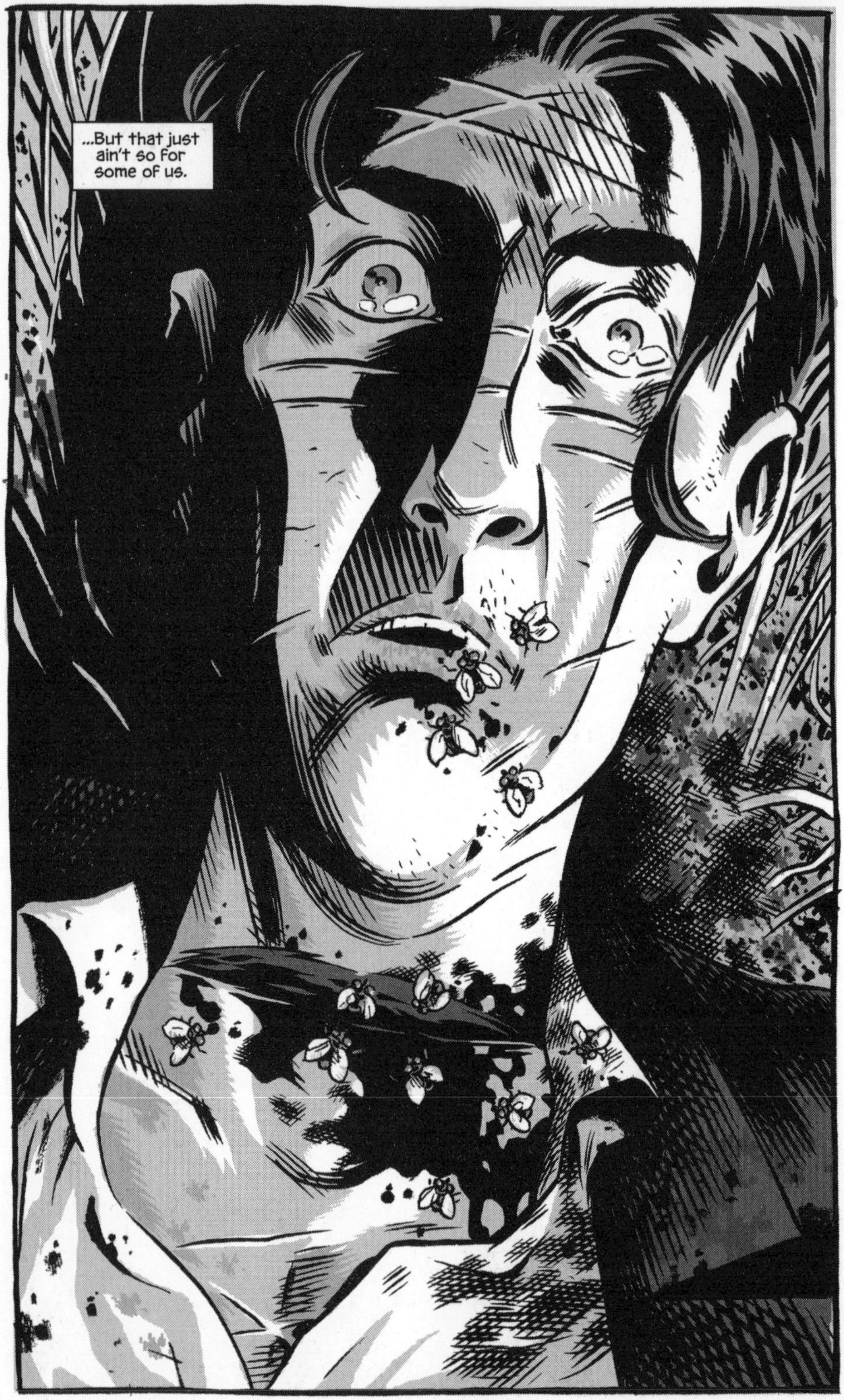
...But that just ain't so for some of us.

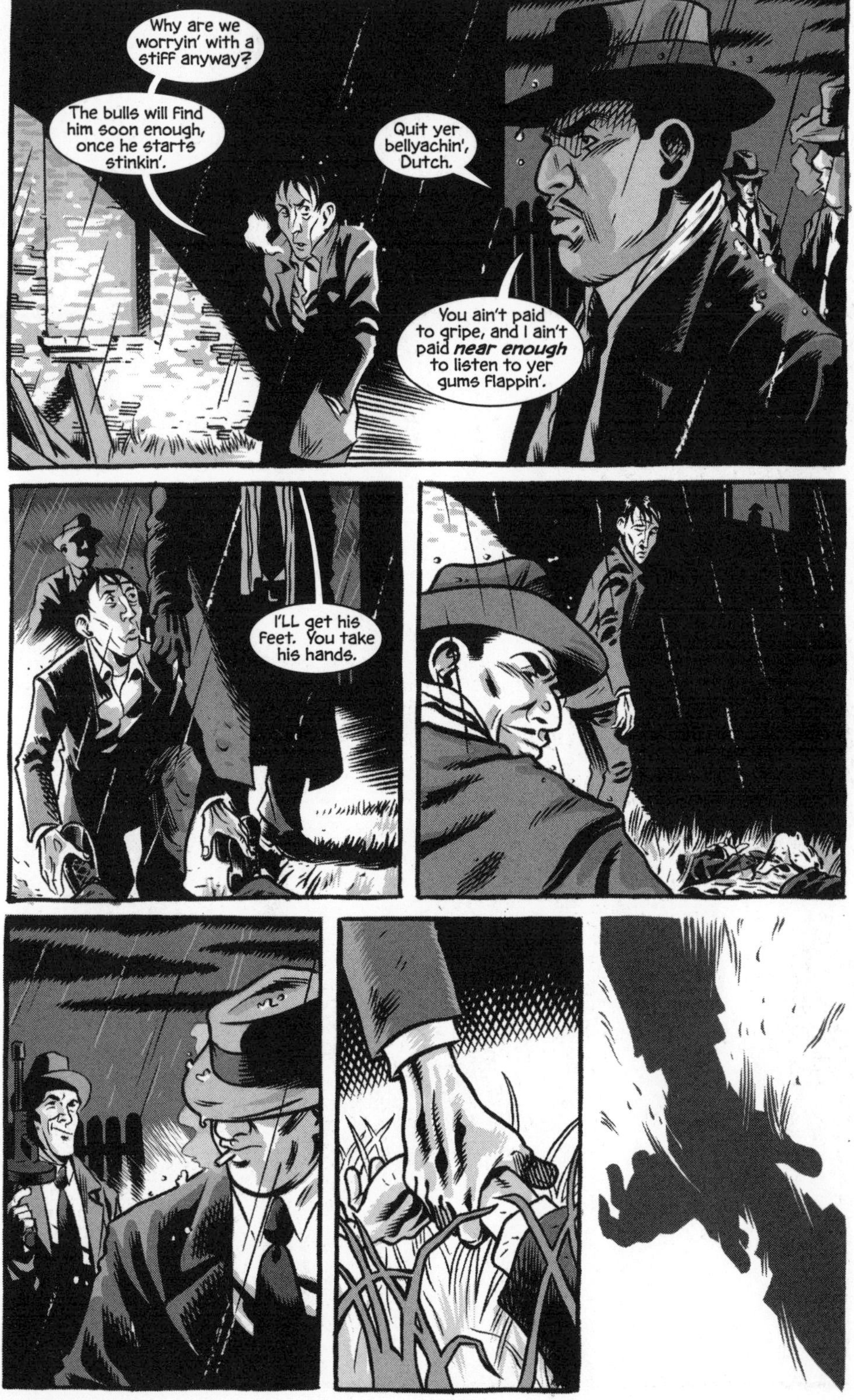
Why are we worryin' with a stiff anyway?
The bulls will find him soon enough, once he starts stinkin'.
Quit yer bellyachin', Dutch.
You ain't paid to gripe, and I ain't paid *near enough* to listen to yer gums flappin'.
I'LL get his feet. You take his hands.

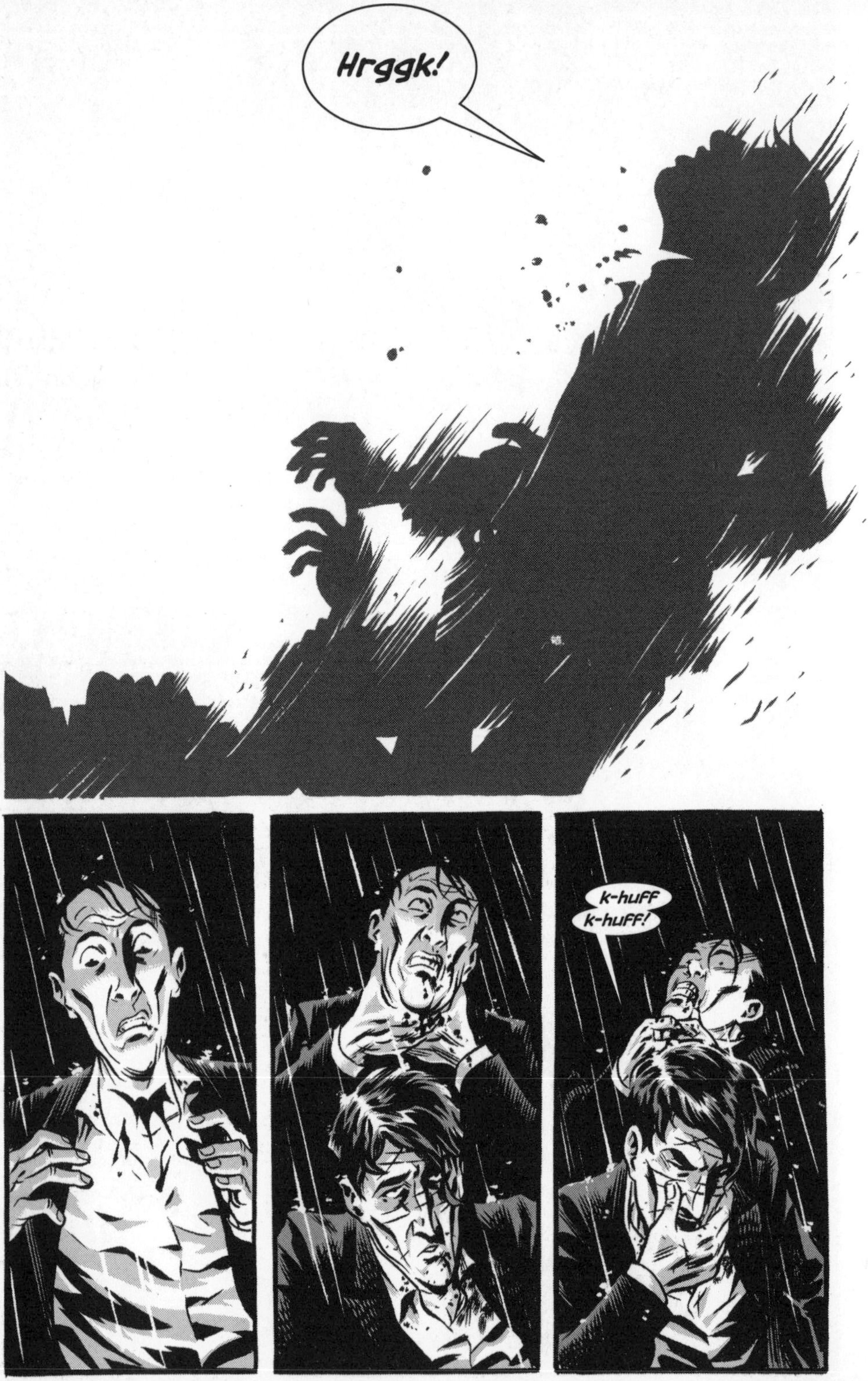
Hrggk!
k-huff
k-huff!

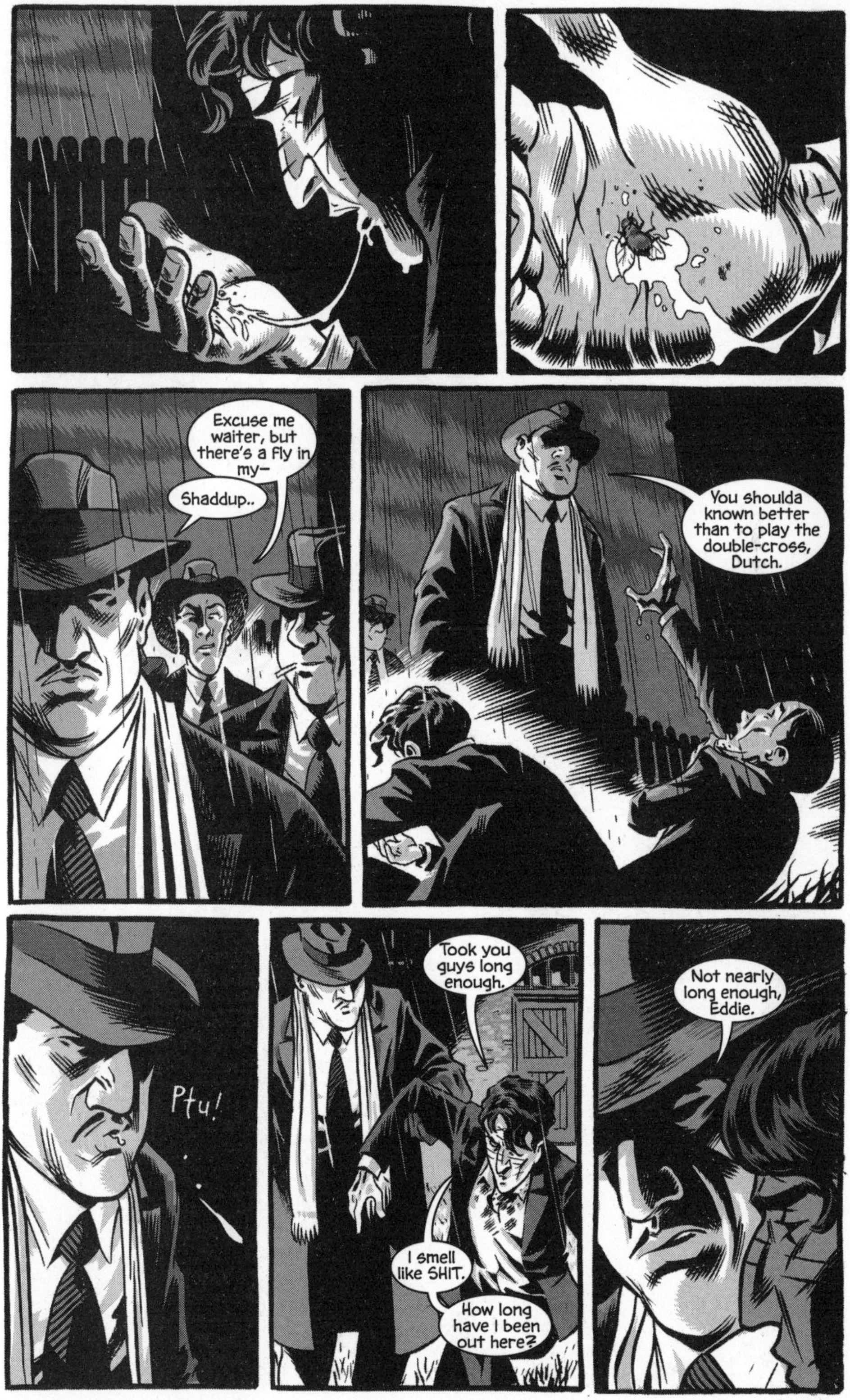

Excuse me waiter, but there's a fly in my—
Shaddup..
You shoulda known better than to play the double-cross, Dutch.
Ptu!
Took you guys long enough.
I smell like SHIT.
How long have I been out here?
Not nearly long enough, Eddie.

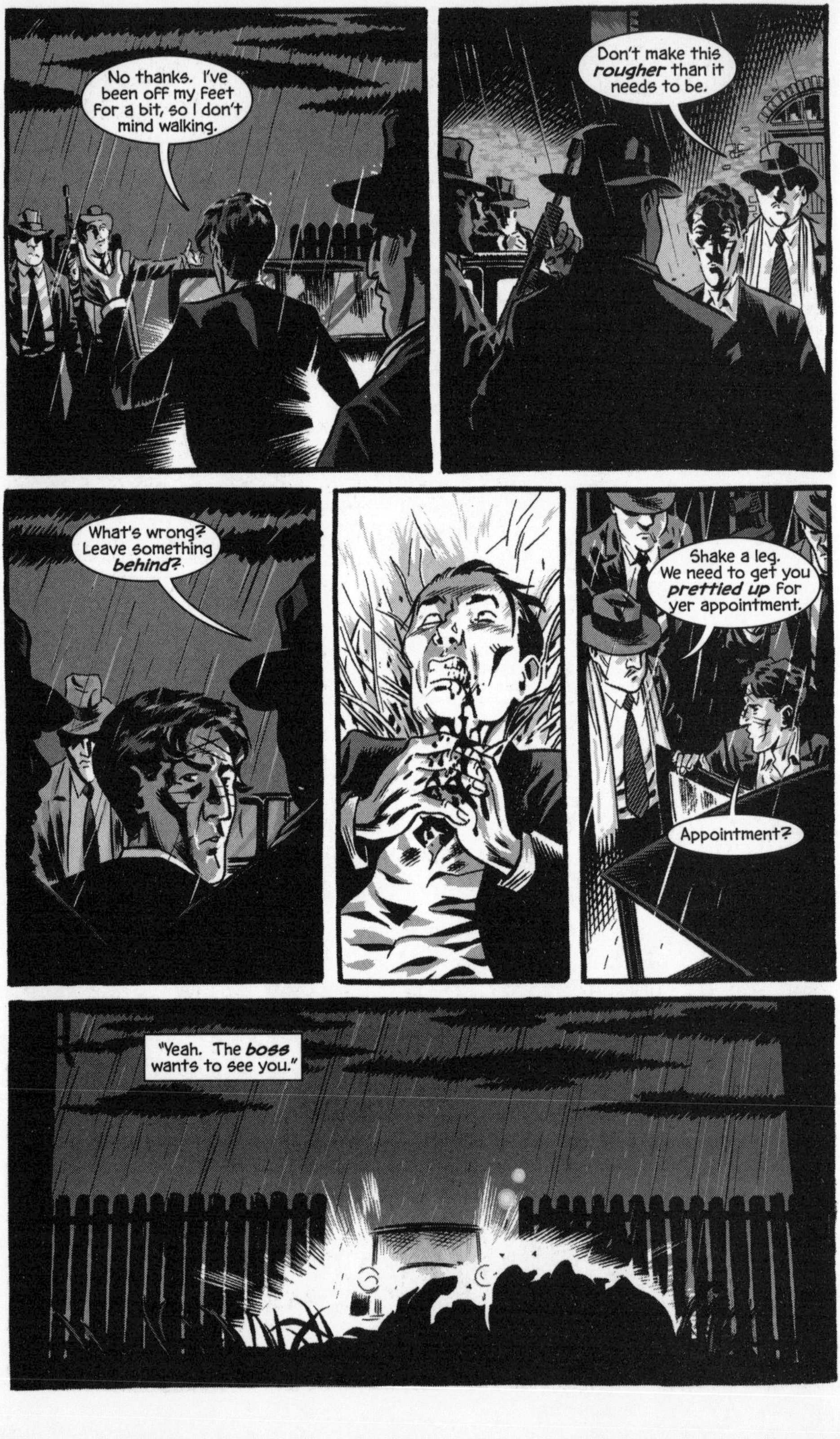

No thanks. I've been off my feet for a bit, so I don't mind walking.
Don't make this **rougher** than it needs to be.
What's wrong? Leave something **behind**?
Shake a leg. We need to get you **prettied up** for yer appointment.
Appointment?
"Yeah. The **boss** wants to see you."

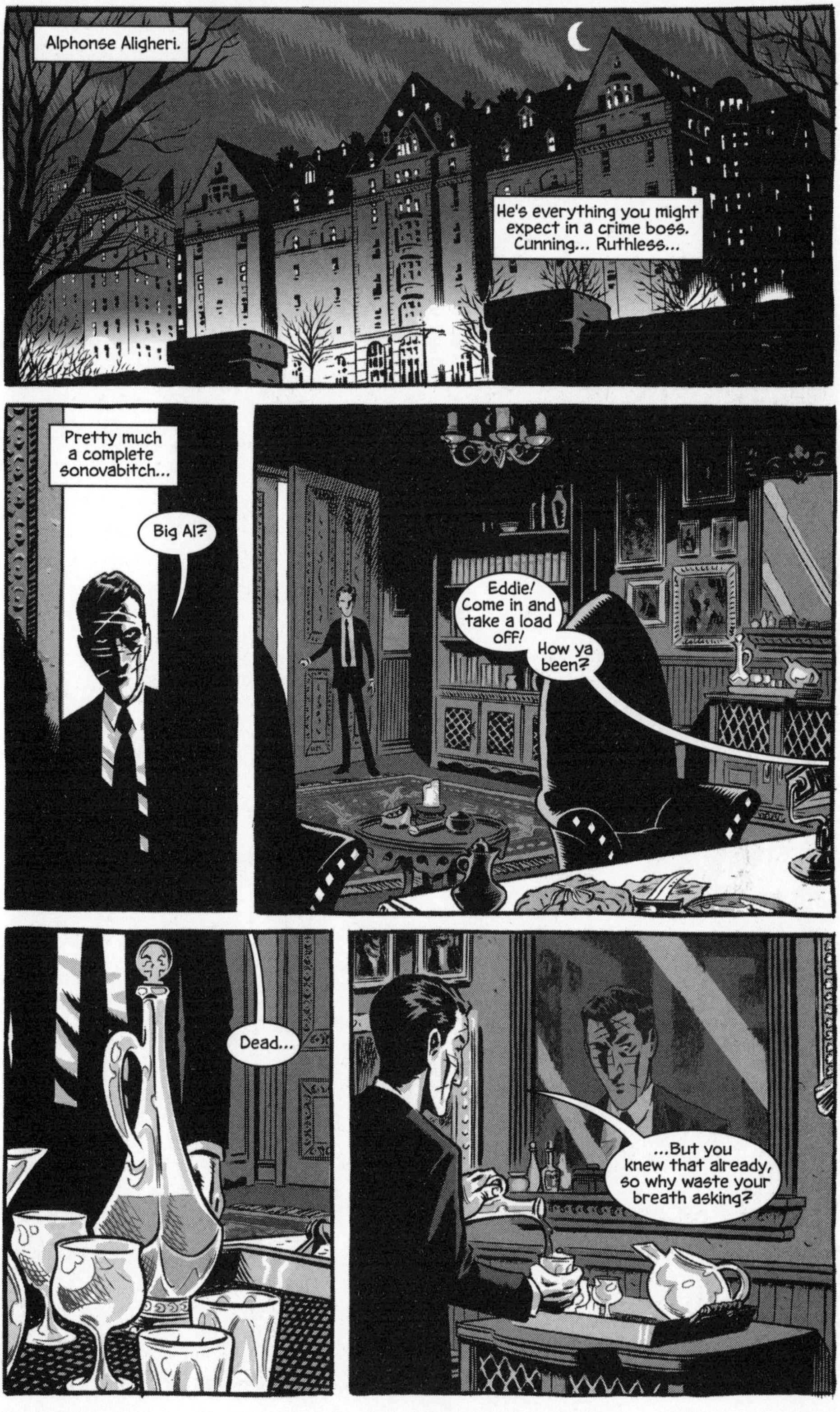

Alphonse Aligheri.
He's everything you might expect in a crime boss. Cunning... Ruthless...
Pretty much a complete sonovabitch...
Big Al?
Eddie! Come in and take a load off!
How ya been?
Dead...
...But you knew that already, so why waste your breath asking?

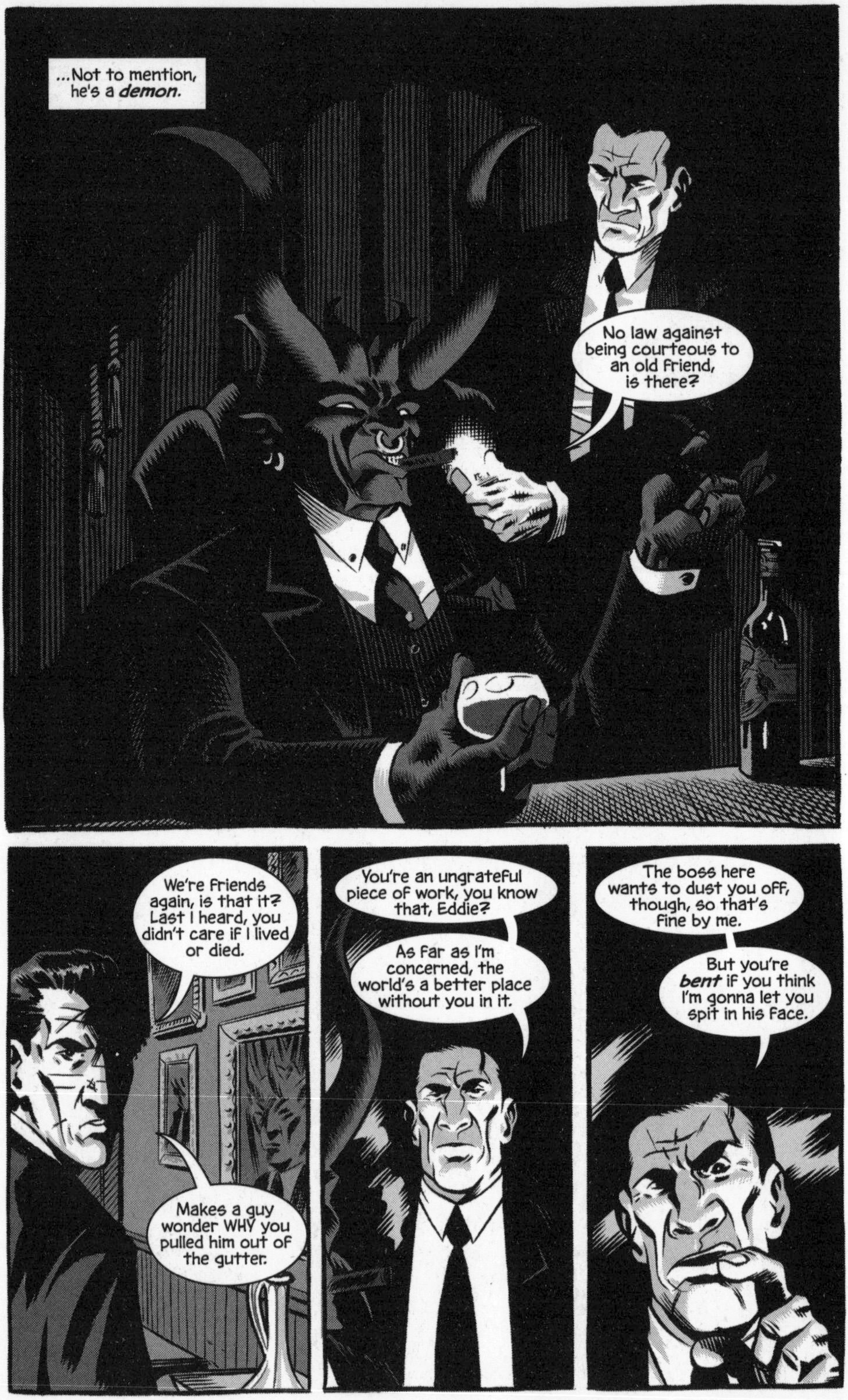

...Not to mention, he's a *demon.*
No law against being courteous to an old friend, is there?
We're friends again, is that it? Last I heard, you didn't care if I lived or died.
Makes a guy wonder WHY you pulled him out of the gutter.
You're an ungrateful piece of work, you know that, Eddie?
As far as I'm concerned, the world's a better place without you in it.
The boss here wants to dust you off, though, so that's fine by me.
But you're *bent* if you think I'm gonna let you spit in his face.

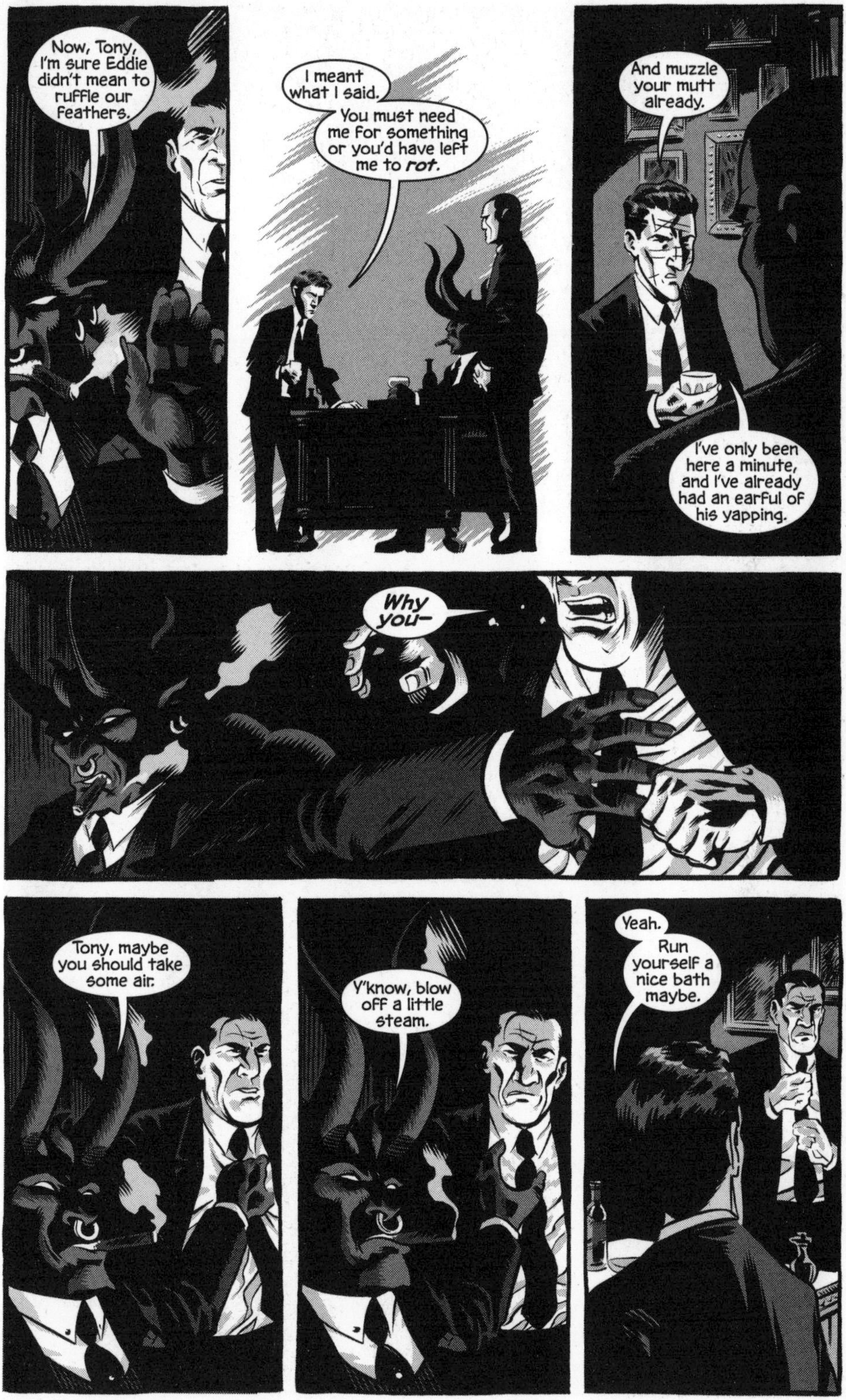
Now, Tony, I'm sure Eddie didn't mean to ruffle our feathers.
I meant what I said.
You must need me for something or you'd have left me to *rot*.
And muzzle your mutt already.
I've only been here a minute, and I've already had an earful of his yapping.
Why you–
Tony, maybe you should take some air.
Y'know, blow off a little steam.
Yeah.
Run yourself a nice bath maybe.

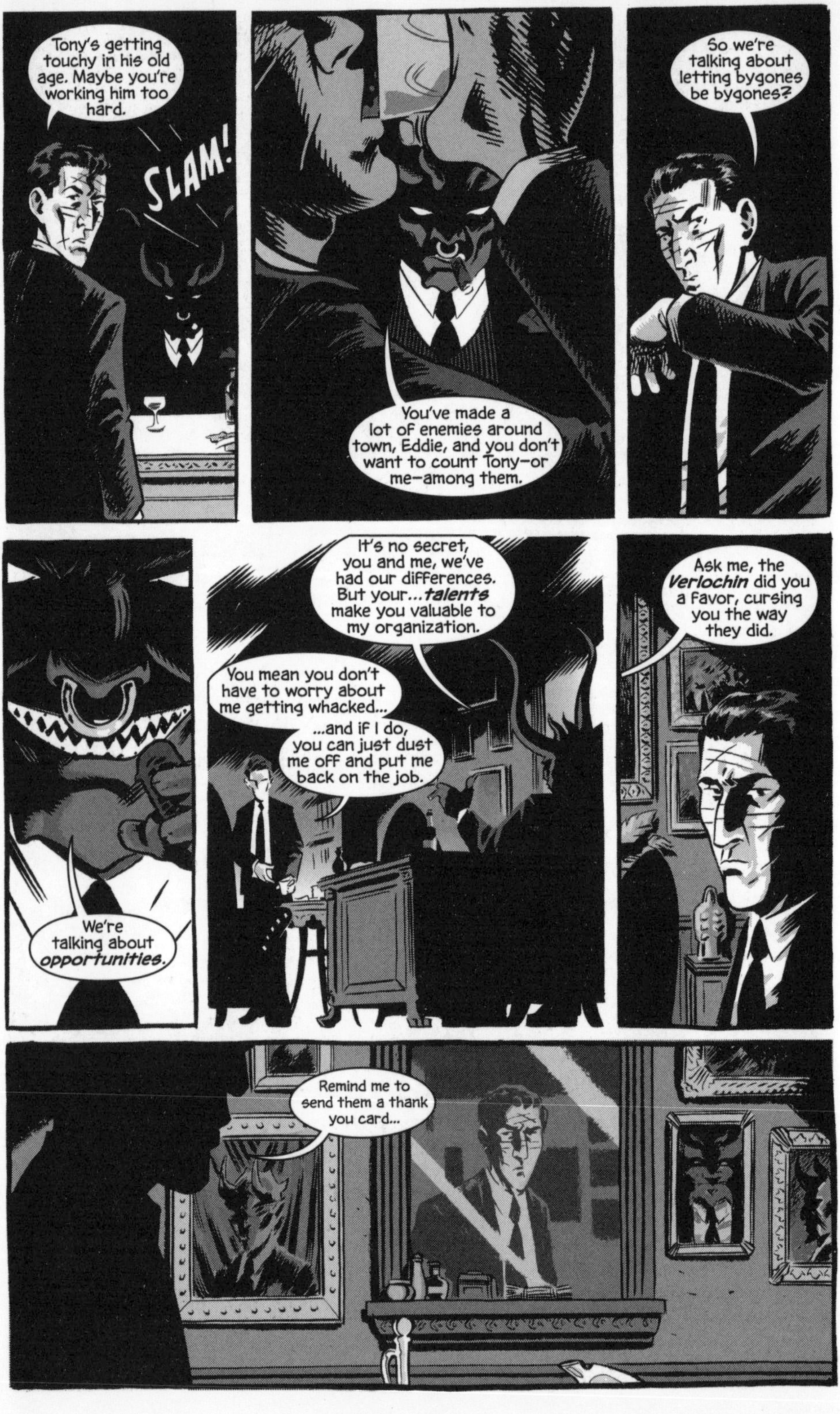

Tony's getting touchy in his old age. Maybe you're working him too hard.
SLAM!
You've made a lot of enemies around town, Eddie, and you don't want to count Tony—or me—among them.
So we're talking about letting bygones be bygones?
We're talking about *opportunities*.
It's no secret, you and me, we've had our differences. But your...*talents* make you valuable to my organization.
You mean you don't have to worry about me getting whacked...
...and if I do, you can just dust me off and put me back on the job.
Ask me, the *Verlochin* did you a favor, cursing you the way they did.
Remind me to send them a thank you card...

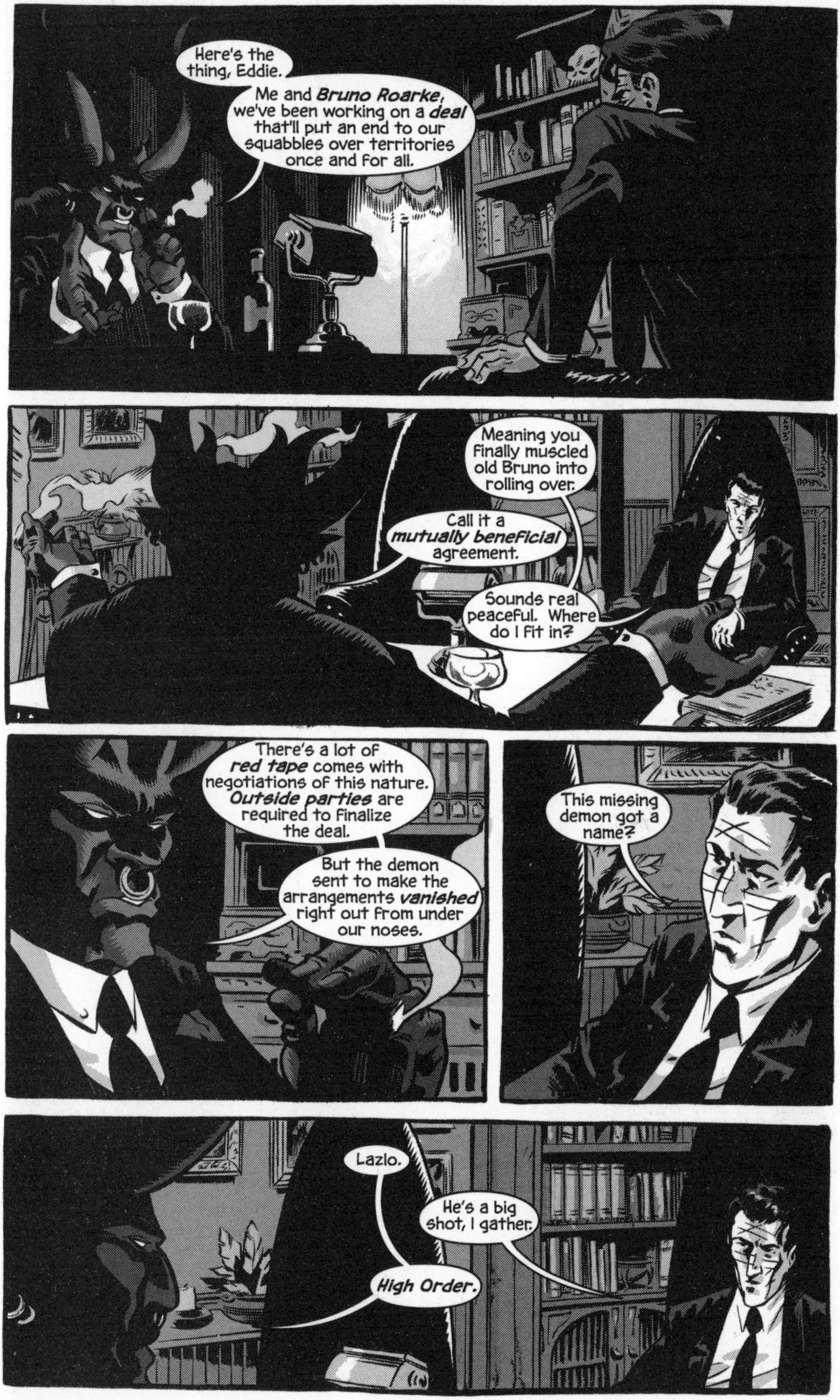
Here's the thing, Eddie.
Me and Bruno Roarke, we've been working on a deal that'll put an end to our squabbles over territories once and for all.
Meaning you finally muscled old Bruno into rolling over.
Call it a mutually beneficial agreement.
Sounds real peaceful. Where do I fit in?
There's a lot of red tape comes with negotiations of this nature. Outside parties are required to finalize the deal.
But the demon sent to make the arrangements vanished right out from under our noses.
This missing demon got a name?
Lazlo.
High Order.
He's a big shot, I gather.

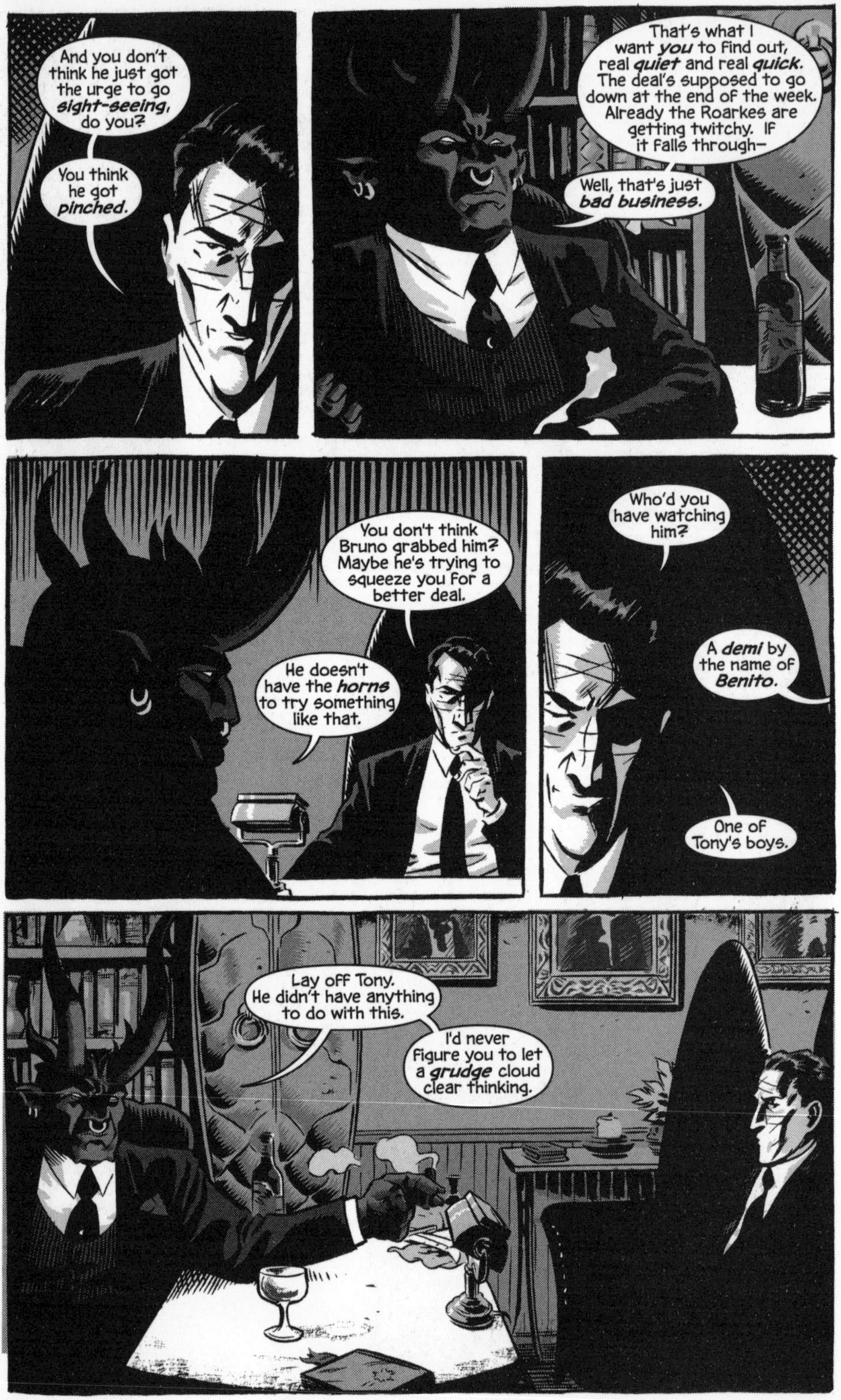
And you don't think he just got the urge to go *sight-seeing*, do you?
You think he got *pinched*.
That's what I want *you* to find out, real *quiet* and real *quick*. The deal's supposed to go down at the end of the week. Already the Roarkes are getting twitchy. If it falls through—
Well, that's just *bad business*.
You don't think Bruno grabbed him? Maybe he's trying to squeeze you for a better deal.
He doesn't have the *horns* to try something like that.
Who'd you have watching him?
A *demi* by the name of *Benito*.
One of Tony's boys.
Lay off Tony. He didn't have anything to do with this.
I'd never figure you to let a *grudge* cloud clear thinking.

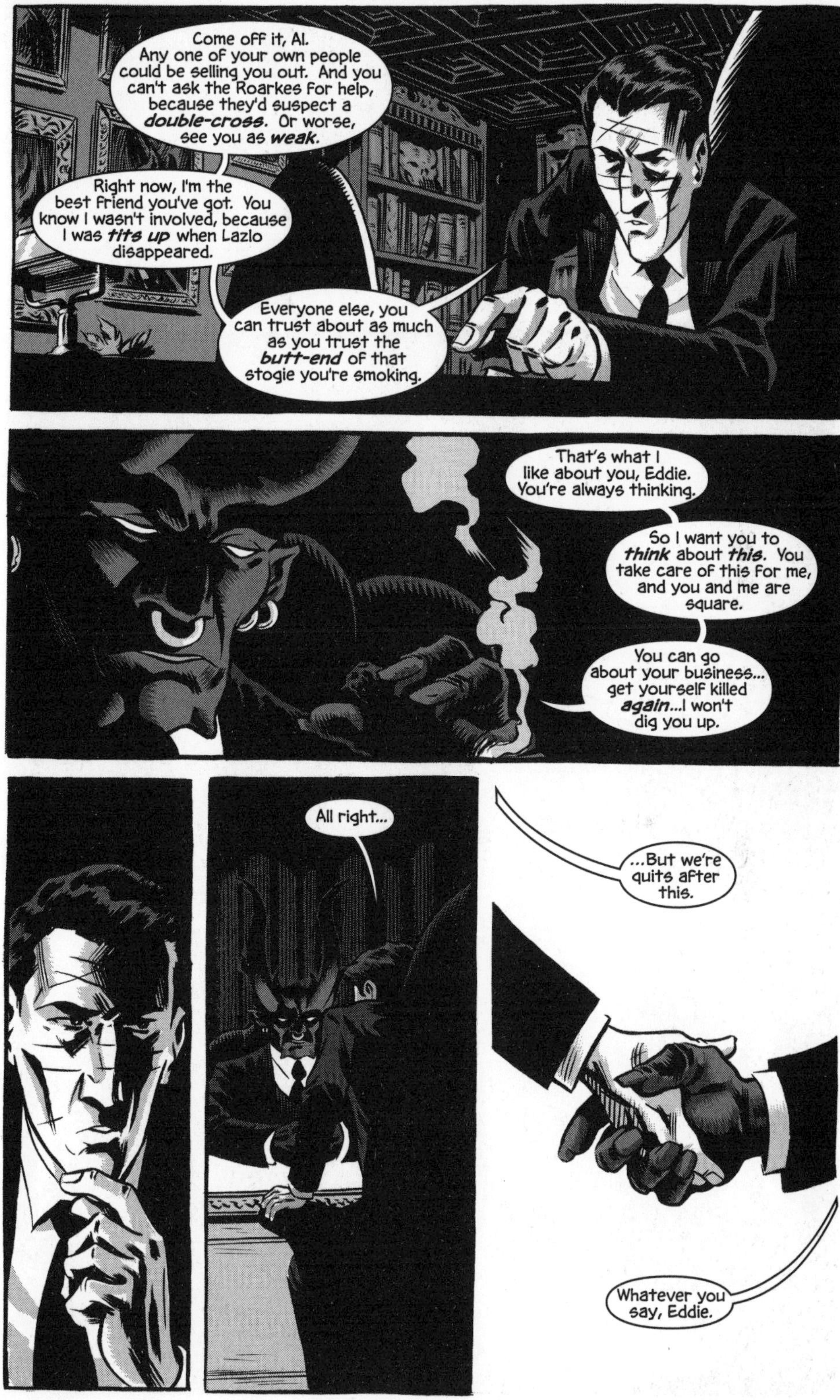
Come off it, Al. Any one of your own people could be selling you out. And you can't ask the Roarkes for help, because they'd suspect a double-cross. Or worse, see you as weak.
Right now, I'm the best friend you've got. You know I wasn't involved, because I was tits up when Lazlo disappeared.
Everyone else, you can trust about as much as you trust the butt-end of that stogie you're smoking.
That's what I like about you, Eddie. You're always thinking.
So I want you to think about this. You take care of this for me, and you and me are square.
You can go about your business... get yourself killed again...I won't dig you up.
All right...
...But we're quits after this.
Whatever you say, Eddie.

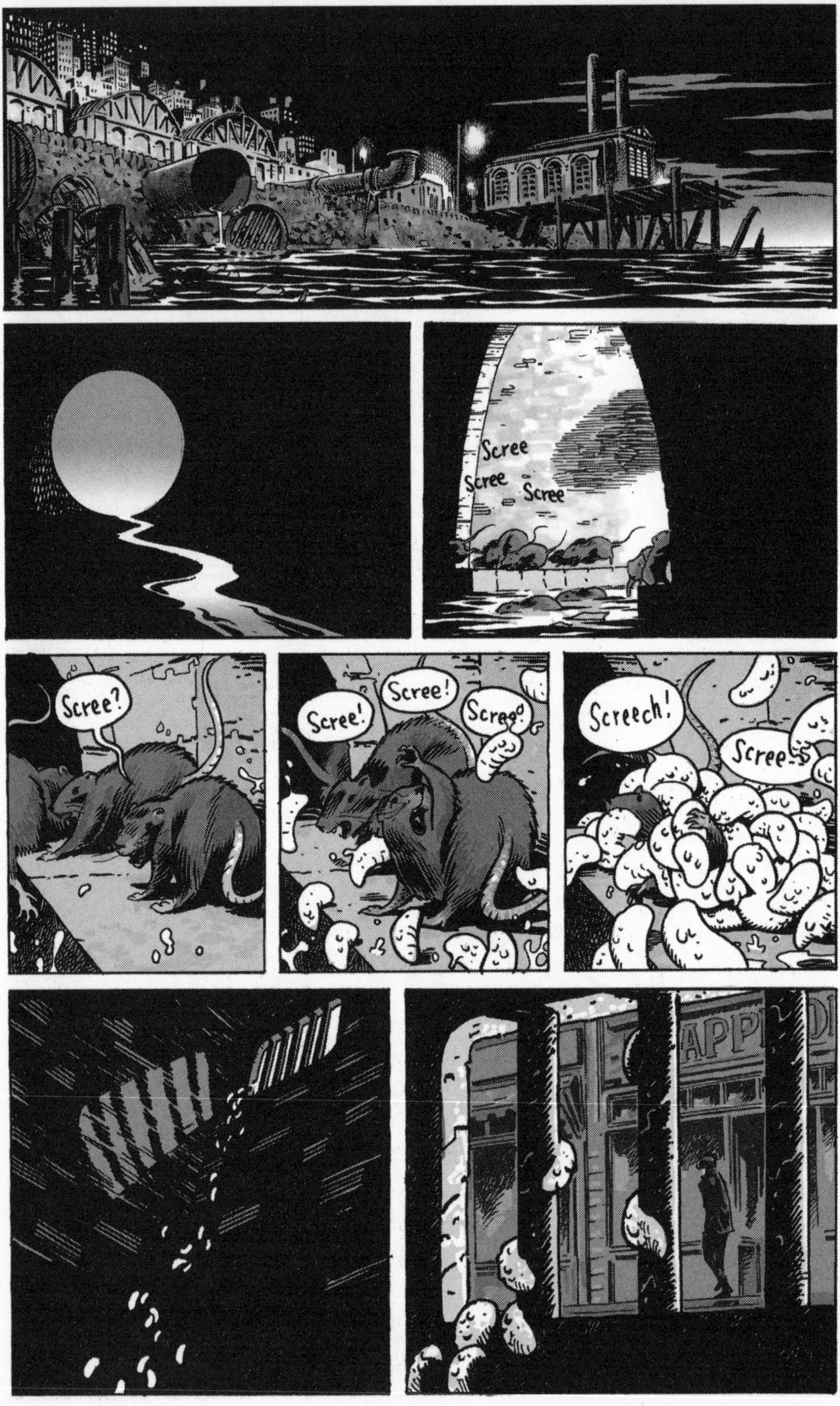
Scree
Scree
Scree
Scree?
Scree!
Scree!
Scree
Screech!
Scree-

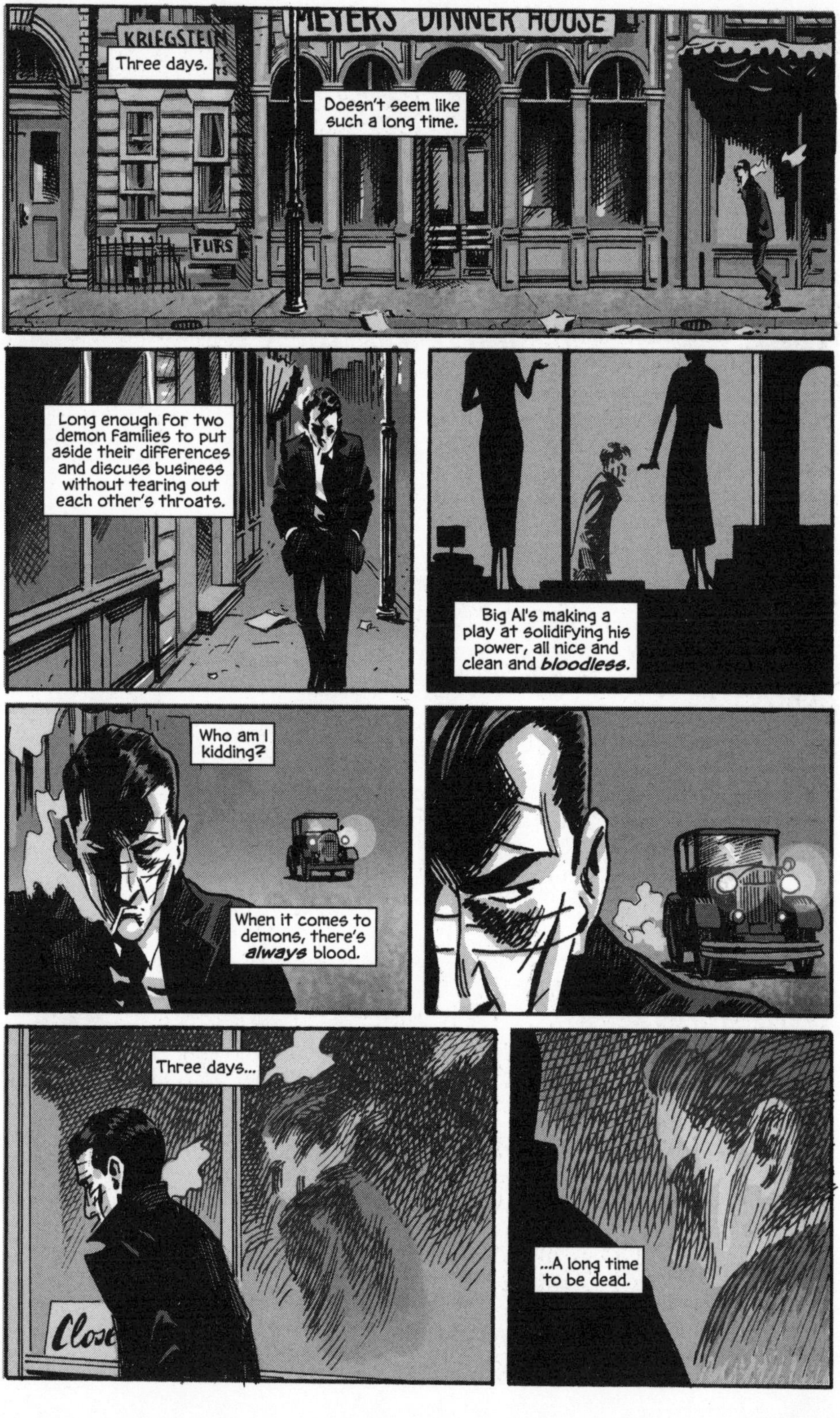
MEYERS DINNER HOUSE
KRIEGSTEIN
Three days.
Doesn't seem like such a long time.
FURS
Long enough for two demon families to put aside their differences and discuss business without tearing out each other's throats.
Big Al's making a play at solidifying his power, all nice and clean and *bloodless.*
Who am I kidding?
When it comes to demons, there's *always* blood.
Three days...
Close
...A long time to be dead.

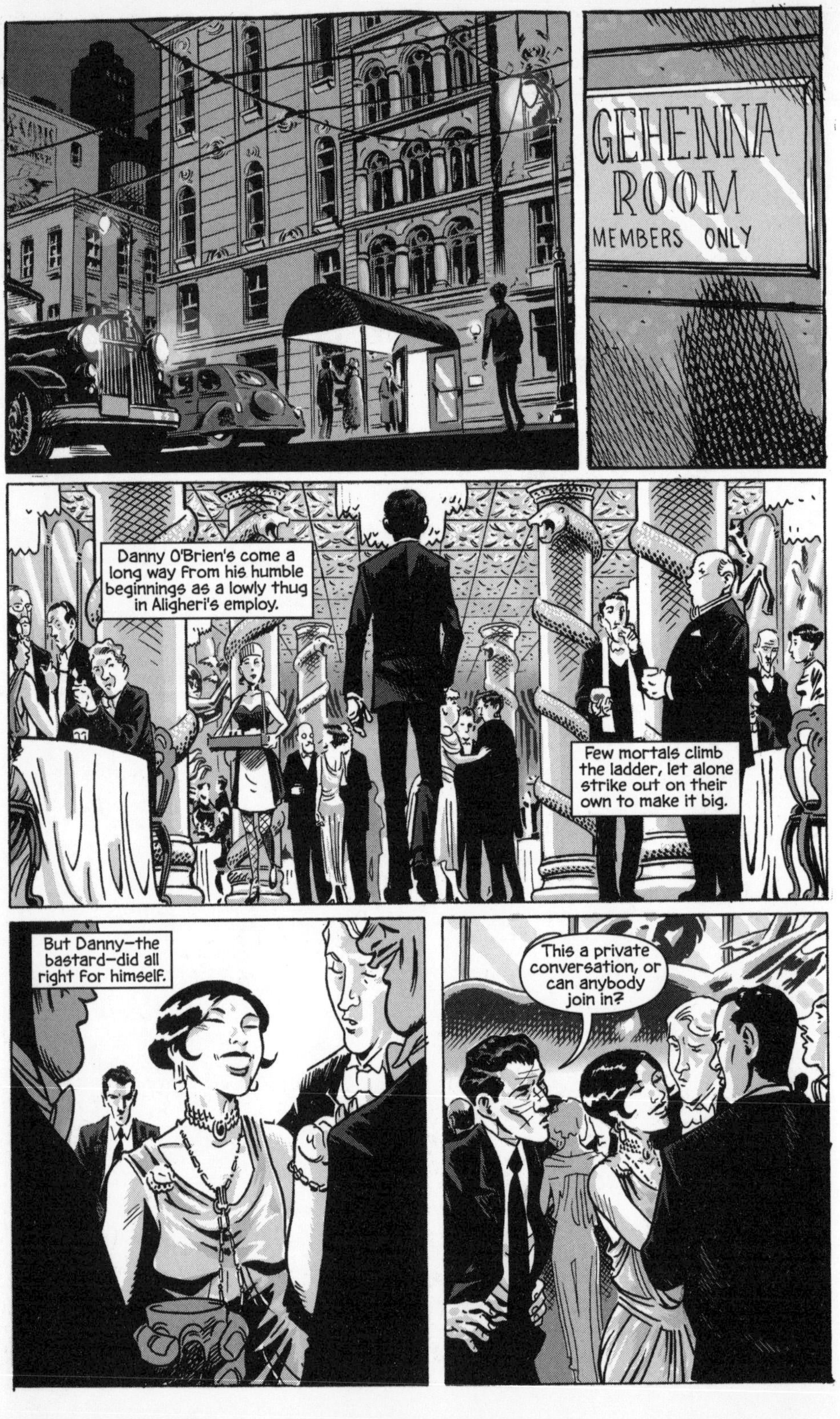
GEHENNA ROOM
MEMBERS ONLY
Danny O'Brien's come a long way from his humble beginnings as a lowly thug in Aligheri's employ.
Few mortals climb the ladder, let alone strike out on their own to make it big.
But Danny—the bastard—did all right for himself.
This a private conversation, or can anybody join in?

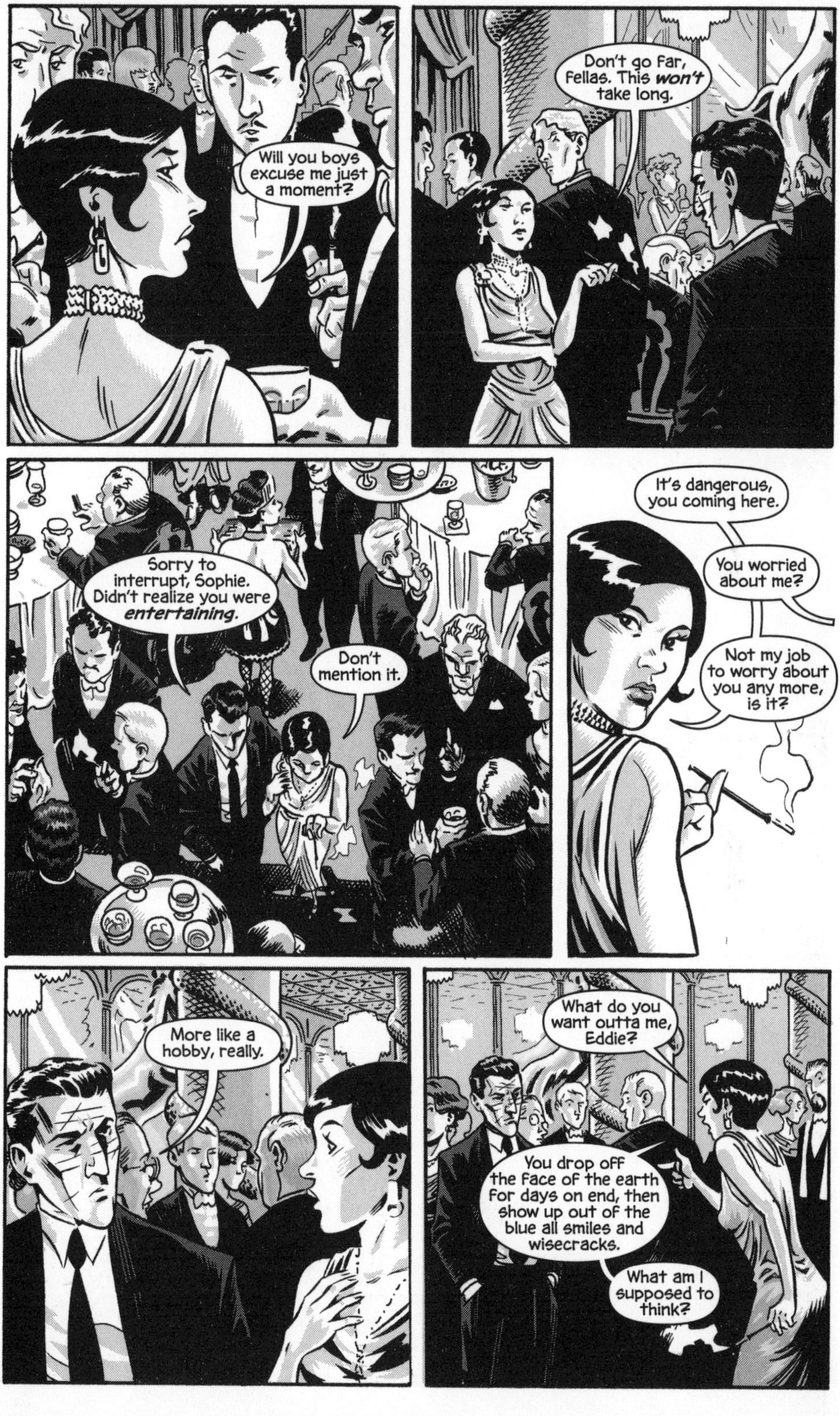
Will you boys excuse me just a moment?
Don't go far, Fellas. This *won't* take long.
Sorry to interrupt, Sophie. Didn't realize you were *entertaining*.
Don't mention it.
It's dangerous, you coming here.
You worried about me?
Not my job to worry about you any more, is it?
More like a hobby, really.
What do you want outta me, Eddie?
You drop off the face of the earth for days on end, then show up out of the blue all smiles and wisecracks.
What am I supposed to think?

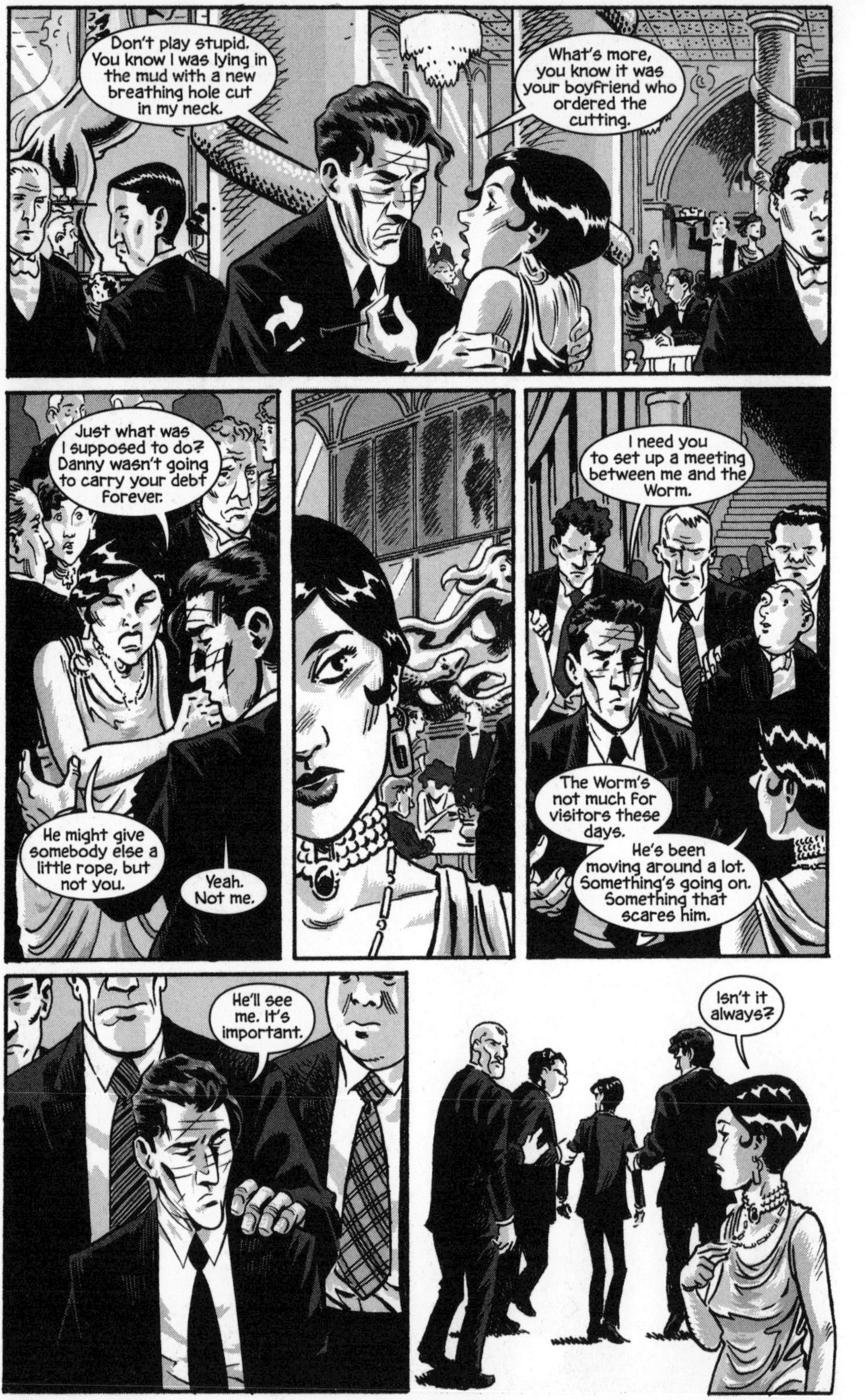

Don't play stupid. You know I was lying in the mud with a new breathing hole cut in my neck.
What's more, you know it was your boyfriend who ordered the cutting.
Just what was I supposed to do? Danny wasn't going to carry your debt forever.
He might give somebody else a little rope, but not you.
Yeah. Not me.
I need you to set up a meeting between me and the Worm.
The Worm's not much for visitors these days.
He's been moving around a lot. Something's going on. Something that scares him.
He'll see me. It's important.
Isn't it always?

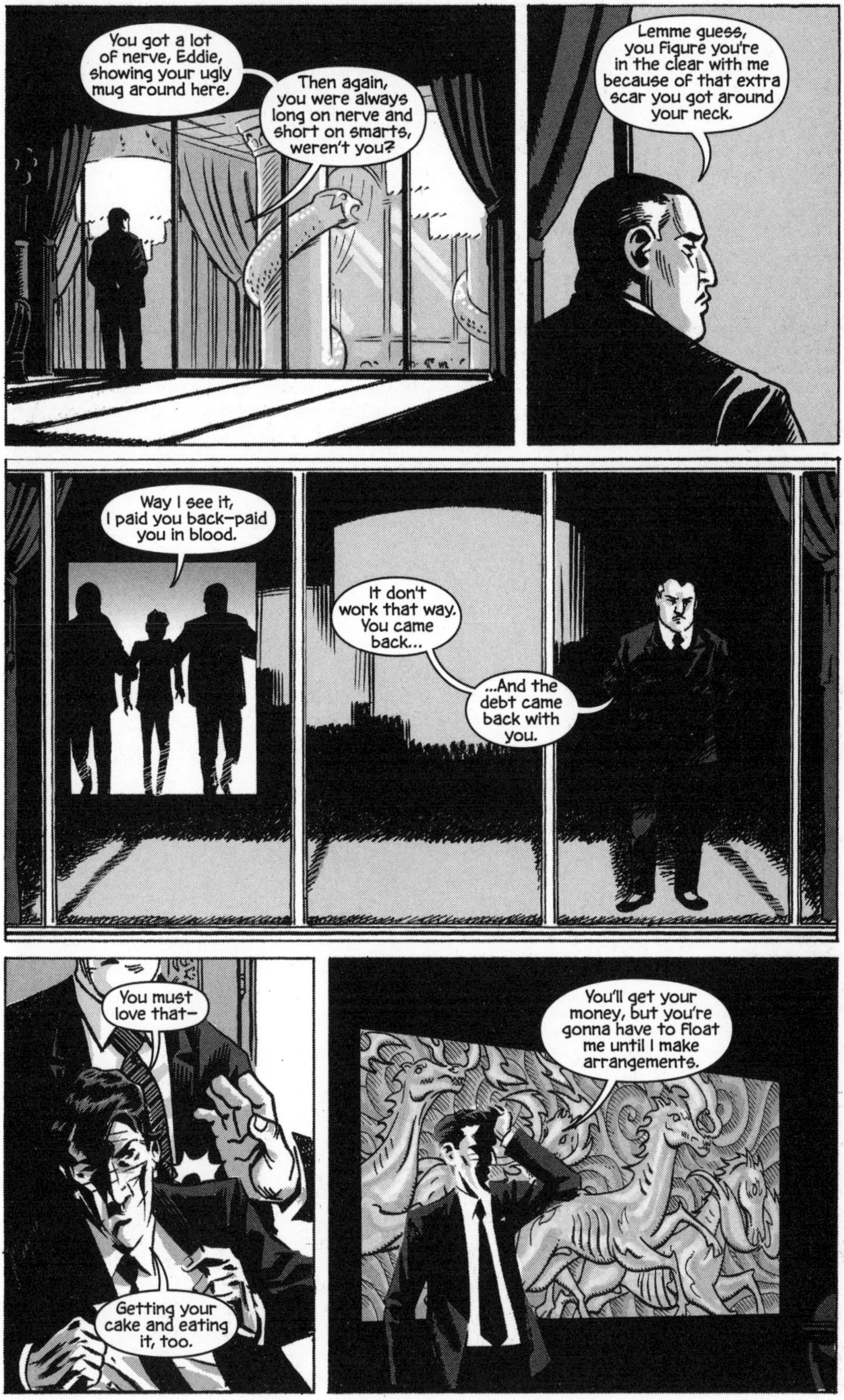
You got a lot of nerve, Eddie, showing your ugly mug around here.
Then again, you were always long on nerve and short on smarts, weren't you?
Lemme guess, you figure you're in the clear with me because of that extra scar you got around your neck.
Way I see it, I paid you back–paid you in blood.
It don't work that way. You came back...
...And the debt came back with you.
You must love that–
Getting your cake and eating it, too.
You'll get your money, but you're gonna have to float me until I make arrangements.

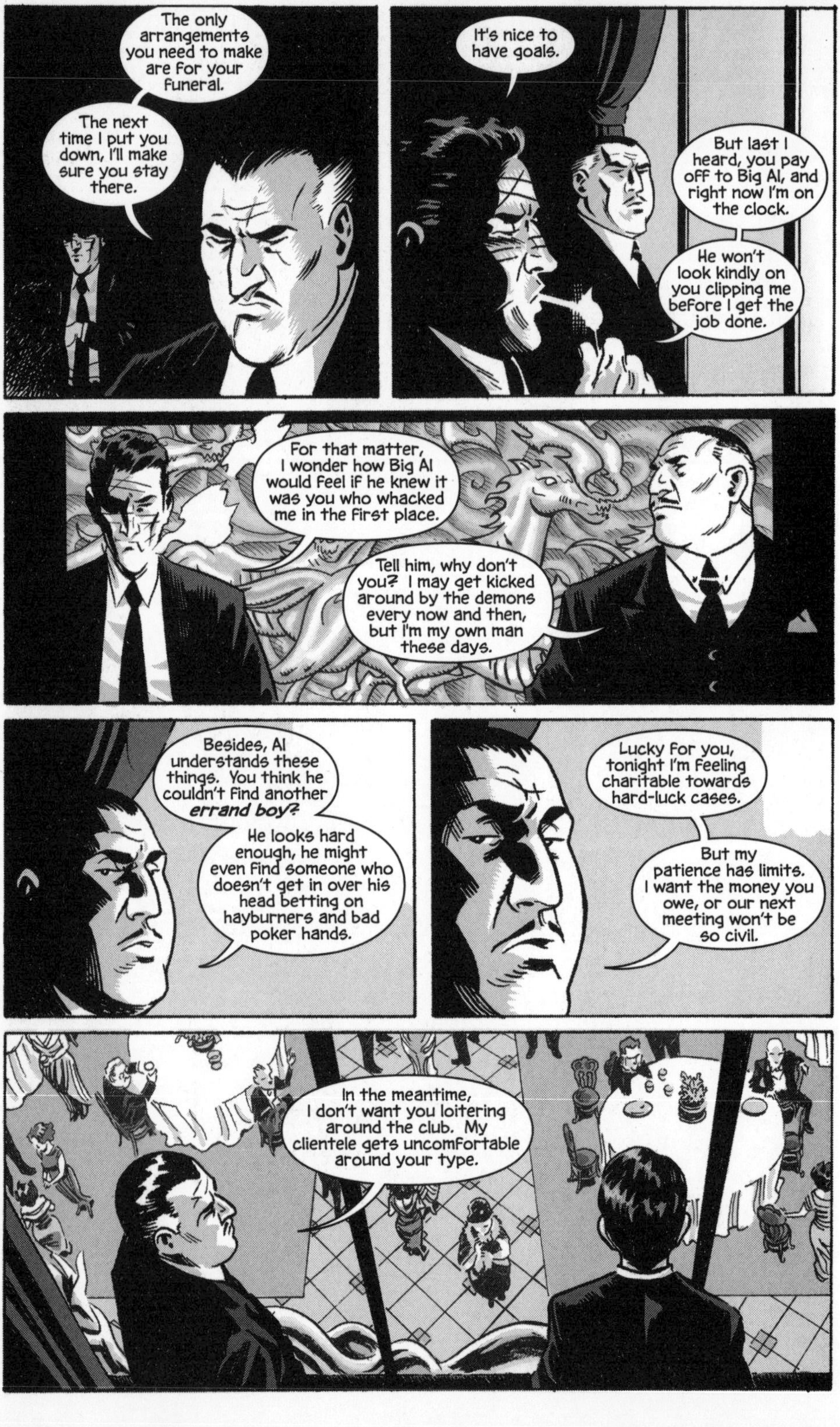
The only arrangements you need to make are for your funeral.
The next time I put you down, I'll make sure you stay there.
It's nice to have goals.
But last I heard, you pay off to Big Al, and right now I'm on the clock.
He won't look kindly on you clipping me before I get the job done.
For that matter, I wonder how Big Al would feel if he knew it was you who whacked me in the first place.
Tell him, why don't you? I may get kicked around by the demons every now and then, but I'm my own man these days.
Besides, Al understands these things. You think he couldn't find another *errand boy?*
He looks hard enough, he might even find someone who doesn't get in over his head betting on hayburners and bad poker hands.
Lucky for you, tonight I'm feeling charitable towards hard-luck cases.
But my patience has limits. I want the money you owe, or our next meeting won't be so civil.
In the meantime, I don't want you loitering around the club. My clientele gets uncomfortable around your type.

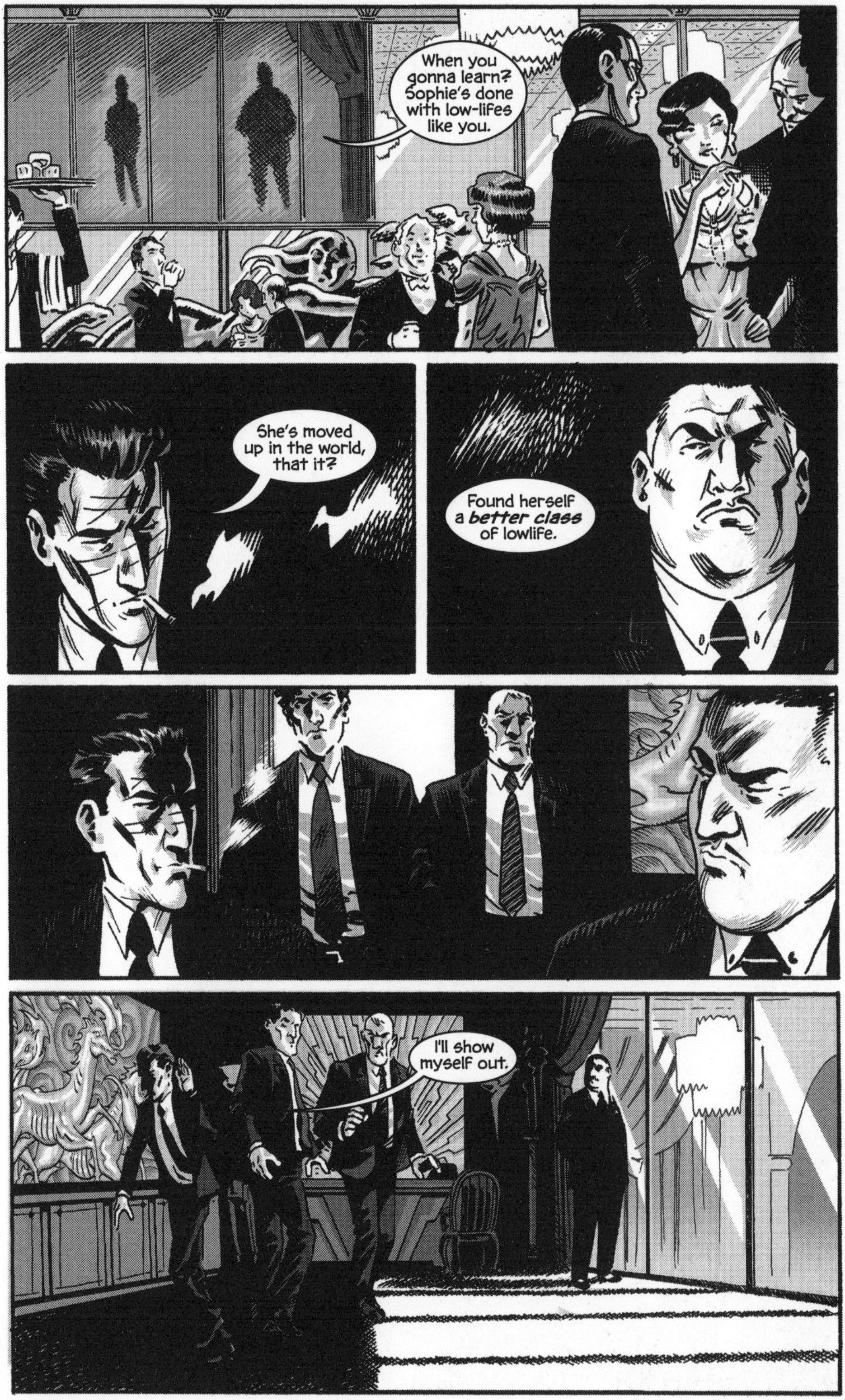
When you gonna learn? Sophie's done with low-lifes like you.
She's moved up in the world, that it?
Found herself a *better class* of lowlife.
I'll show myself out.

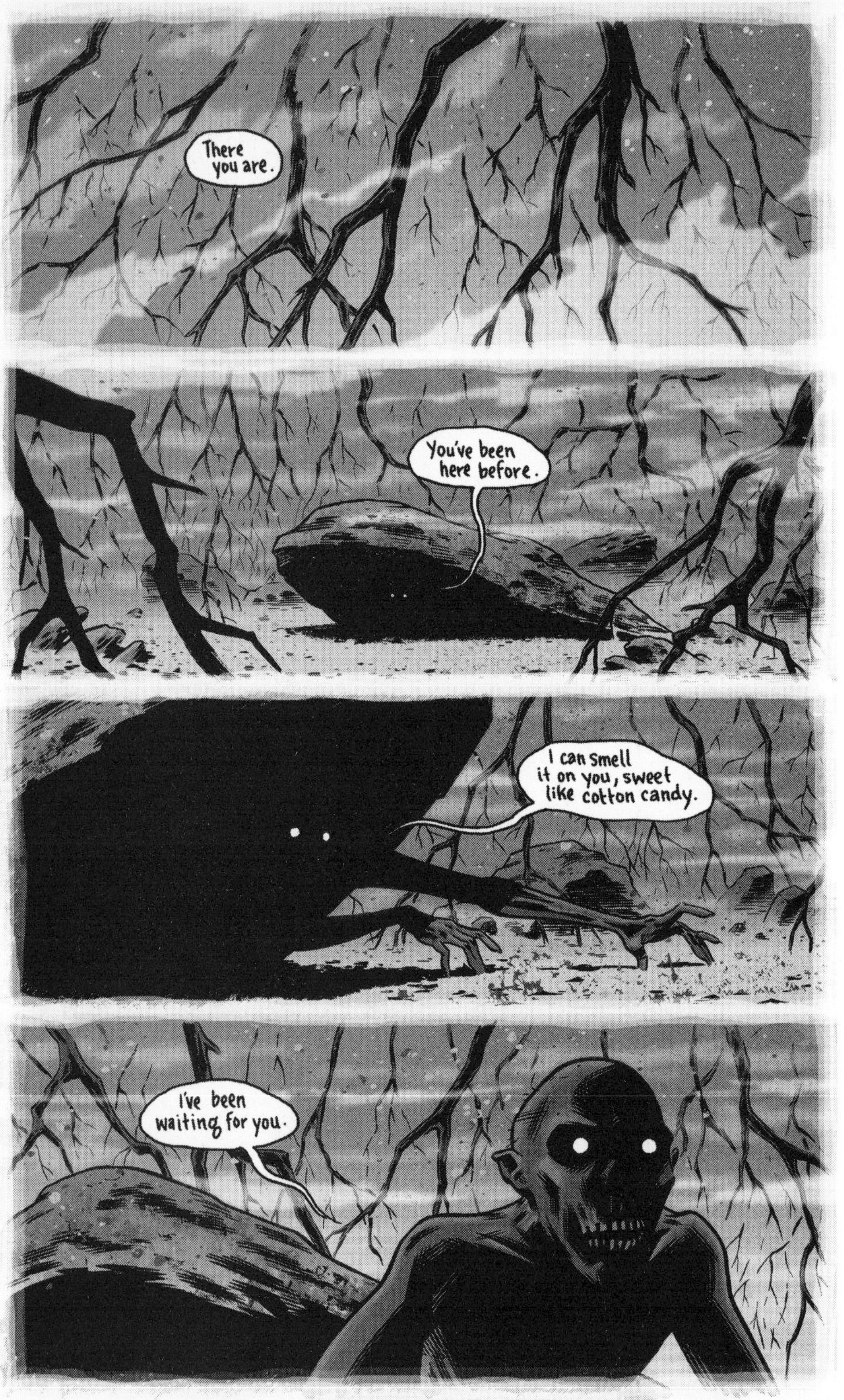
There you are.
You've been here before.
I can smell it on you, sweet like cotton candy.
I've been waiting for you.

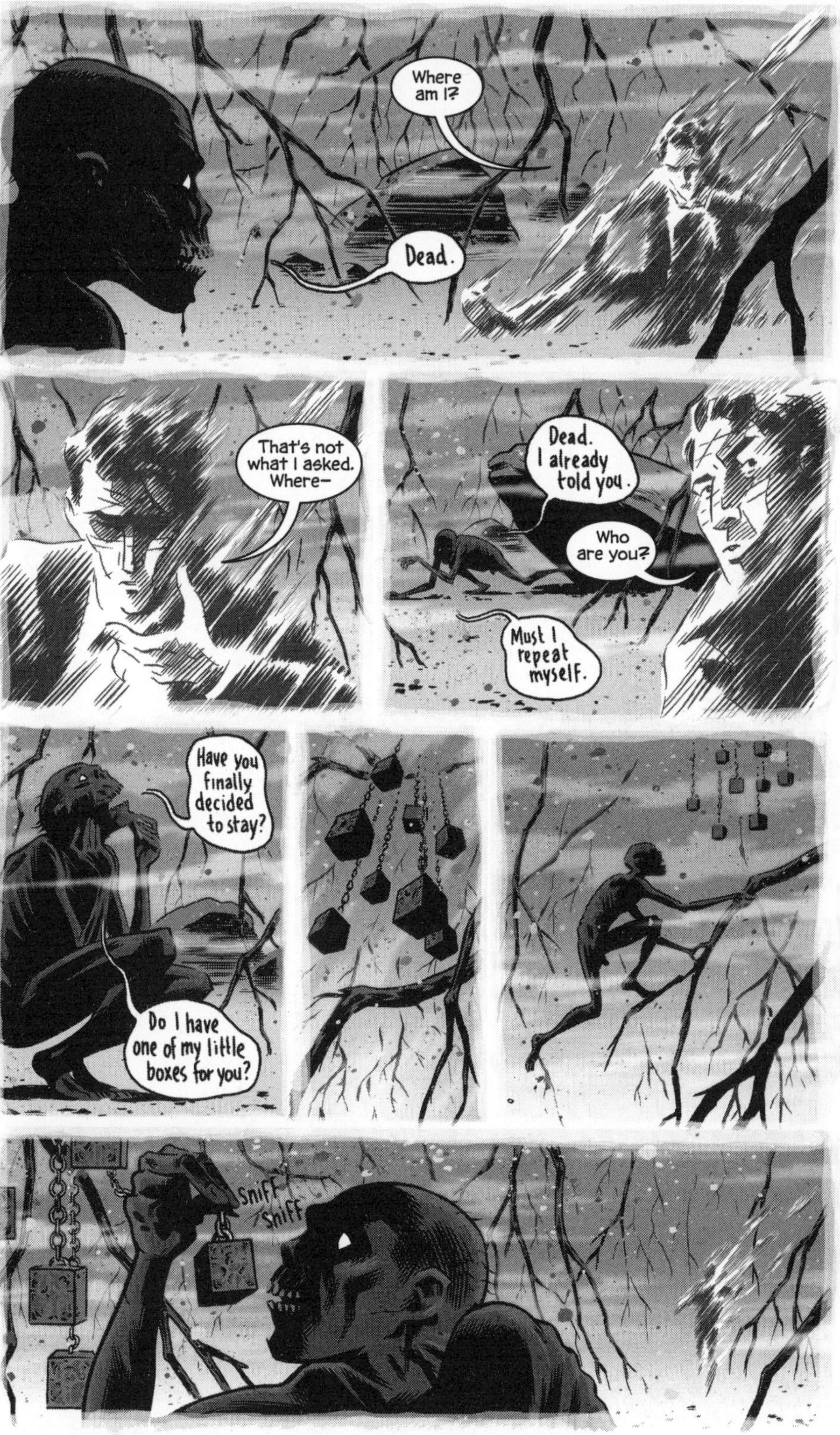
Where am I?
Dead.
That's not what I asked. Where–
Dead. I already told you.
Who are you?
Must I repeat myself.
Have you finally decided to stay?
Do I have one of my little boxes for you?
Sniff
Sniff

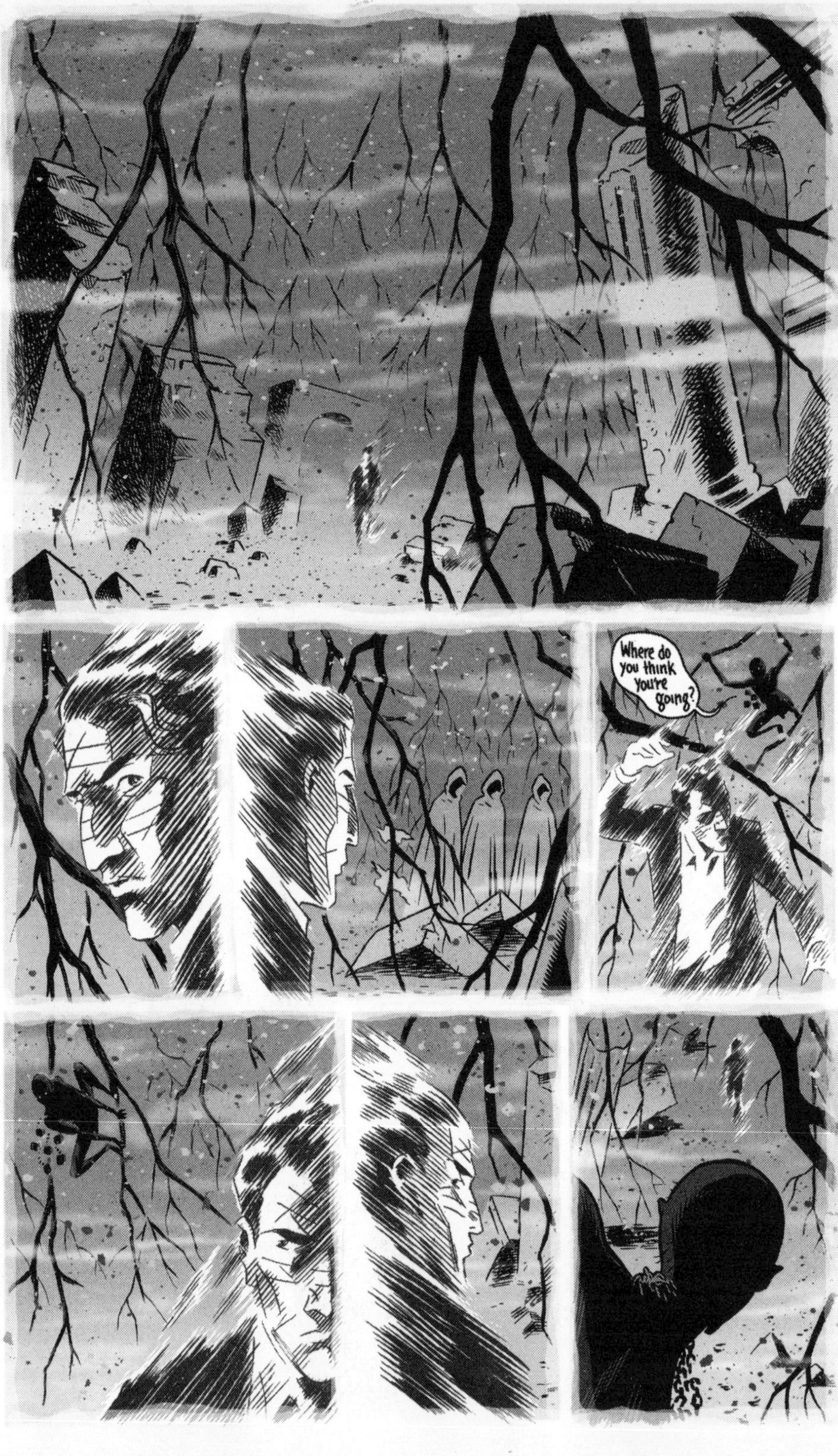
Where do you think you're going?

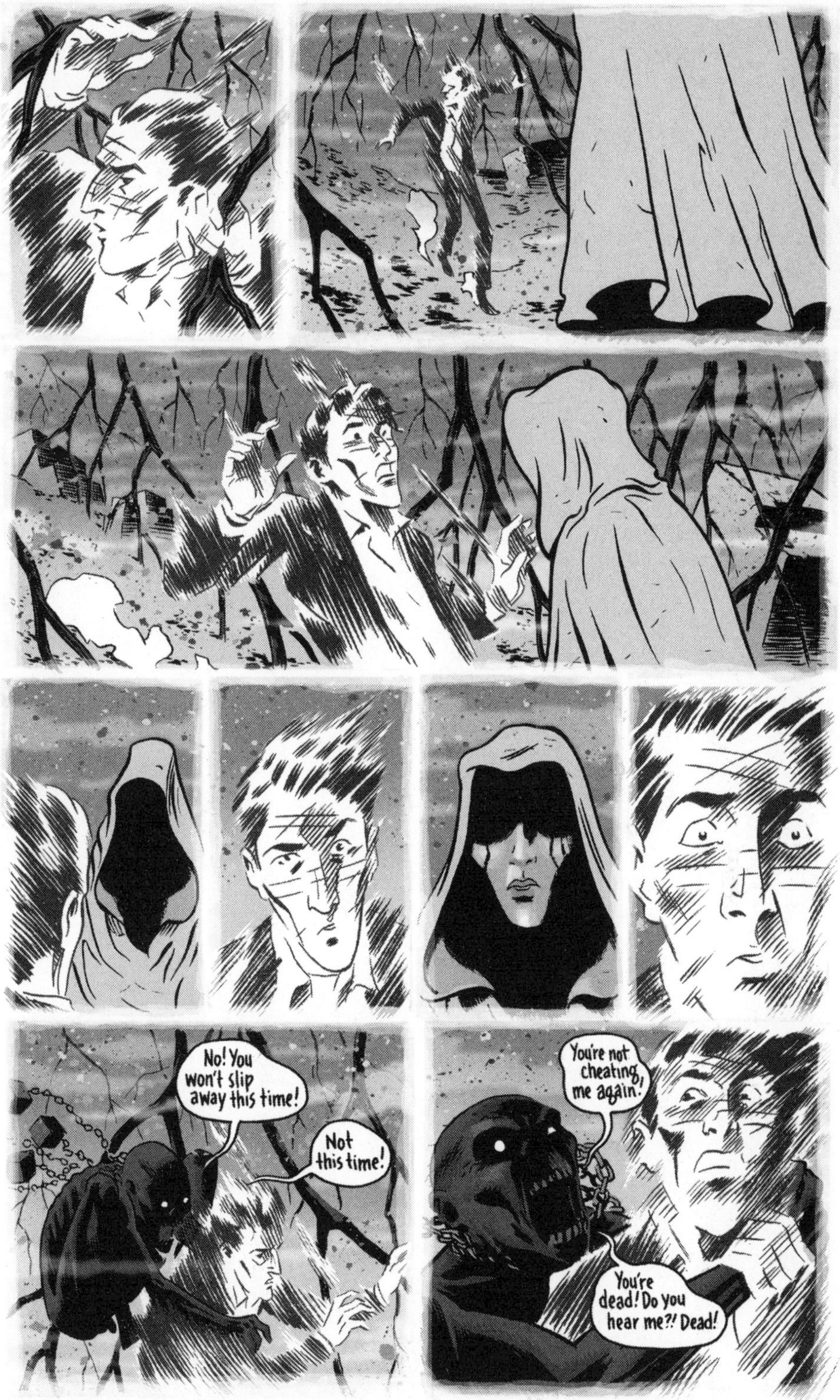

No! You won't slip away this time!
Not this time!
You're not cheating me again.
You're dead! Do you hear me?! Dead!

Three days.

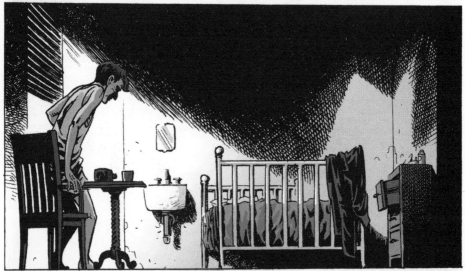

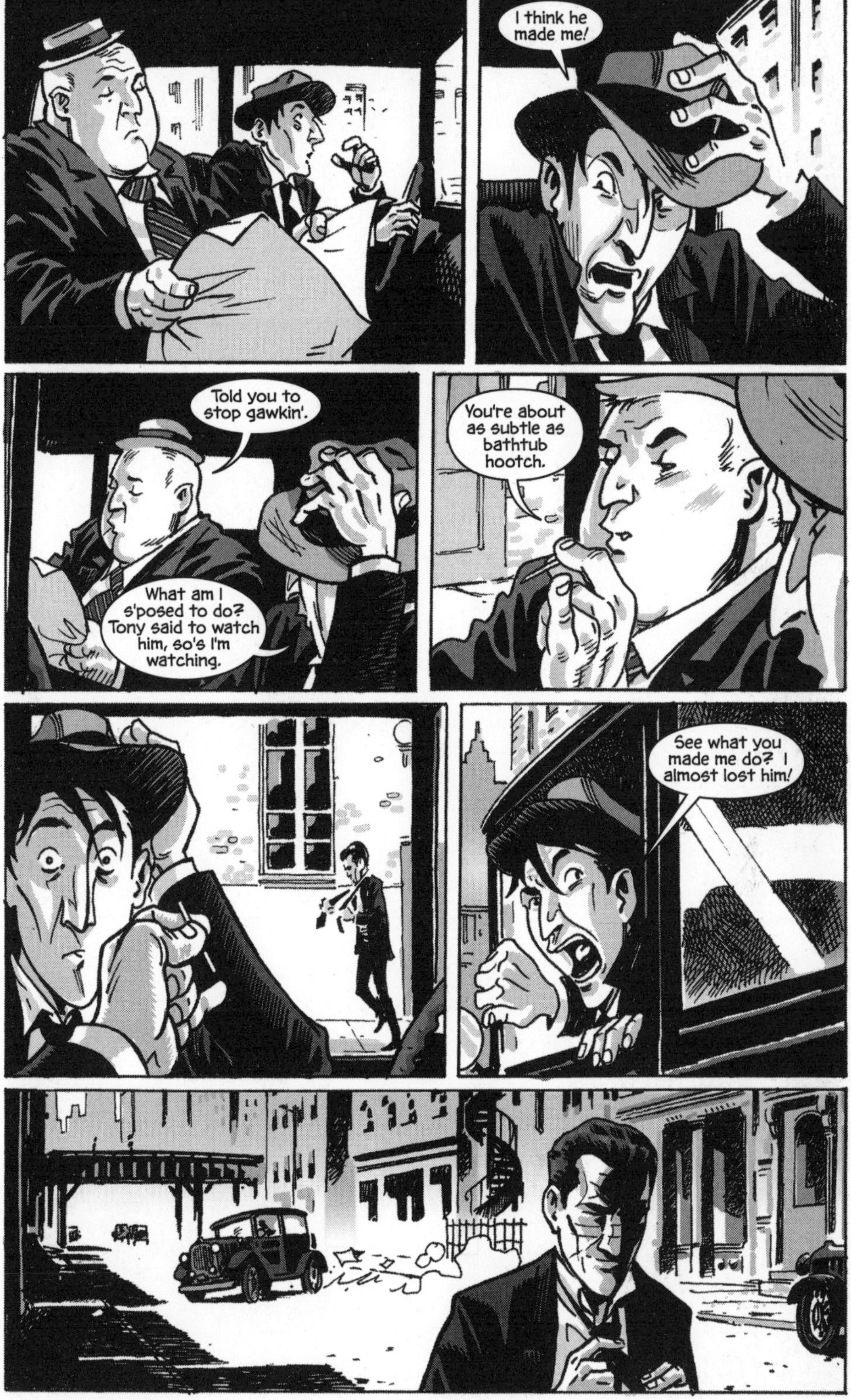
I think he made me!
Told you to stop gawkin'.
What am I s'posed to do? Tony said to watch him, so's I'm watching.
You're about as subtle as bathtub hootch.
See what you made me do? I almost lost him!

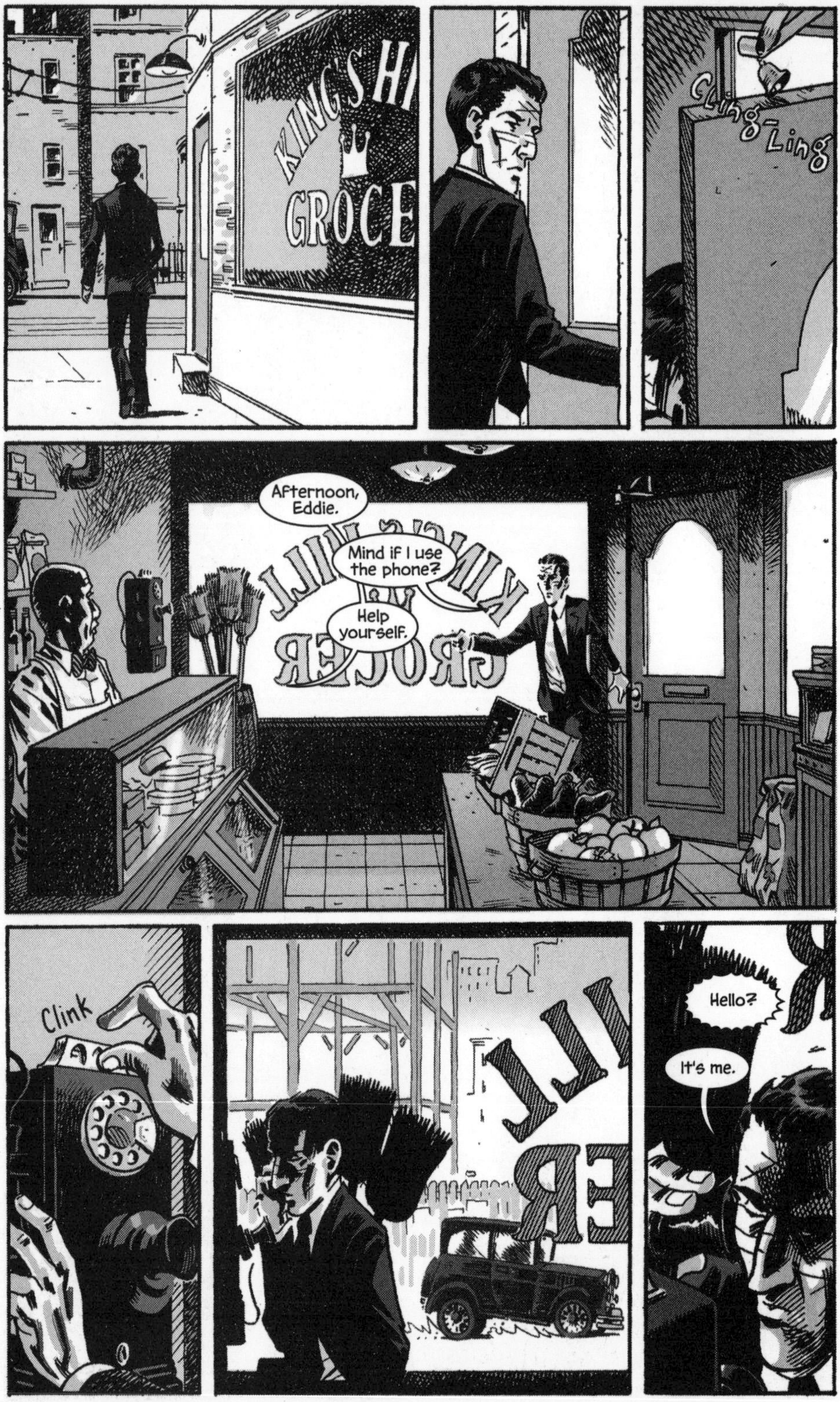
KING'S HI
GROCE
Cling-Ling
Afternoon, Eddie.
Mind if I use the phone?
Help yourself.
Clink
Hello?
It's me.

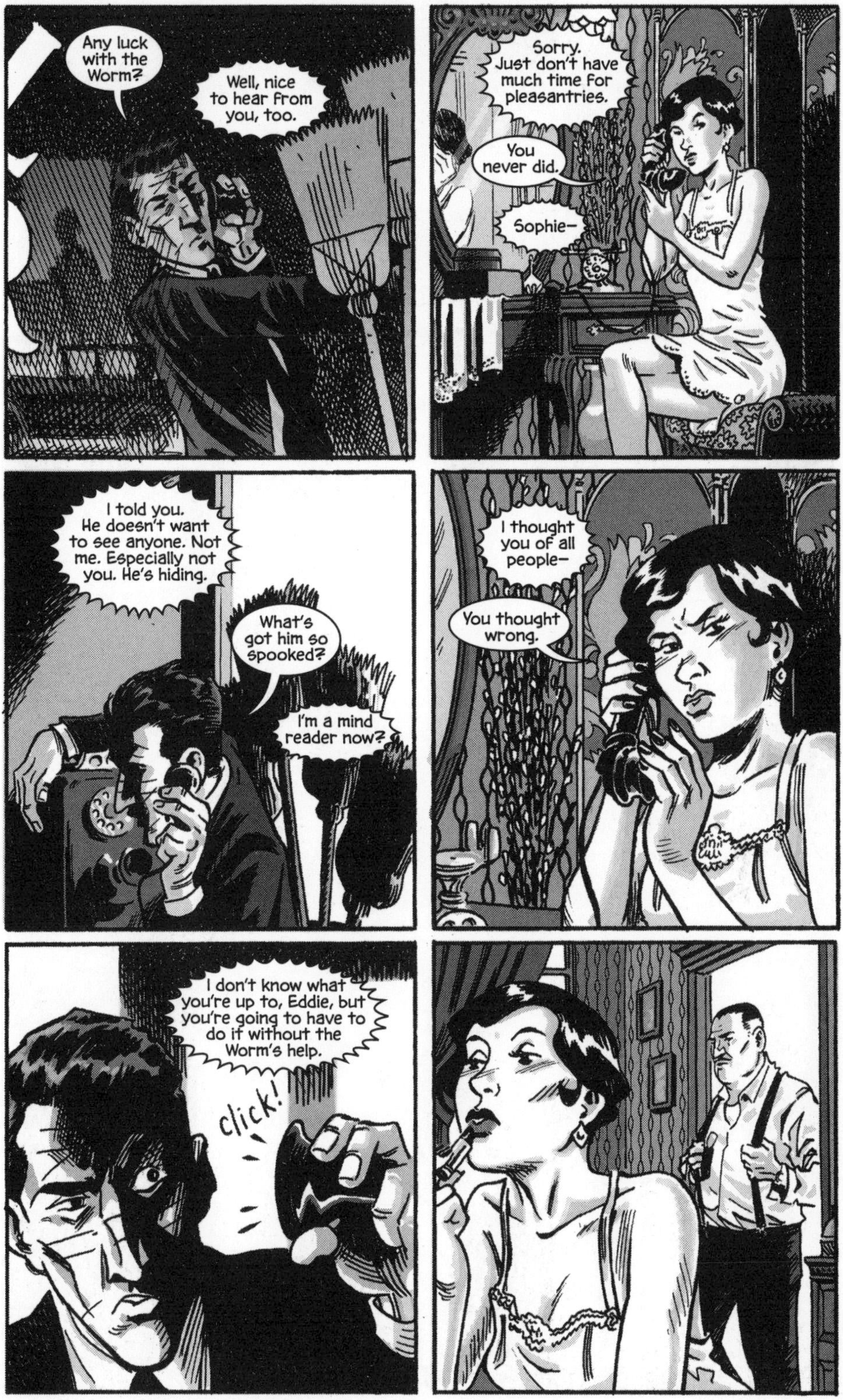
Any luck with the Worm?
Well, nice to hear from you, too.
Sorry. Just don't have much time for pleasantries.
You never did.
Sophie—
I told you. He doesn't want to see anyone. Not me. Especially not you. He's hiding.
What's got him so spooked?
I'm a mind reader now?
I thought you of all people—
You thought wrong.
I don't know what you're up to, Eddie, but you're going to have to do it without the Worm's help.
click!

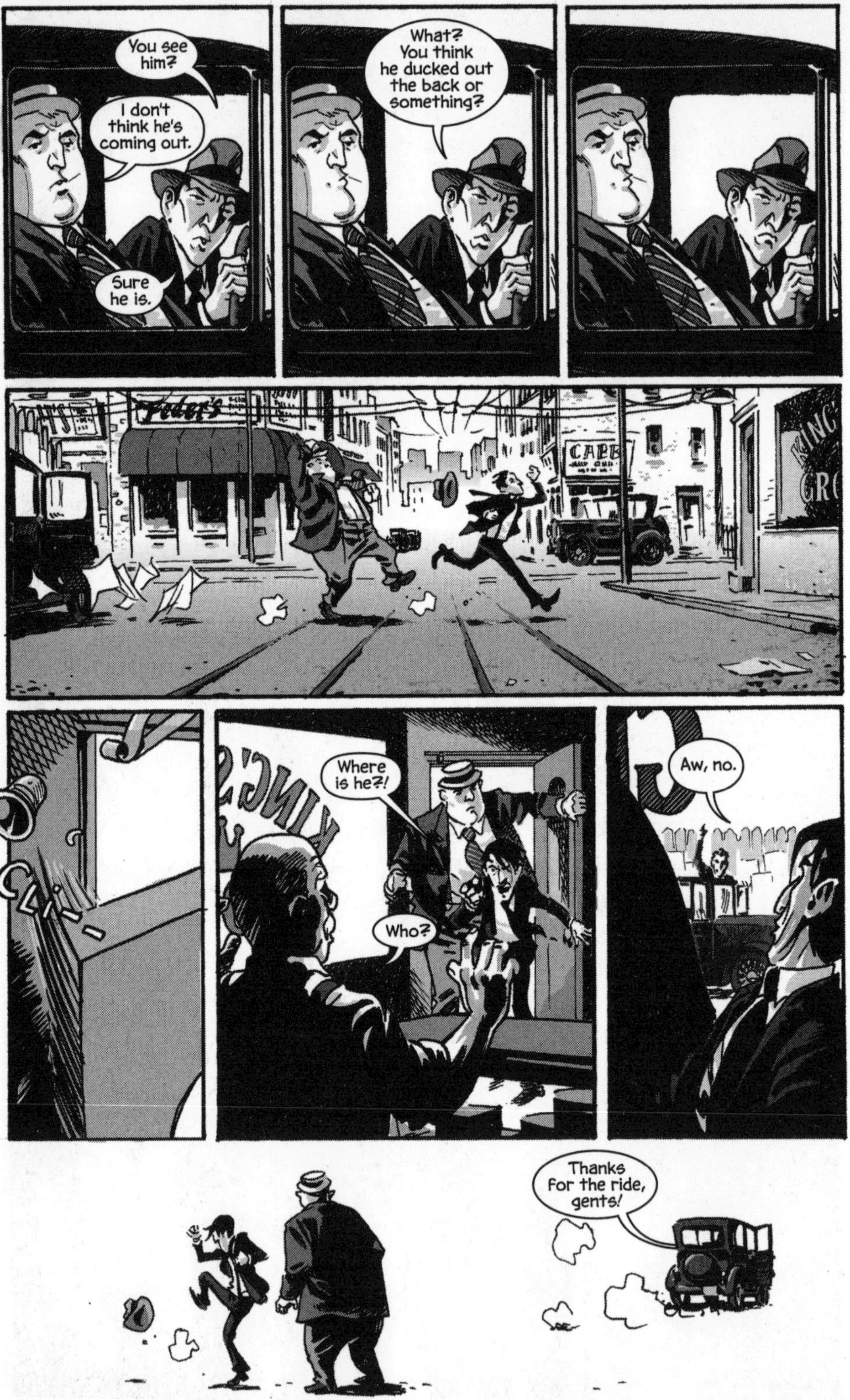
You see him?
I don't think he's coming out.
Sure he is.
What? You think he ducked out the back or something?
Where is he?!
Who?
Aw, no.
Thanks for the ride, gents!

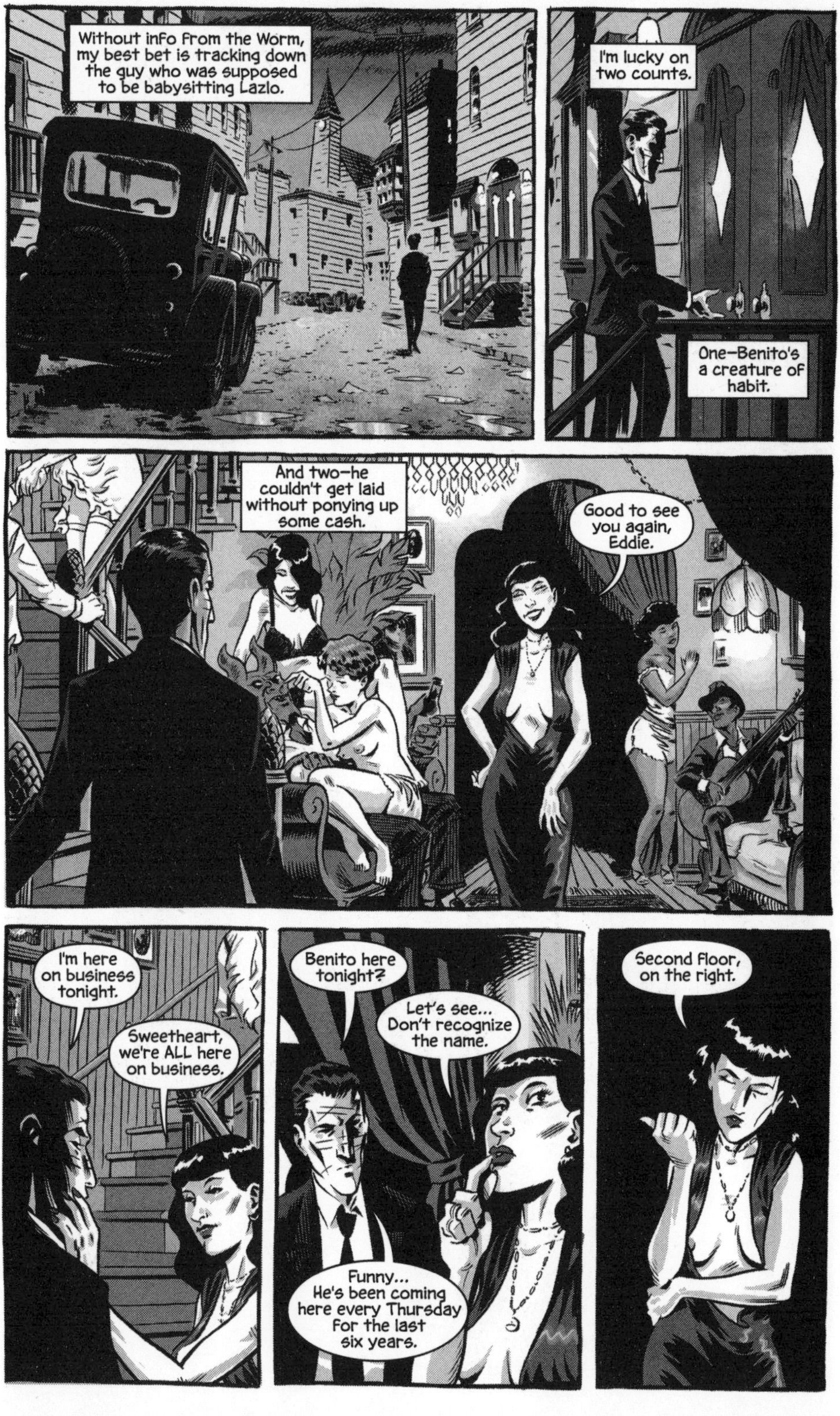
Without info from the Worm, my best bet is tracking down the guy who was supposed to be babysitting Lazlo.
I'm lucky on two counts.
One—Benito's a creature of habit.
And two—he couldn't get laid without ponying up some cash.
Good to see you again, Eddie.
I'm here on business tonight.
Sweetheart, we're ALL here on business.
Benito here tonight?
Let's see... Don't recognize the name.
Funny... He's been coming here every Thursday for the last six years.
Second floor, on the right.

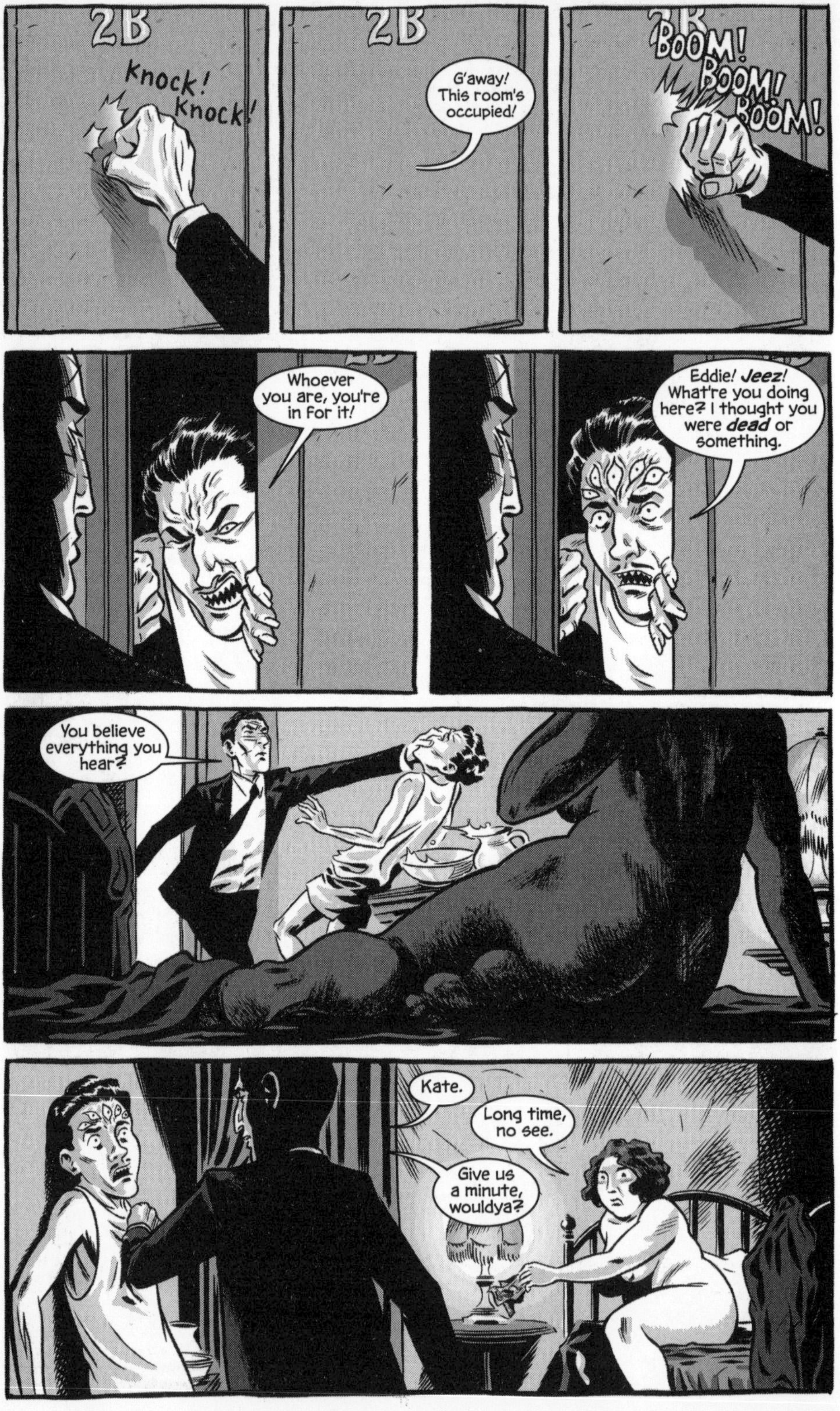
2B
knock! knock!
2B
G'away! This room's occupied!
BOOM! BOOM! BOOM!
Whoever you are, you're in for it!
Eddie! Jeez! What're you doing here? I thought you were dead or something.
You believe everything you hear?
Kate.
Long time, no see.
Give us a minute, wouldya?

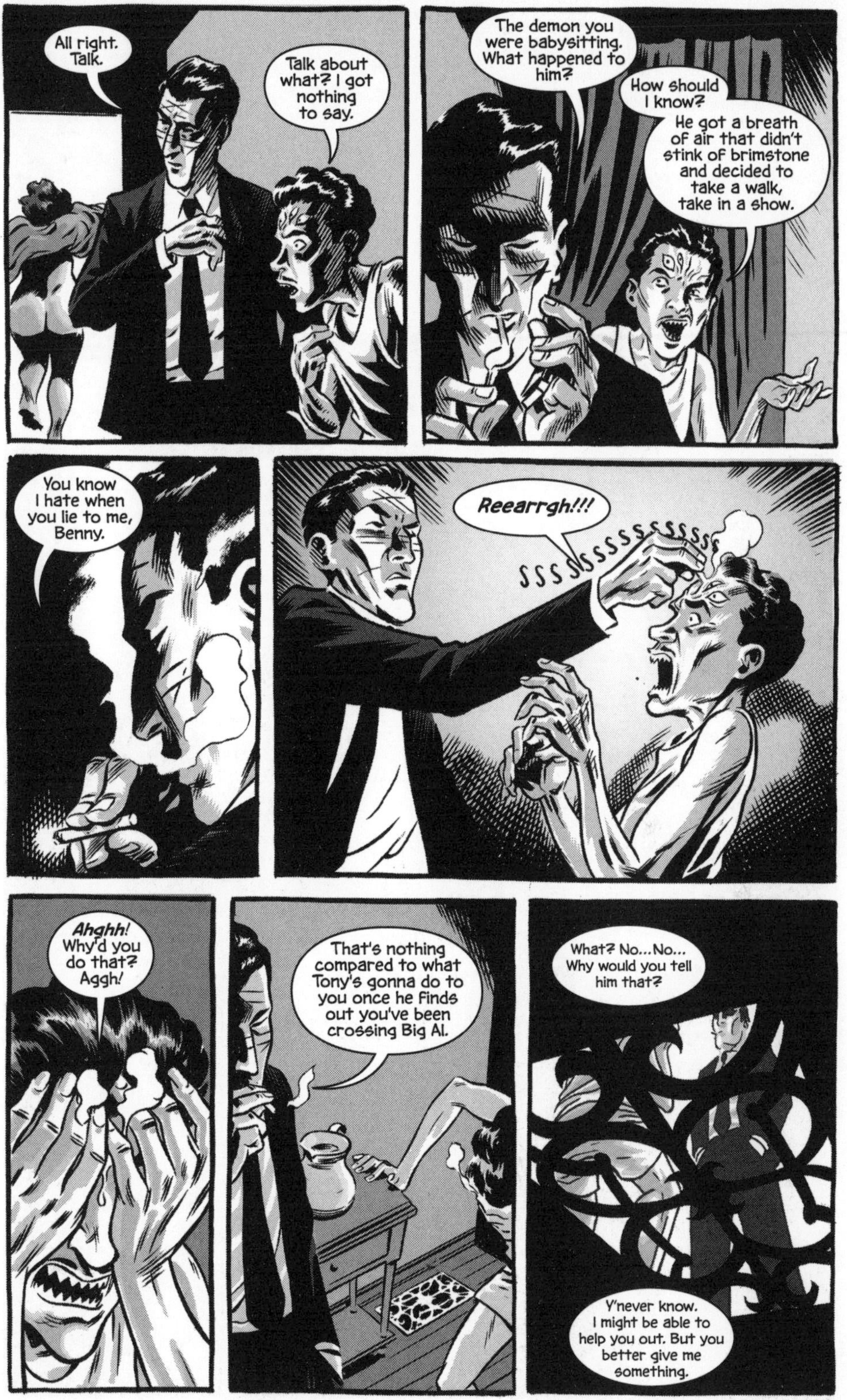
All right. Talk.
Talk about what? I got nothing to say.
The demon you were babysitting. What happened to him?
How should I know?
He got a breath of air that didn't stink of brimstone and decided to take a walk, take in a show.
You know I hate when you lie to me, Benny.
Reearrgh!!!
SSSSSSSSSSSSSS
Ahghh! Why'd you do that? Agghh!
That's nothing compared to what Tony's gonna do to you once he finds out you've been crossing Big Al.
What? No...No... Why would you tell him that?
Y'never know. I might be able to help you out. But you better give me something.

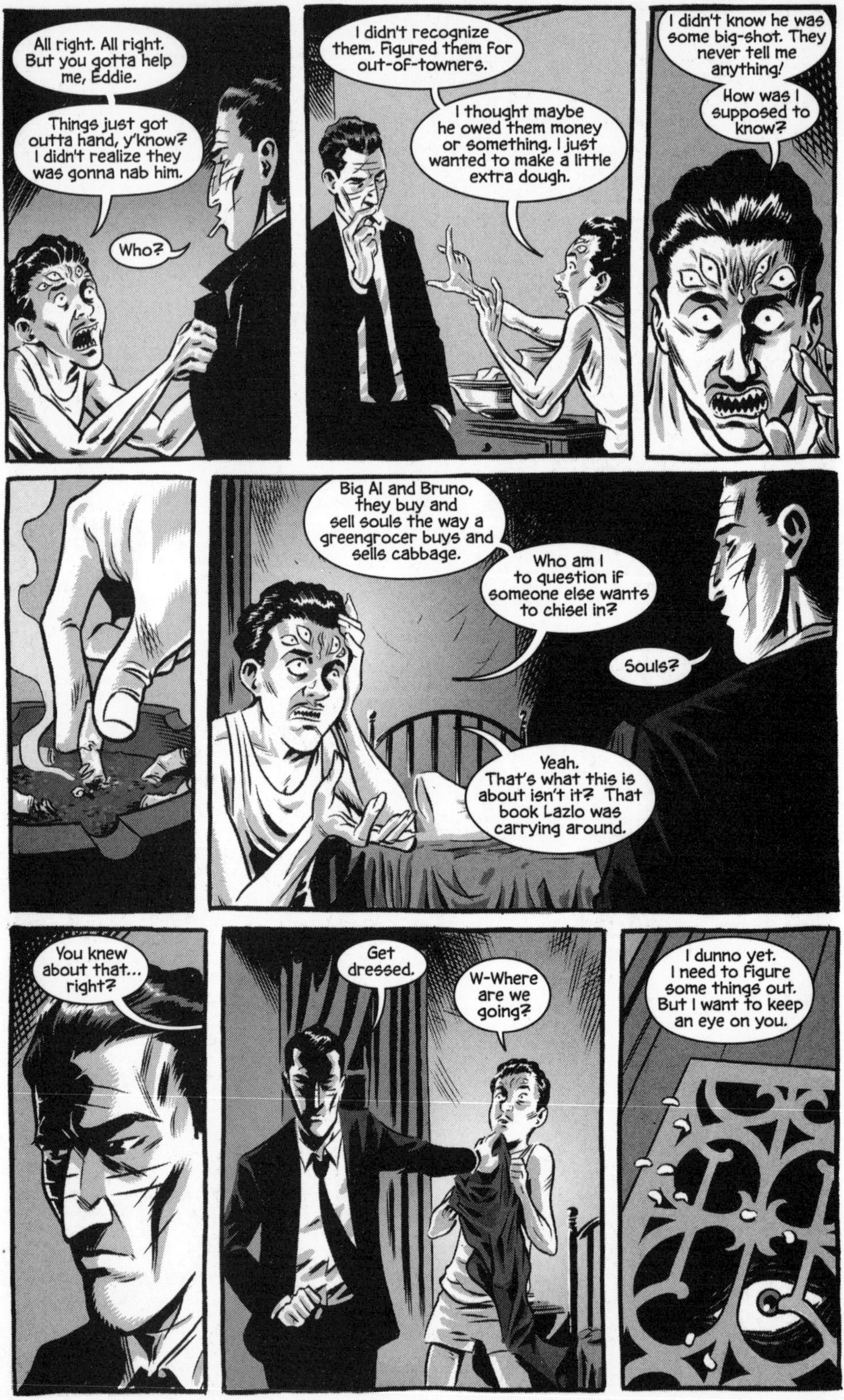

All right. All right. But you gotta help me, Eddie.
Things just got outta hand, y'know? I didn't realize they was gonna nab him.
Who?
I didn't recognize them. Figured them for out-of-towners.
I thought maybe he owed them money or something. I just wanted to make a little extra dough.
I didn't know he was some big-shot. They never tell me anything!
How was I supposed to know?
Big Al and Bruno, they buy and sell souls the way a greengrocer buys and sells cabbage.
Who am I to question if someone else wants to chisel in?
Souls?
Yeah. That's what this is about isn't it? That book Lazlo was carrying around.
You knew about that... right?
Get dressed.
W-Where are we going?
I dunno yet. I need to figure some things out. But I want to keep an eye on you.

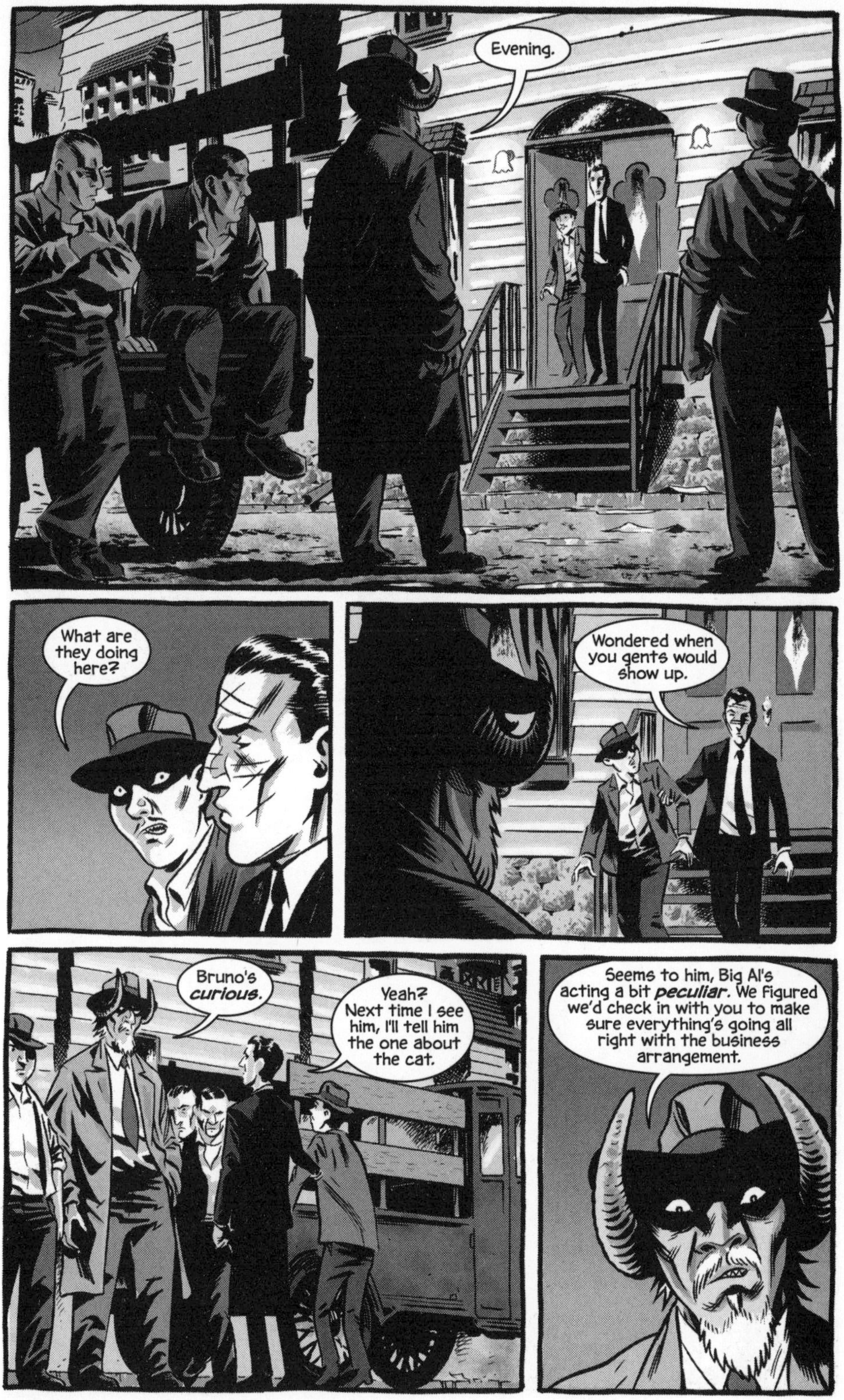
Evening.
What are they doing here?
Wondered when you gents would show up.
Bruno's *curious.*
Yeah? Next time I see him, I'll tell him the one about the cat.
Seems to him, Big Al's acting a bit *peculiar.* We figured we'd check in with you to make sure everything's going all right with the business arrangement.

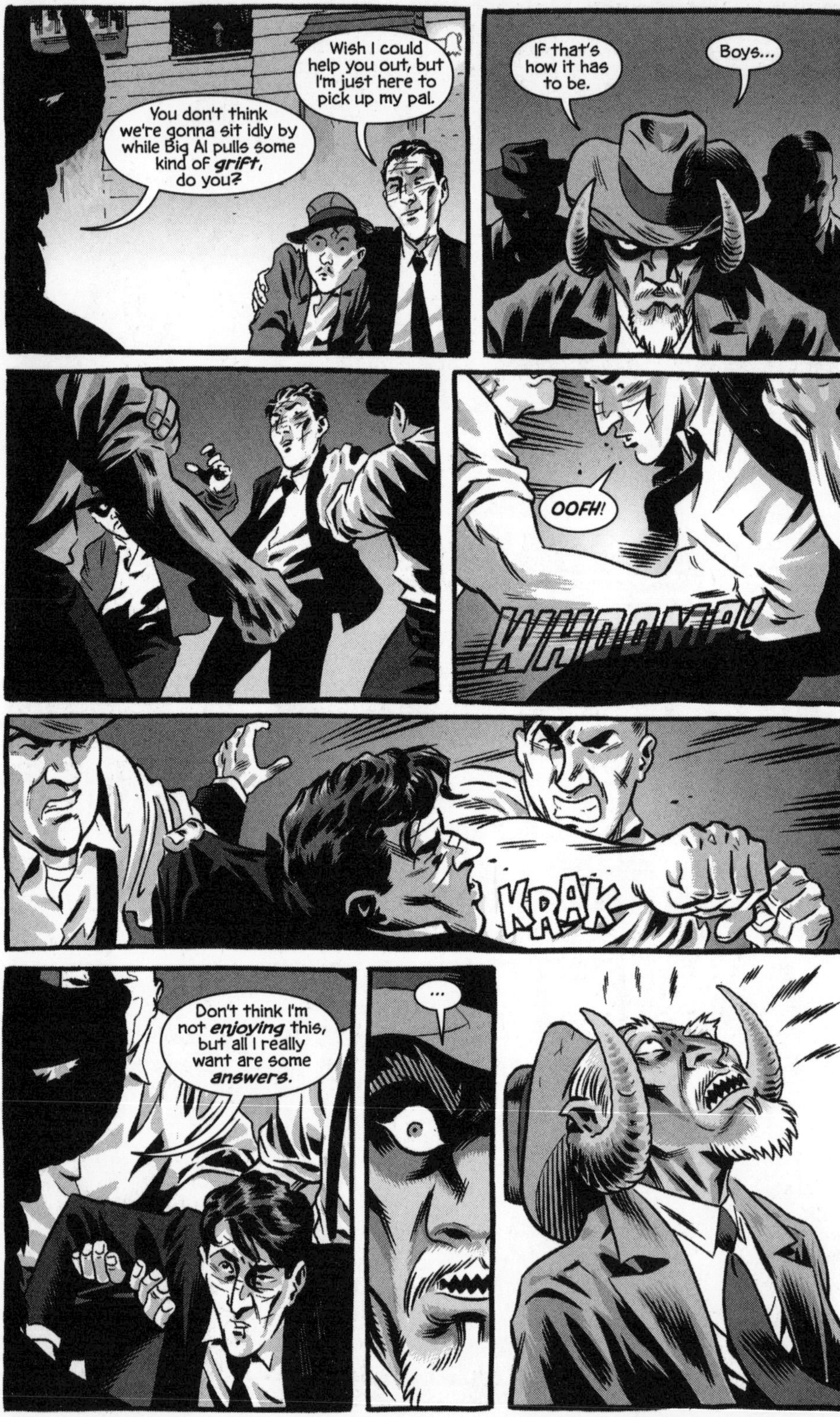
You don't think we're gonna sit idly by while Big Al pulls some kind of *grift*, do you?
Wish I could help you out, but I'm just here to pick up my pal.
If that's how it has to be.
Boys...
OOFH!
KRAK
Don't think I'm not *enjoying* this, but all I really want are some *answers*.
...

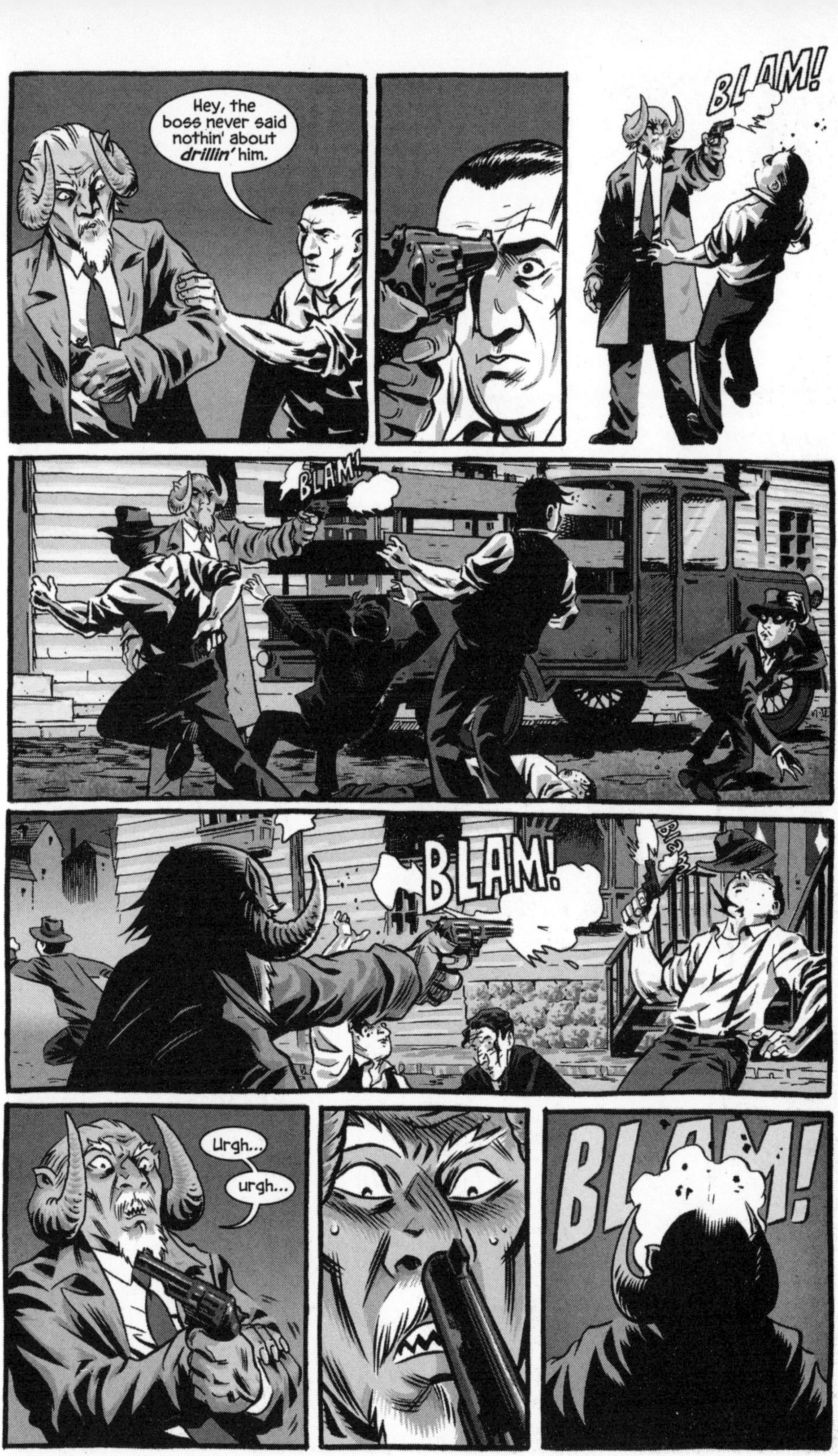
Hey, the boss never said nothin' about *drillin'* him.
BLAM!
BLAM!
BLAM!
BLAM
Urgh...
urgh...
BLAM!

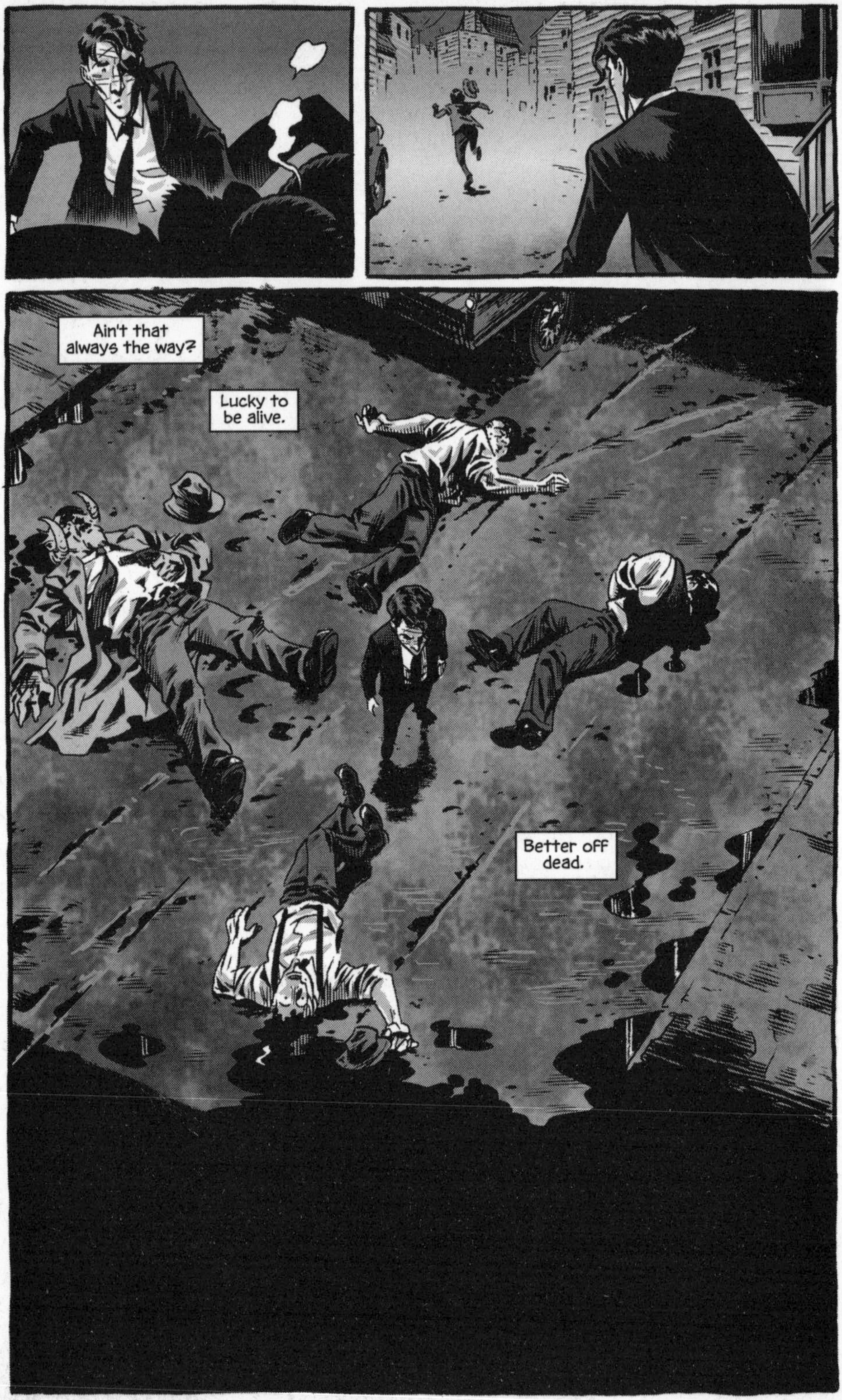
Ain't that always the way?
Lucky to be alive.
Better off dead.

CHAPTER 2

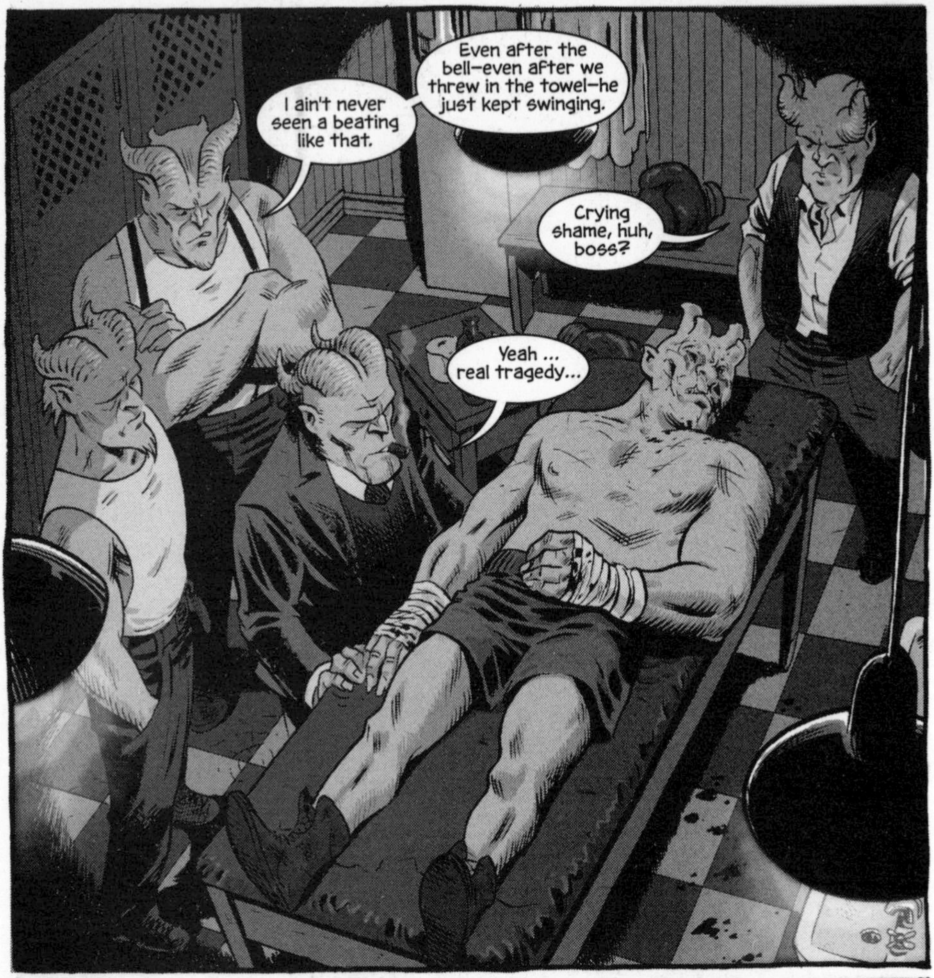
I ain't never seen a beating like that.
Even after the bell—even after we threw in the towel—he just kept swinging.
Crying shame, huh, boss?
Yeah ... real tragedy...

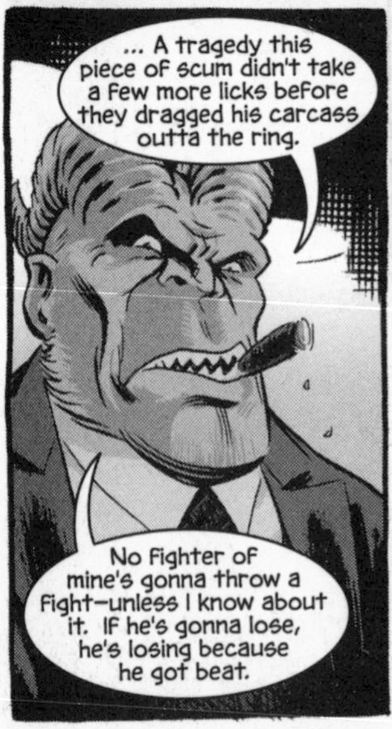
... A tragedy this piece of scum didn't take a few more licks before they dragged his carcass outta the ring.
No fighter of mine's gonna throw a fight—unless I know about it. If he's gonna lose, he's losing because he got beat.

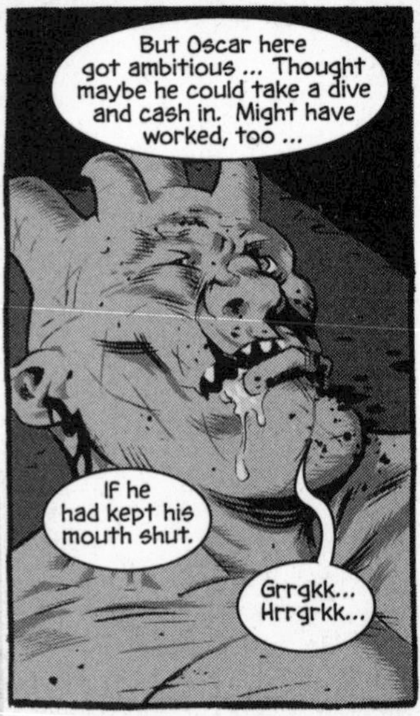
But Oscar here got ambitious ... Thought maybe he could take a dive and cash in. Might have worked, too ...
If he had kept his mouth shut.
Grrgkk... Hrrgrkk...

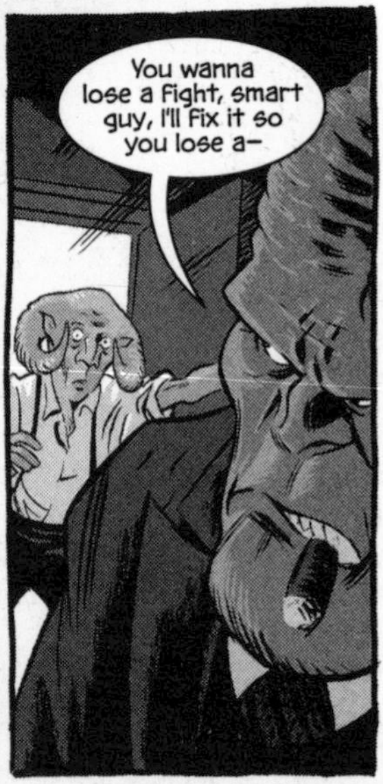
You wanna lose a fight, smart guy, I'll fix it so you lose a—

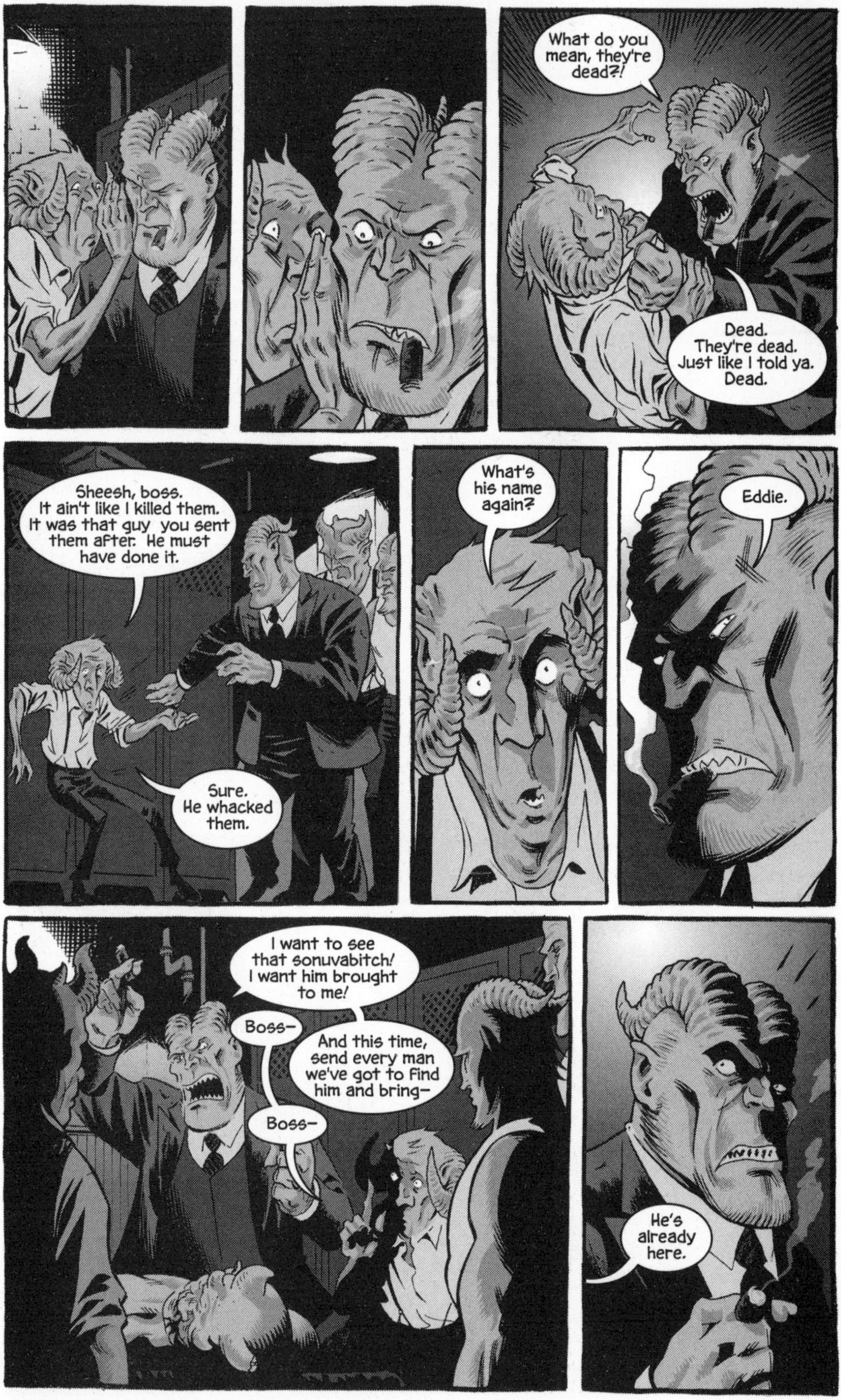
What do you mean, they're dead?!
Dead. They're dead. Just like I told ya. Dead.
Sheesh, boss. It ain't like I killed them. It was that guy you sent them after. He must have done it.
Sure. He whacked them.
What's his name again?
Eddie.
I want to see that sonuvabitch! I want him brought to me!
Boss—
And this time, send every man we've got to find him and bring—
Boss—
He's already here.

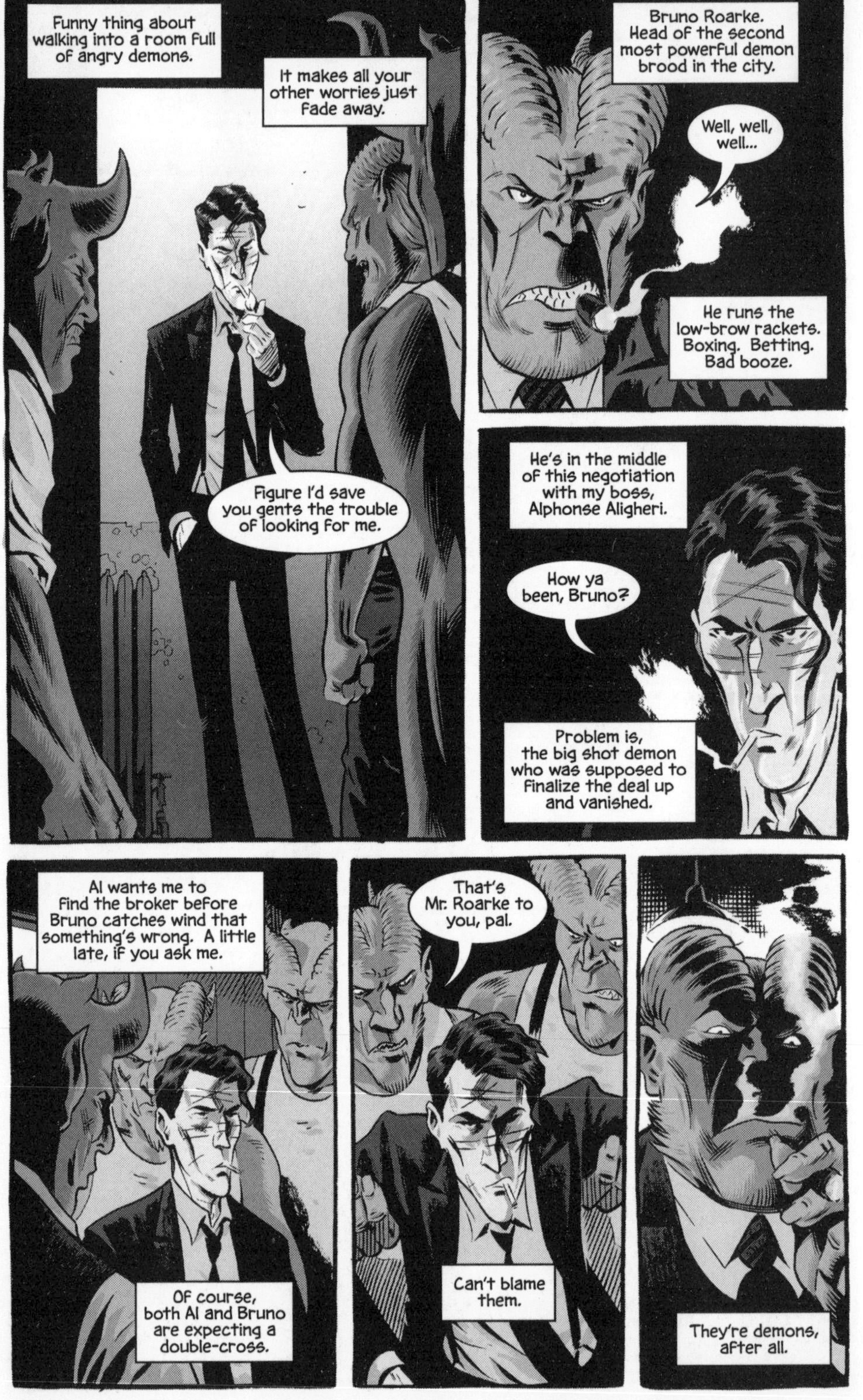
Funny thing about walking into a room full of angry demons.
It makes all your other worries just fade away.
Figure I'd save you gents the trouble of looking for me.
Bruno Roarke. Head of the second most powerful demon brood in the city.
Well, well, well...
He runs the low-brow rackets. Boxing. Betting. Bad booze.
He's in the middle of this negotiation with my boss, Alphonse Aligheri.
How ya been, Bruno?
Problem is, the big shot demon who was supposed to finalize the deal up and vanished.
Al wants me to find the broker before Bruno catches wind that something's wrong. A little late, if you ask me.
Of course, both Al and Bruno are expecting a double-cross.
That's Mr. Roarke to you, pal.
Can't blame them.
They're demons, after all.

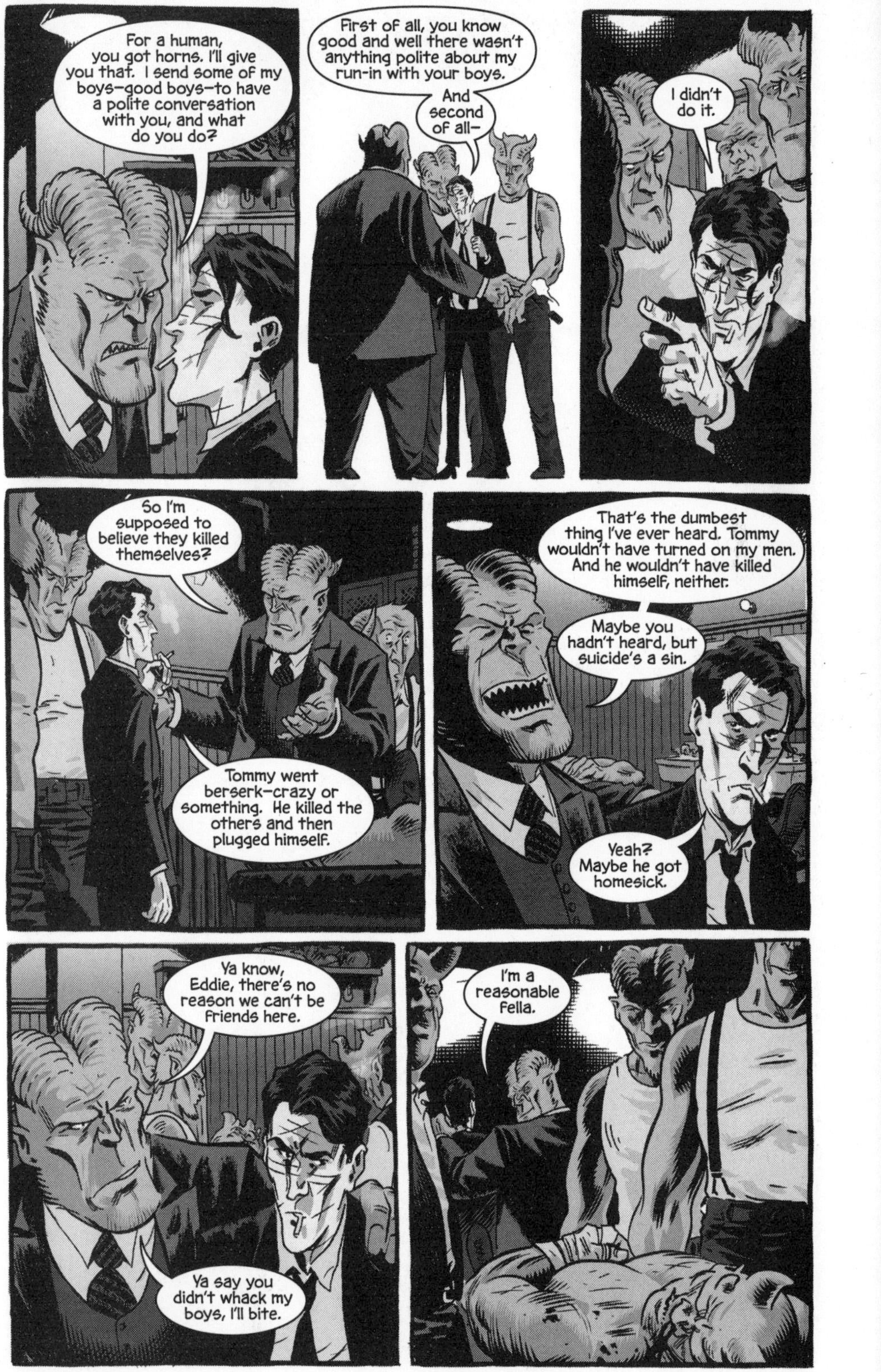
For a human, you got horns. I'll give you that. I send some of my boys—good boys—to have a polite conversation with you, and what do you do?
First of all, you know good and well there wasn't anything polite about my run-in with your boys.
And second of all–
I didn't do it.
So I'm supposed to believe they killed themselves?
Tommy went berserk–crazy or something. He killed the others and then plugged himself.
That's the dumbest thing I've ever heard. Tommy wouldn't have turned on my men. And he wouldn't have killed himself, neither.
Maybe you hadn't heard, but suicide's a sin.
Yeah? Maybe he got homesick.
Ya know, Eddie, there's no reason we can't be friends here.
Ya say you didn't whack my boys, I'll bite.
I'm a reasonable fella.

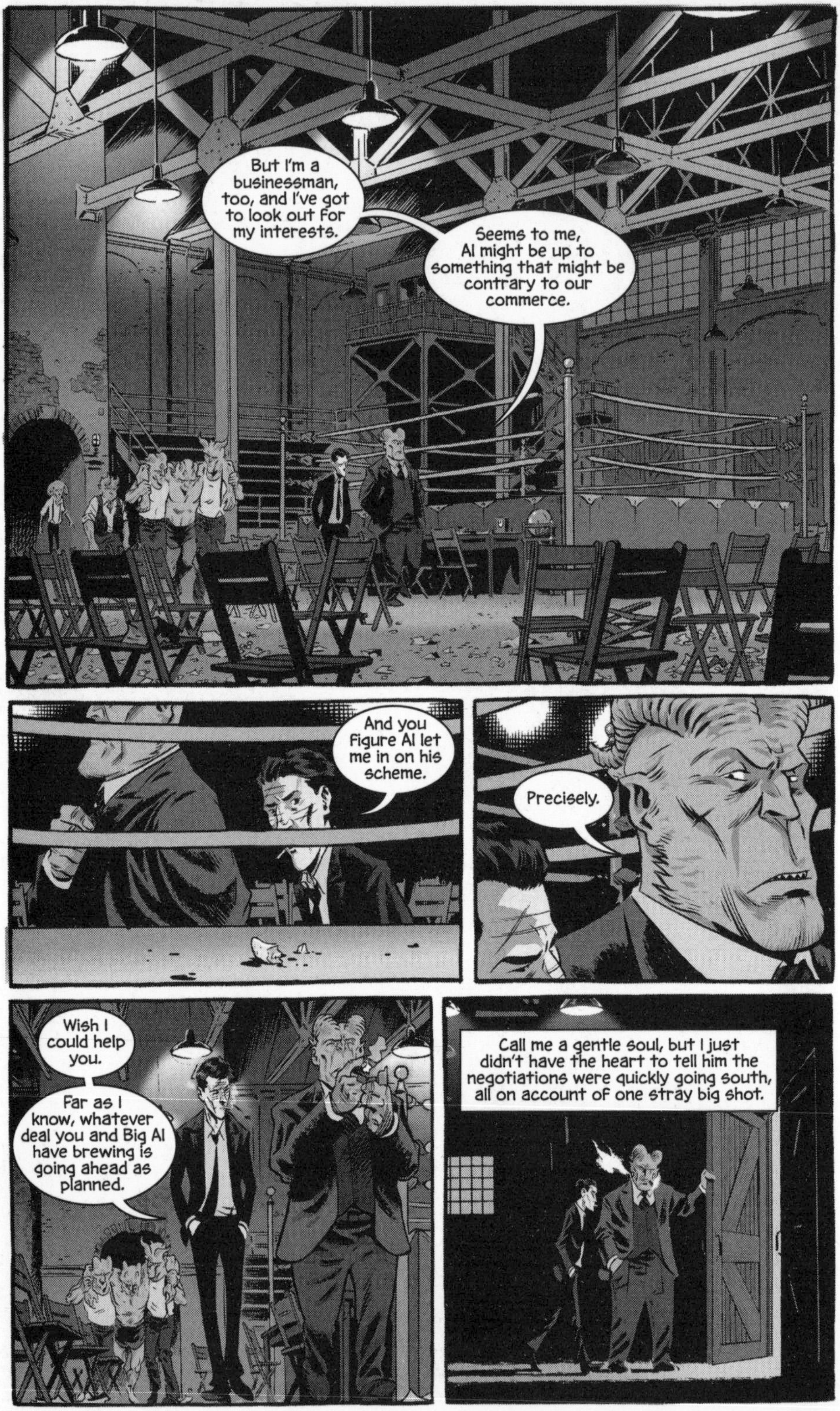
But I'm a businessman, too, and I've got to look out for my interests.
Seems to me, Al might be up to something that might be contrary to our commerce.
And you figure Al let me in on his scheme.
Precisely.
Wish I could help you.
Far as I know, whatever deal you and Big Al have brewing is going ahead as planned.
Call me a gentle soul, but I just didn't have the heart to tell him the negotiations were quickly going south, all on account of one stray big shot.

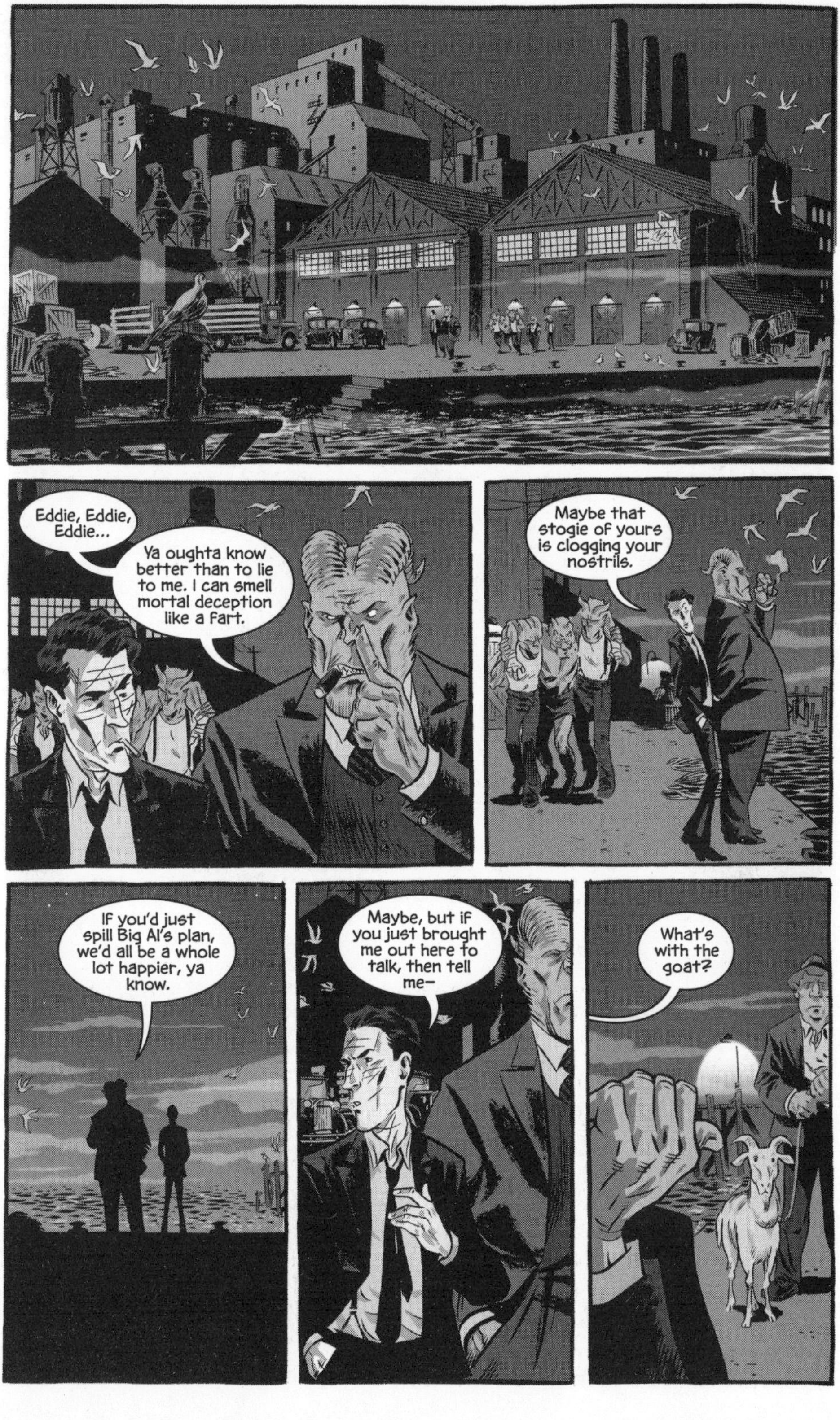
Eddie, Eddie, Eddie...
Ya oughta know better than to lie to me. I can smell mortal deception like a fart.
Maybe that stogie of yours is clogging your nostrils.
If you'd just spill Big Al's plan, we'd all be a whole lot happier, ya know.
Maybe, but if you just brought me out here to talk, then tell me–
What's with the goat?

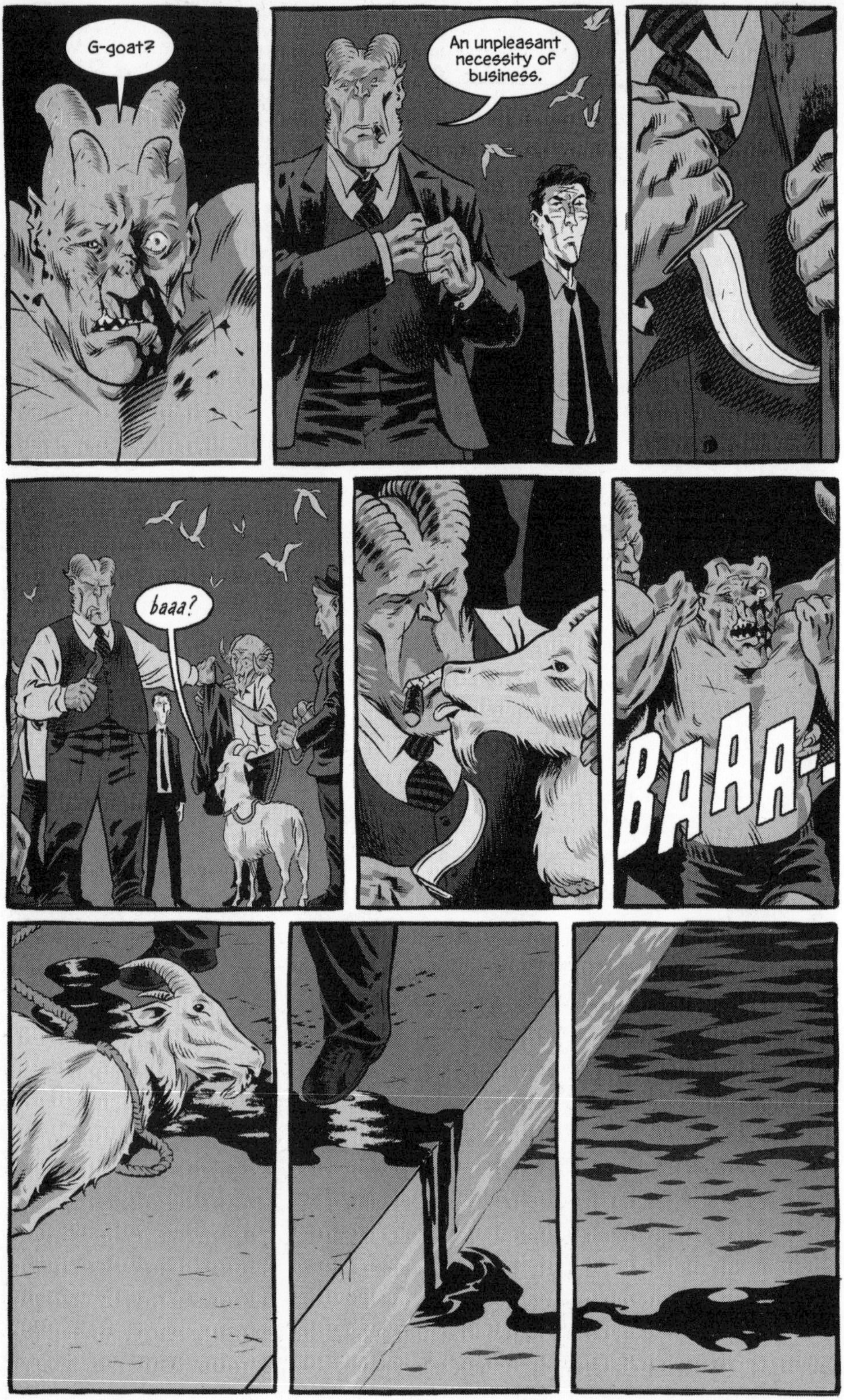

G-goat?
An unpleasant necessity of business.
baaa?
BAAA-

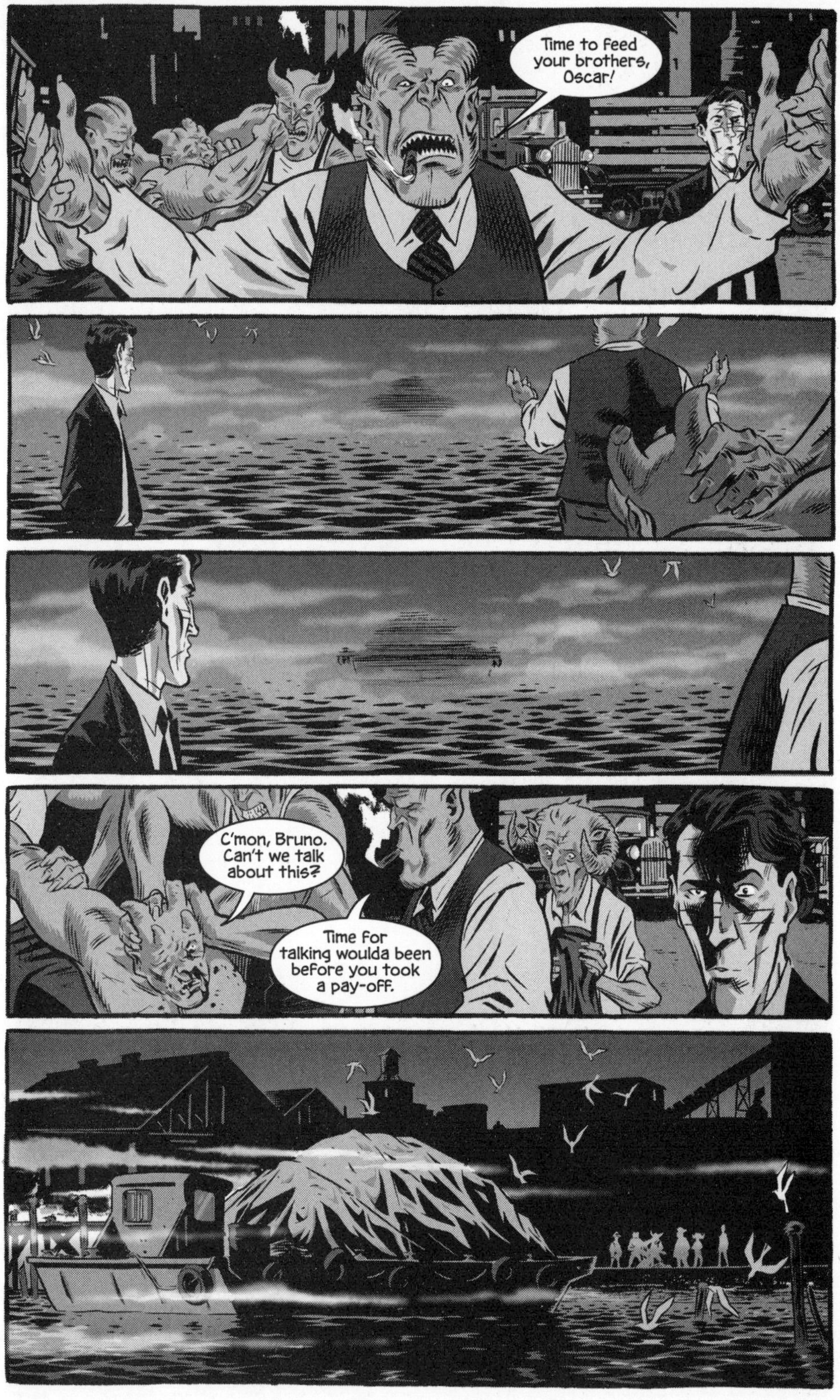
Time to feed your brothers, Oscar!
C'mon, Bruno. Can't we talk about this?
Time for talking woulda been before you took a pay-off.

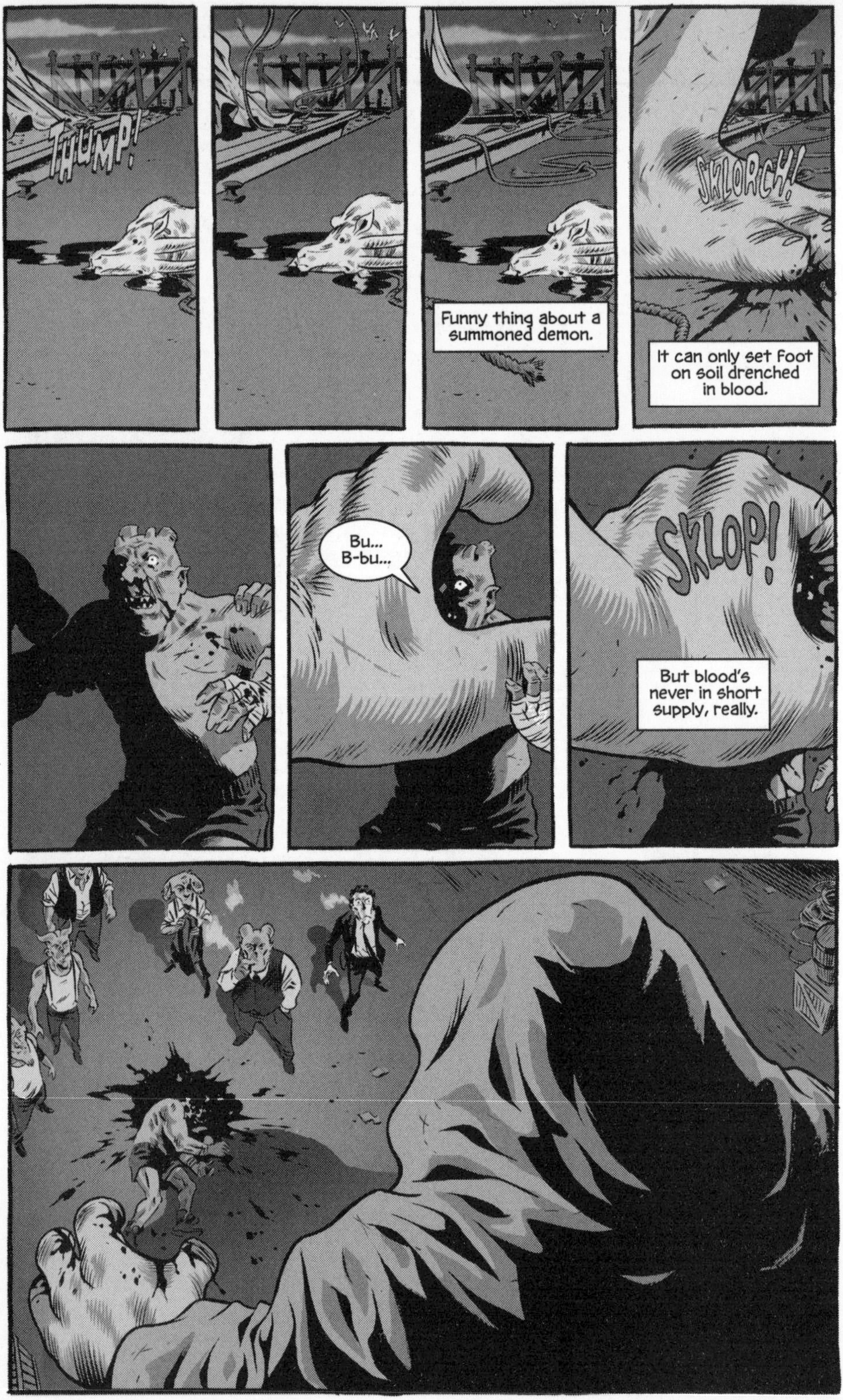
THUMP!
Funny thing about a summoned demon.
SKLORCH!
It can only set foot on soil drenched in blood.
Bu... B-bu...
SKLOP!
But blood's never in short supply, really.

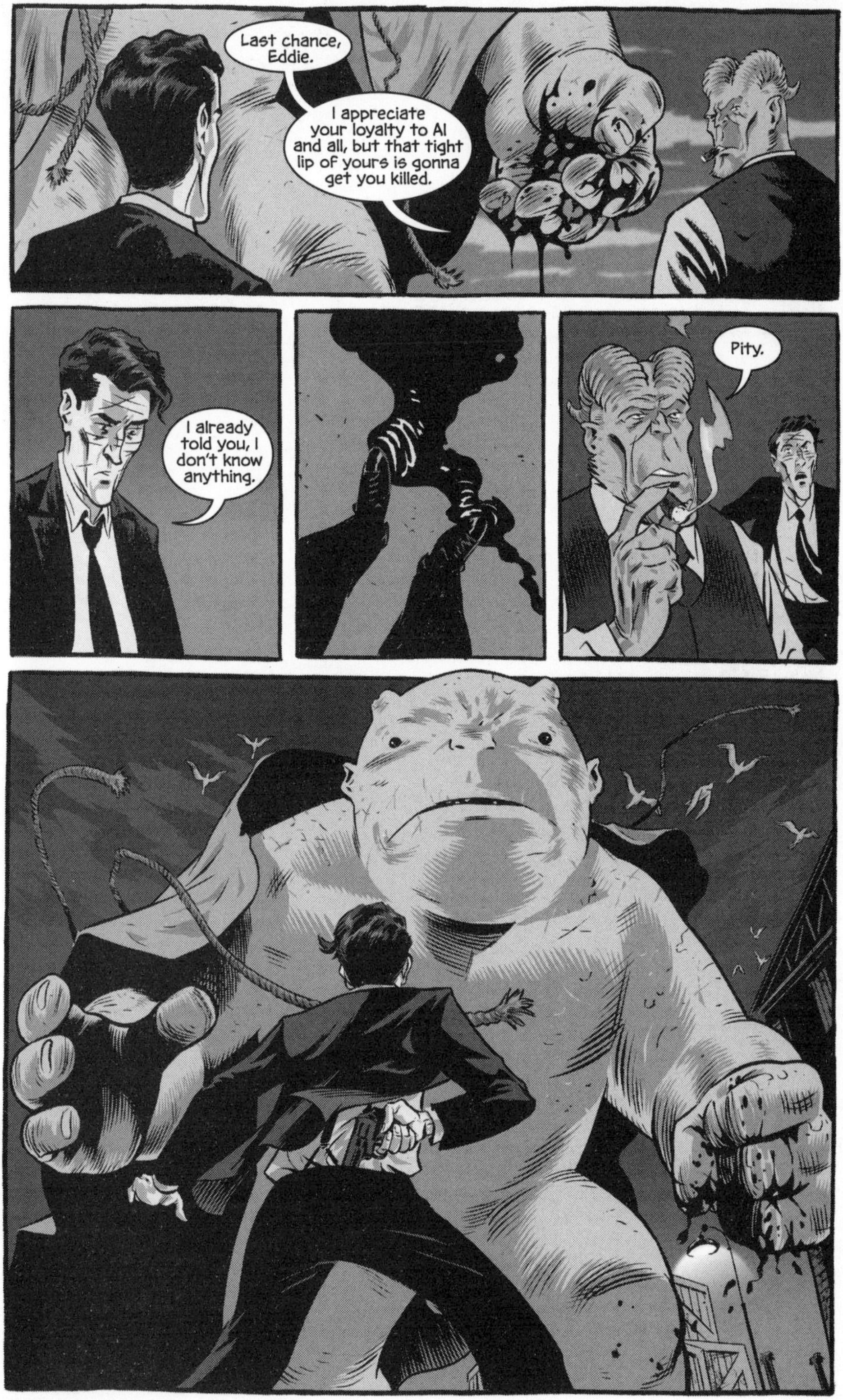
Last chance, Eddie.
I appreciate your loyalty to Al and all, but that tight lip of yours is gonna get you killed.
I already told you, I don't know anything.
Pity.

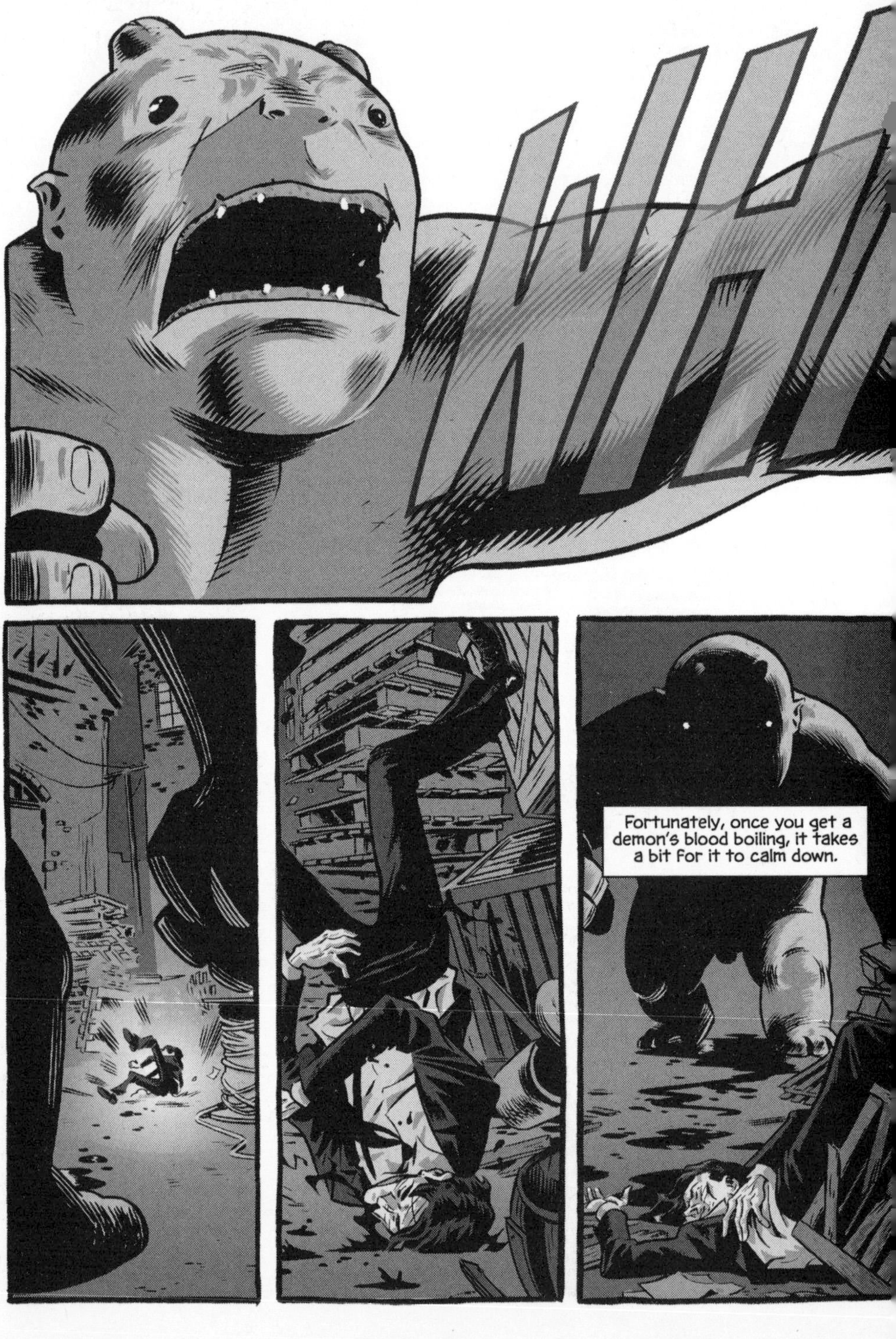

WHA
Fortunately, once you get a demon's blood boiling, it takes a bit for it to calm down.

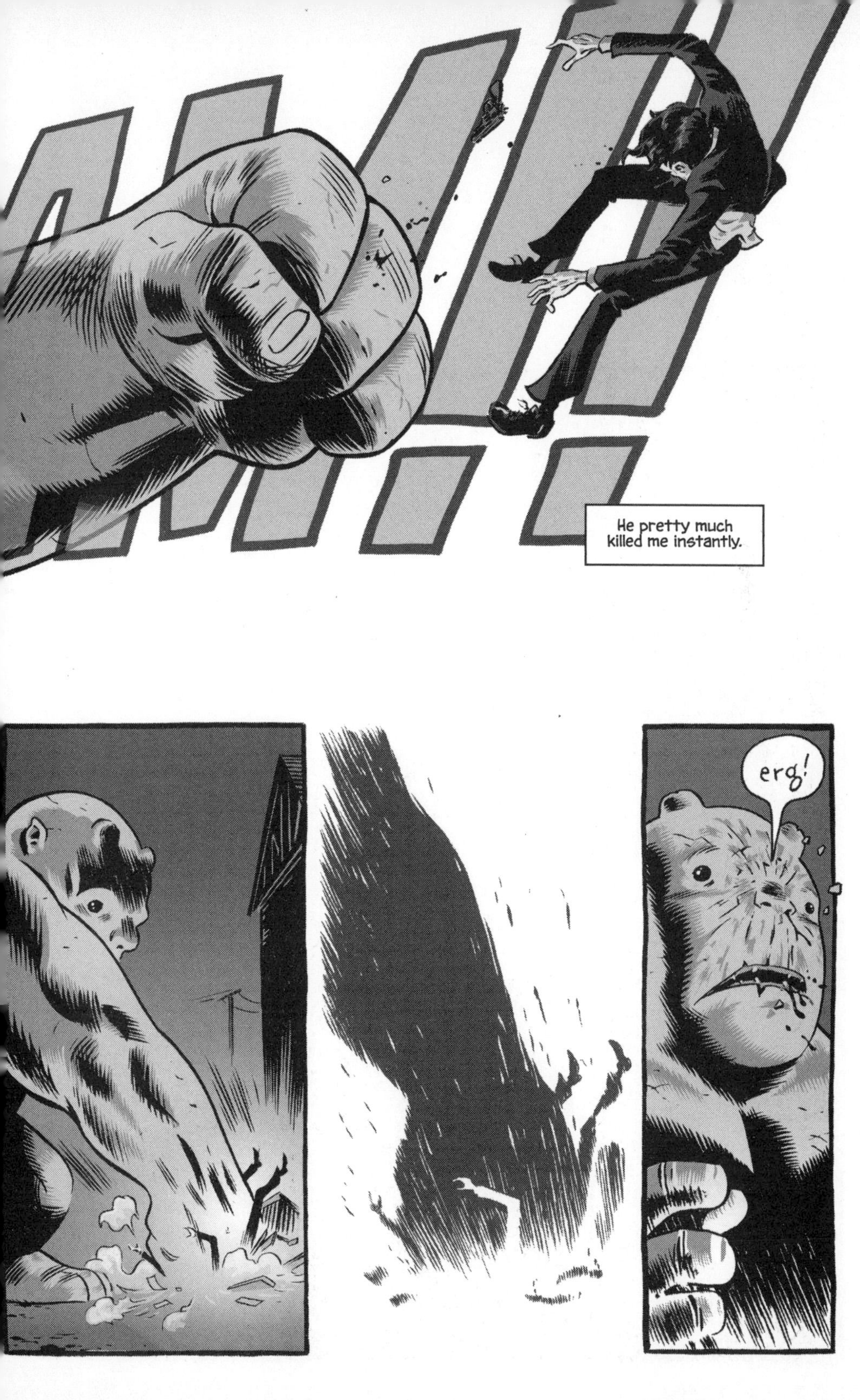
He pretty much killed me instantly.
erg!

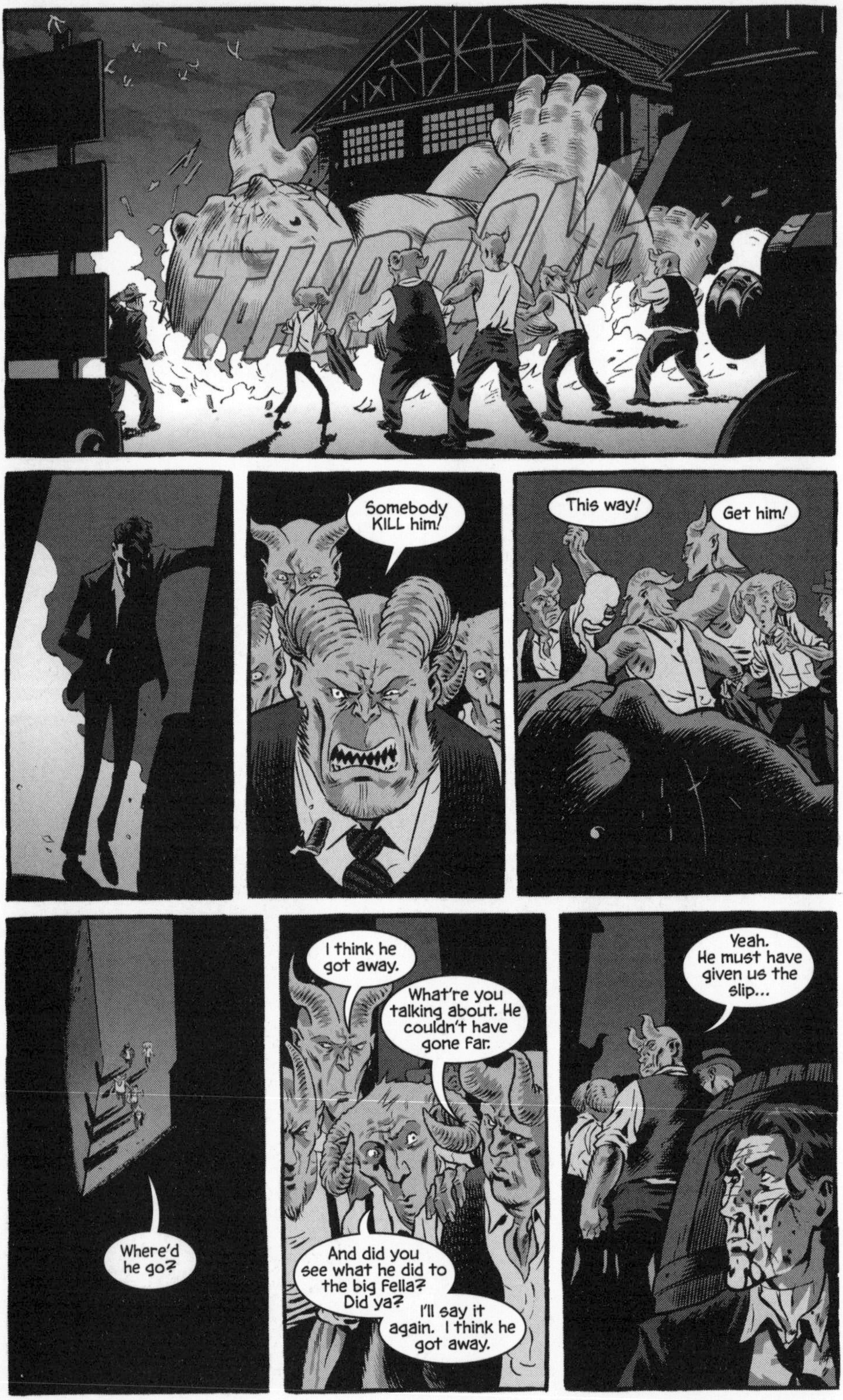
THOOOM!
Somebody KILL him!
This way!
Get him!
Where'd he go?
I think he got away.
What're you talking about. He couldn't have gone far.
And did you see what he did to the big Fella? Did ya?
I'll say it again. I think he got away.
Yeah. He must have given us the slip...

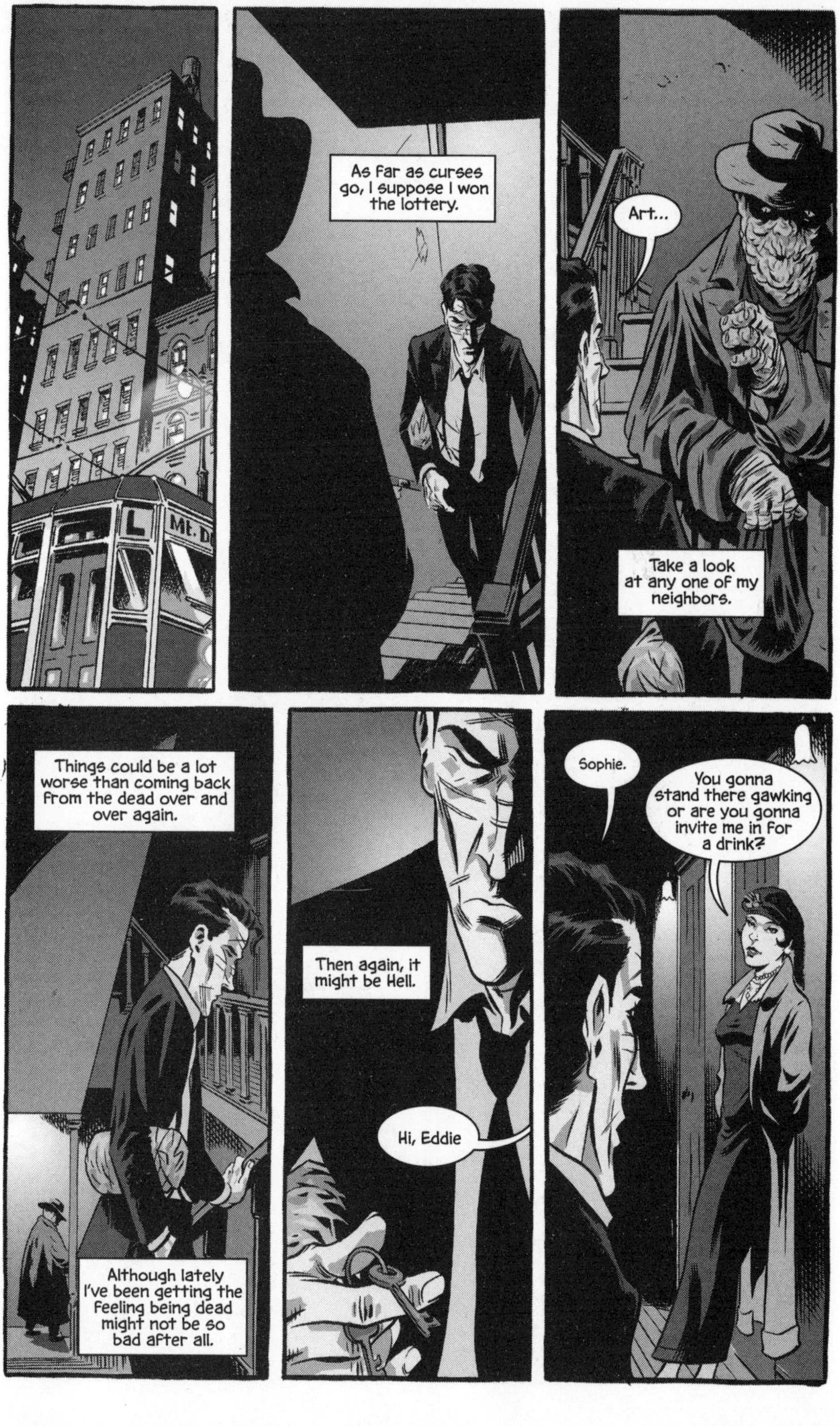
Mt. D
As far as curses go, I suppose I won the lottery.
Art...
Take a look at any one of my neighbors.
Things could be a lot worse than coming back from the dead over and over again.
Although lately I've been getting the feeling being dead might not be so bad after all.
Then again, it might be Hell.
Hi, Eddie
Sophie.
You gonna stand there gawking or are you gonna invite me in for a drink?

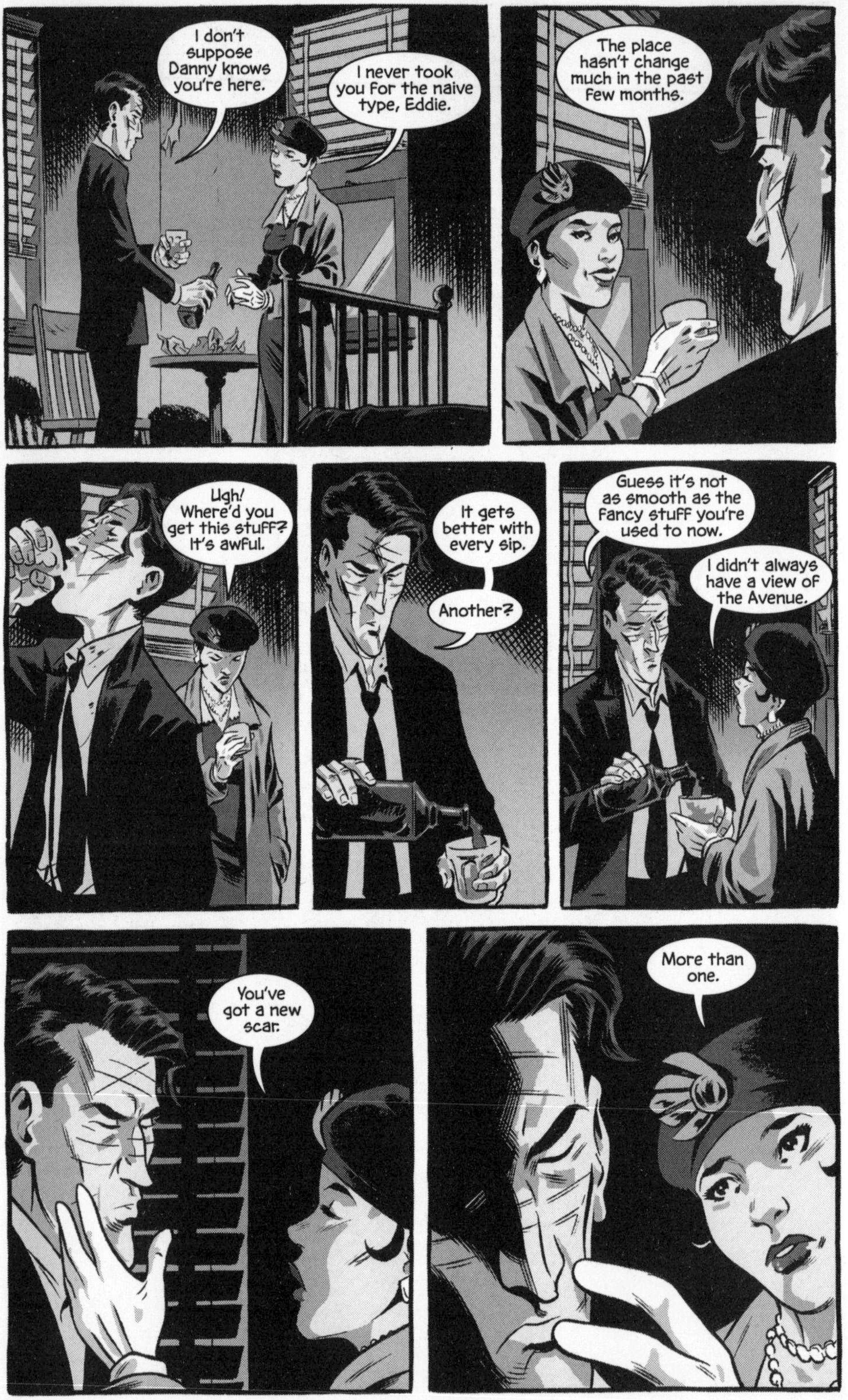
I don't suppose Danny knows you're here.
I never took you for the naive type, Eddie.
The place hasn't change much in the past few months.
Ugh! Where'd you get this stuff? It's awful.
It gets better with every sip.
Another?
Guess it's not as smooth as the fancy stuff you're used to now.
I didn't always have a view of the Avenue.
You've got a new scar.
More than one.

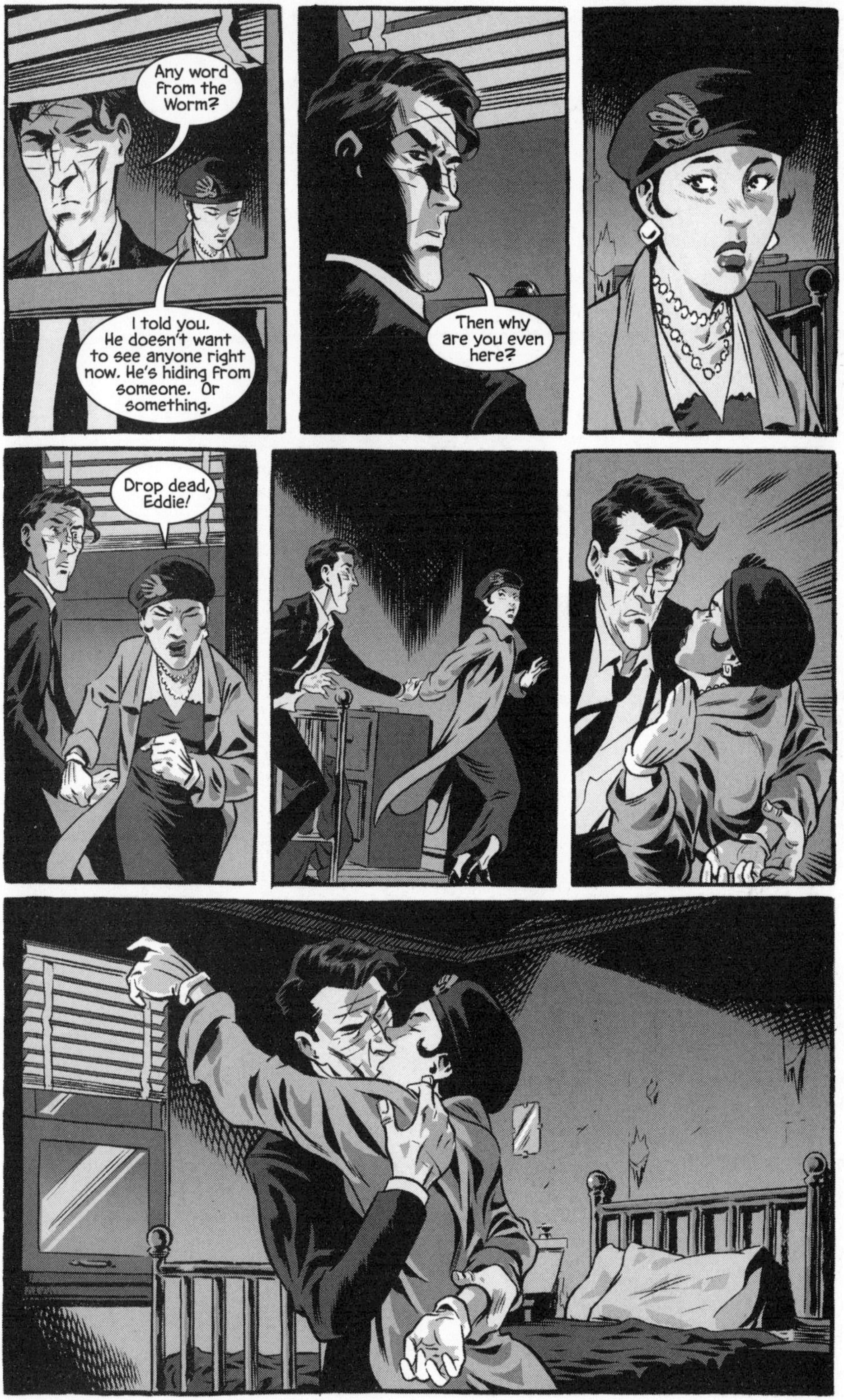
Any word from the Worm?
I told you. He doesn't want to see anyone right now. He's hiding from someone. Or something.
Then why are you even here?
Drop dead, Eddie!

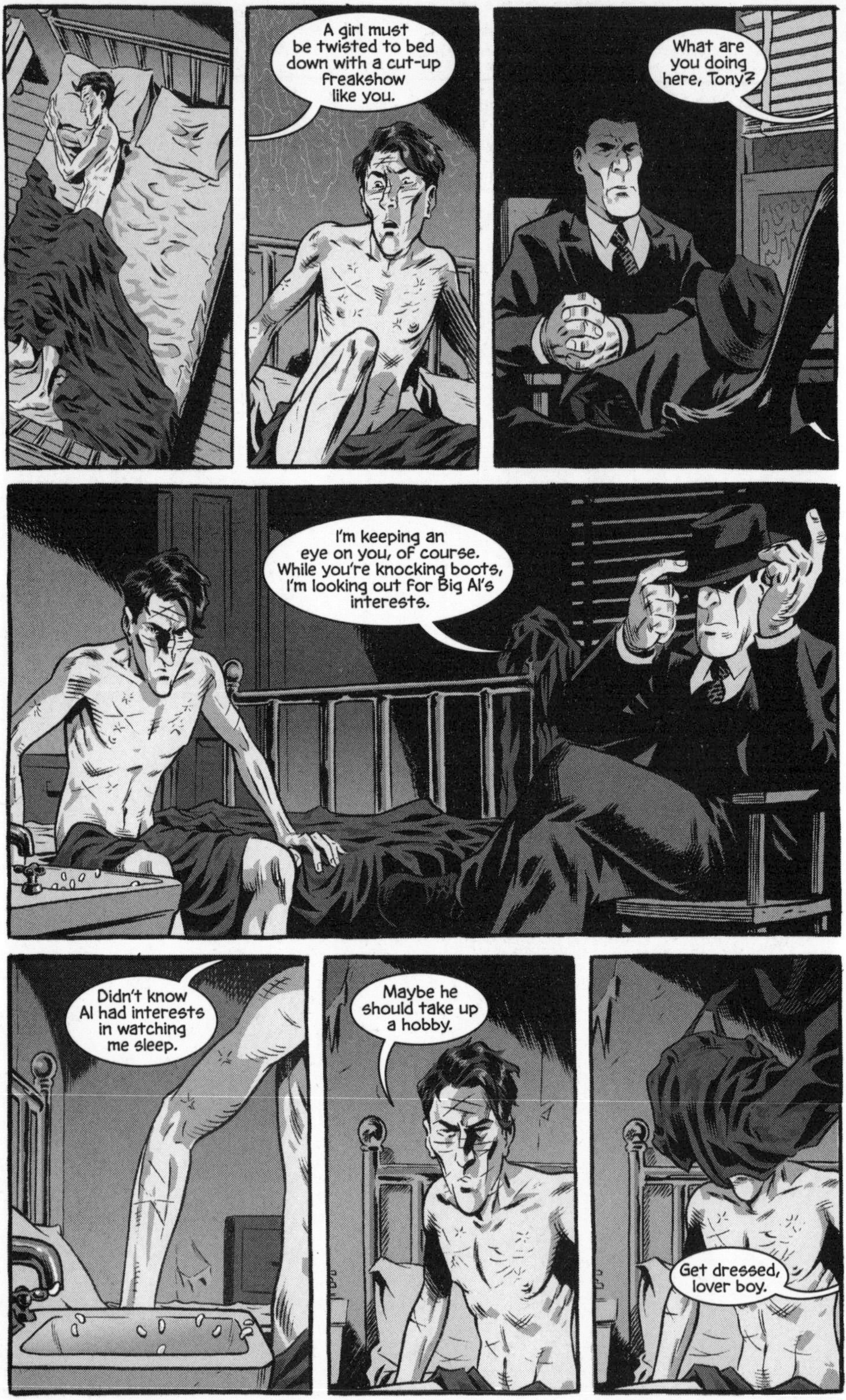
A girl must be twisted to bed down with a cut-up freakshow like you.
What are you doing here, Tony?
I'm keeping an eye on you, of course. While you're knocking boots, I'm looking out for Big Al's interests.
Didn't know Al had interests in watching me sleep.
Maybe he should take up a hobby.
Get dressed, lover boy.

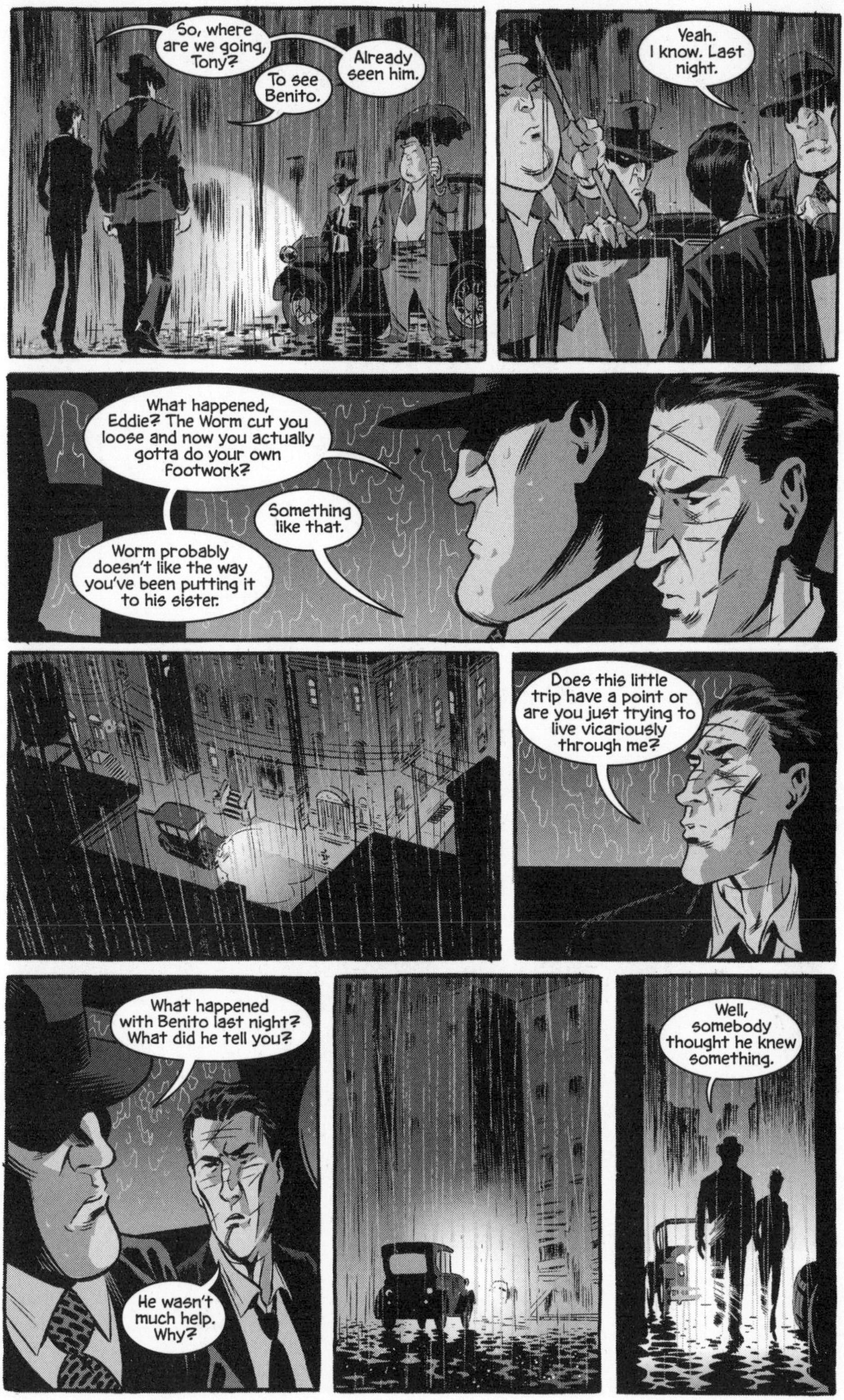
So, where are we going, Tony?
To see Benito.
Already seen him.
Yeah. I know. Last night.
What happened, Eddie? The Worm cut you loose and now you actually gotta do your own footwork?
Worm probably doesn't like the way you've been putting it to his sister.
Something like that.
Does this little trip have a point or are you just trying to live vicariously through me?
What happened with Benito last night? What did he tell you?
He wasn't much help. Why?
Well, somebody thought he knew something.

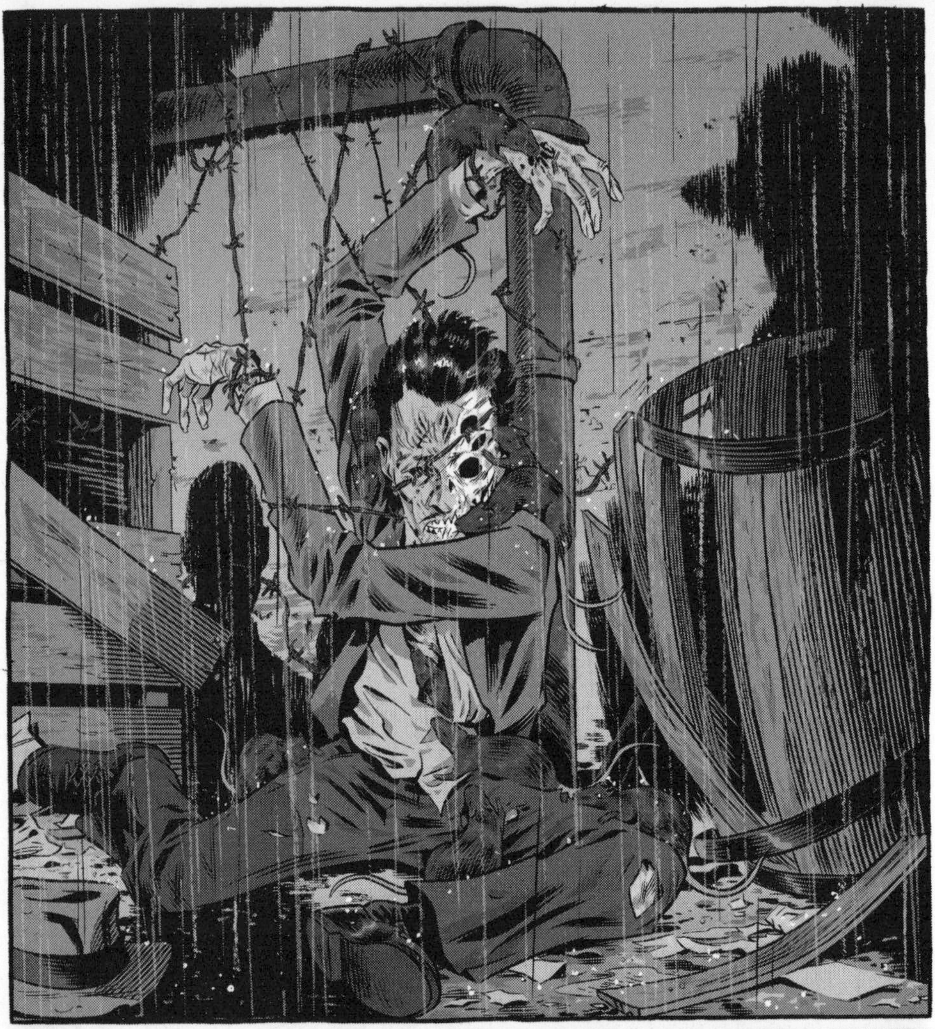
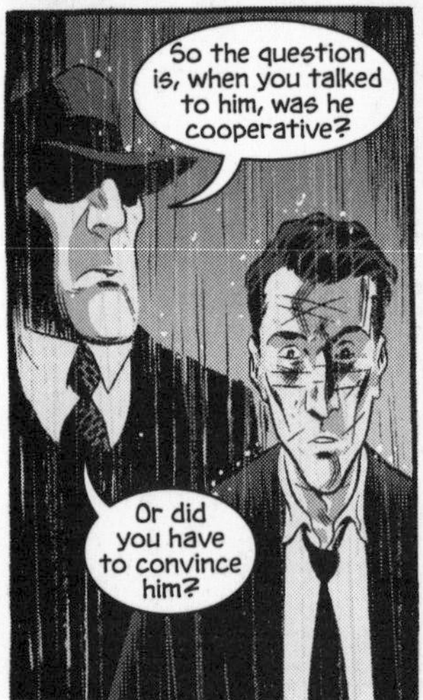
So the question is, when you talked to him, was he cooperative?
Or did you have to convince him?
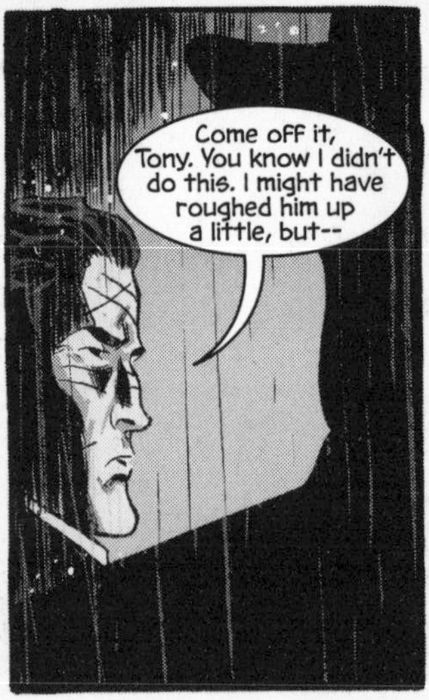
Come off it, Tony. You know I didn't do this. I might have roughed him up a little, but--
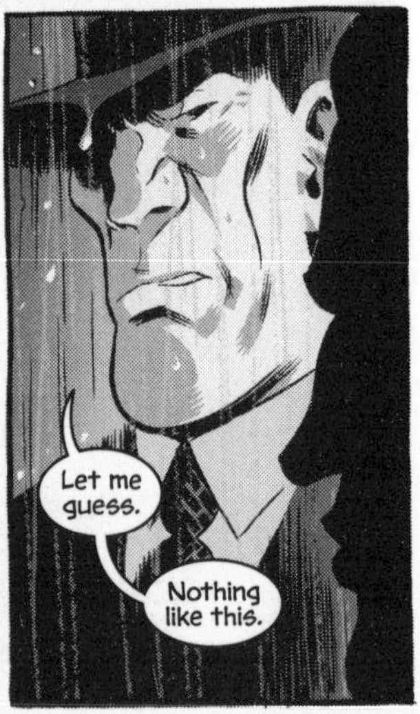
Let me guess.
Nothing like this.

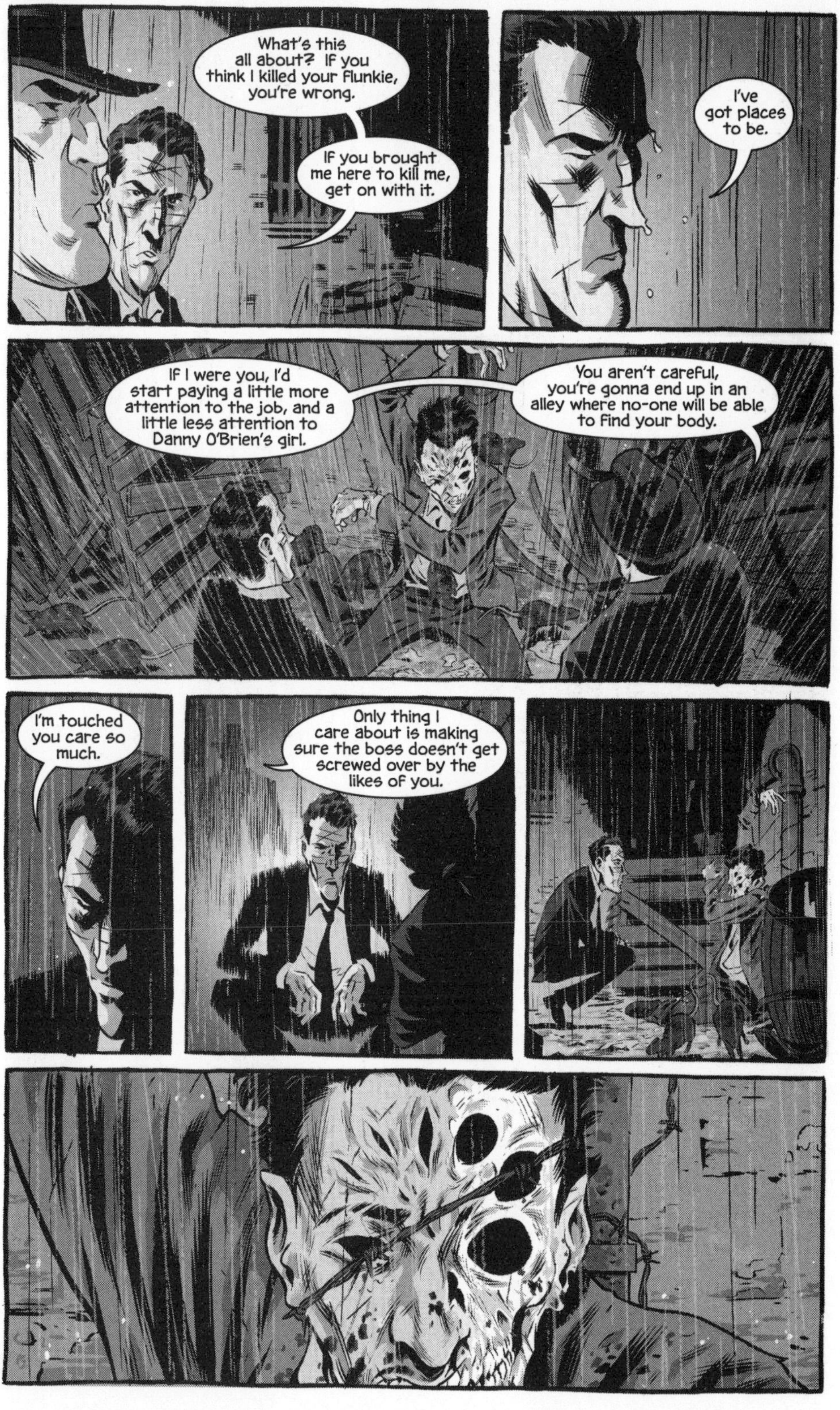
What's this all about? If you think I killed your Flunkie, you're wrong.
If you brought me here to kill me, get on with it.
I've got places to be.
If I were you, I'd start paying a little more attention to the job, and a little less attention to Danny O'Brien's girl.
You aren't careful, you're gonna end up in an alley where no-one will be able to find your body.
I'm touched you care so much.
Only thing I care about is making sure the boss doesn't get screwed over by the likes of you.

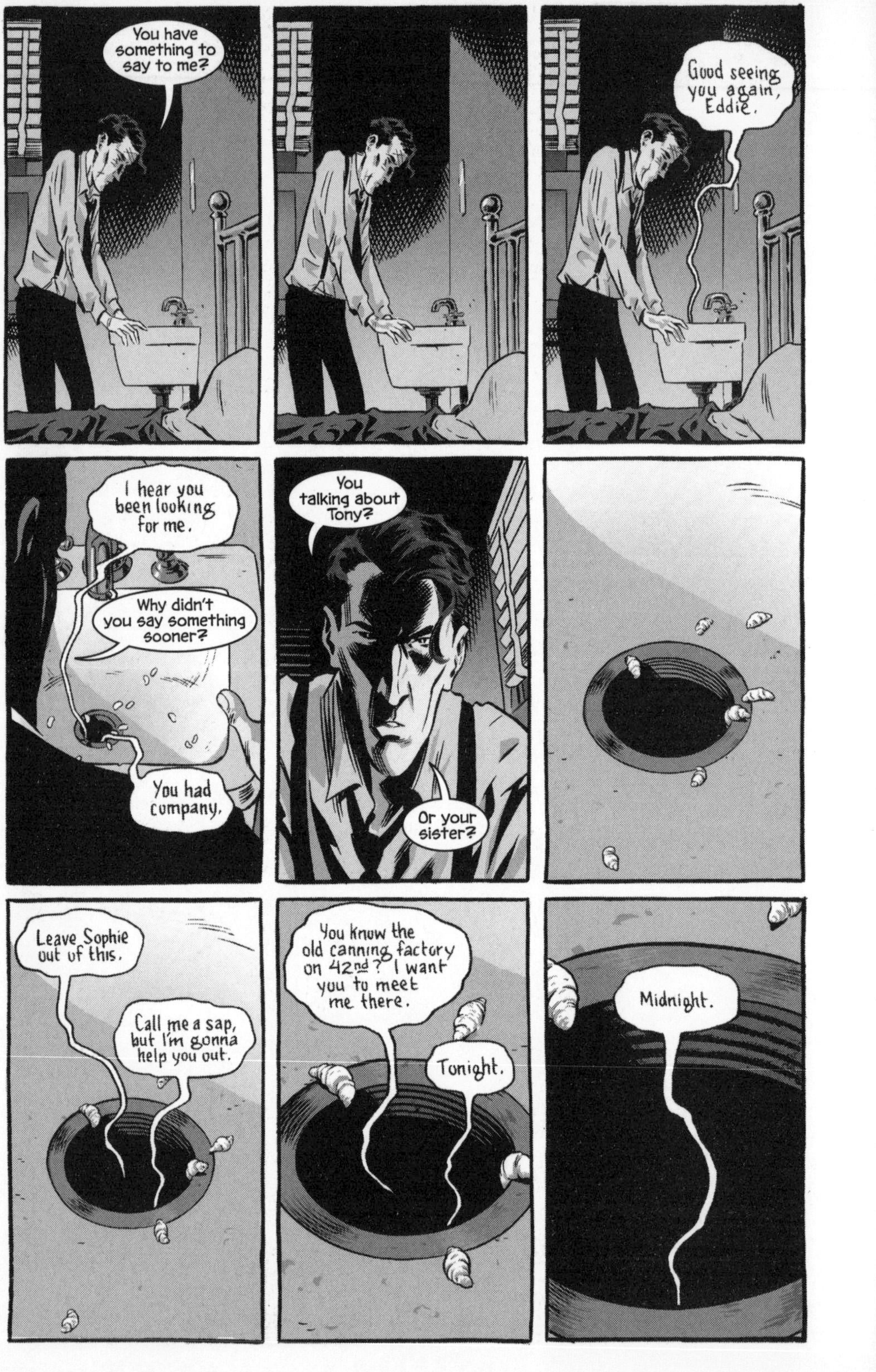
You have something to say to me?
Good seeing you again, Eddie.
I hear you been looking for me.
Why didn't you say something sooner?
You had company.
You talking about Tony?
Or your sister?
Leave Sophie out of this.
Call me a sap, but I'm gonna help you out.
You know the old canning factory on 42nd? I want you to meet me there.
Tonight.
Midnight.

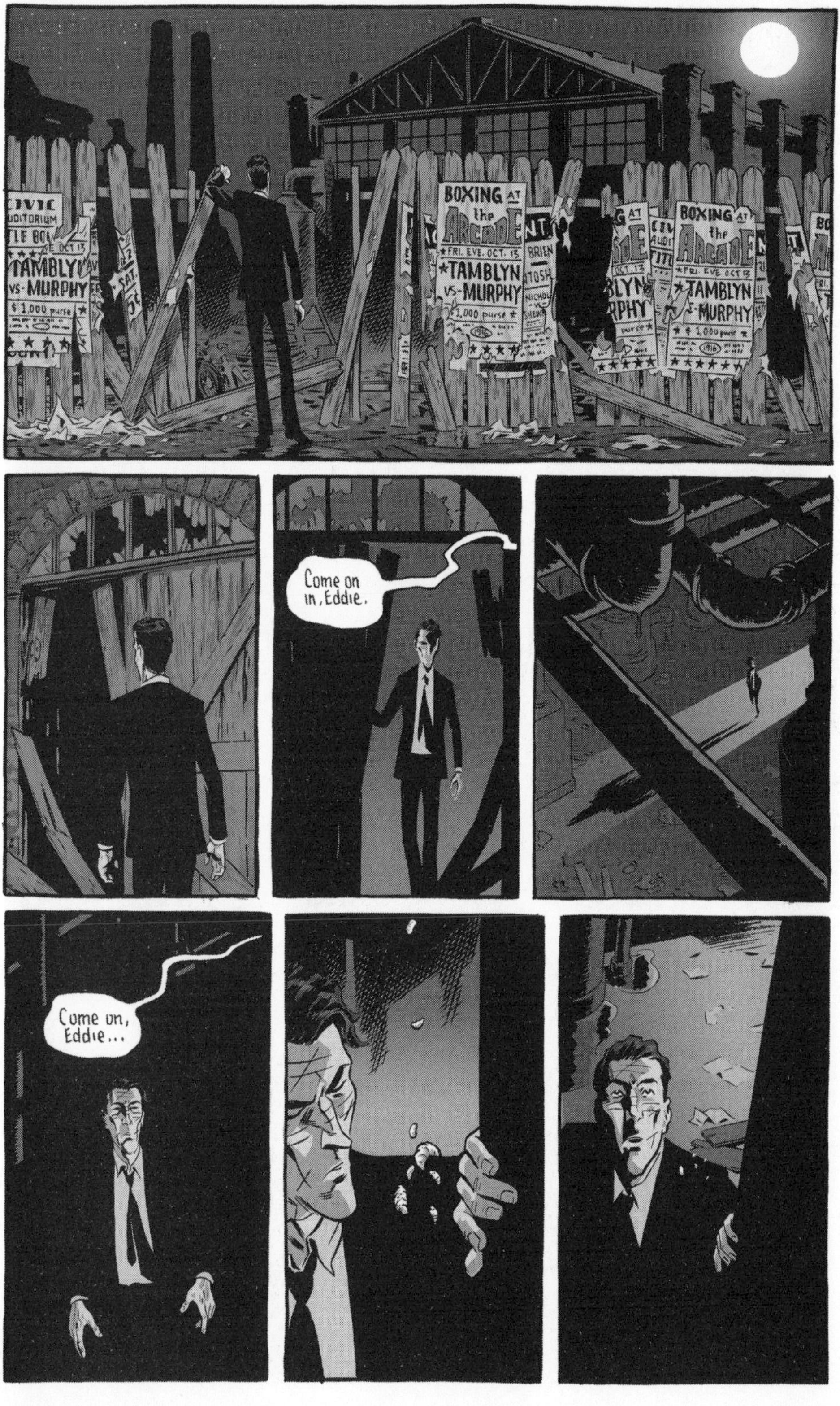
CIVIC
AUDITORIUM
TAMBLYN
vs-MURPHY
$1,000 purse
BOXING AT the ARCADE
FRI. EVE. OCT. 13
TAMBLYN
vs-MURPHY
1,000 purse
BOXING AT the ARCADE
FRI. EVE. OCT. 13
TAMBLYN
-MURPHY
$1,000 purse
Come on in, Eddie.
Come on, Eddie...

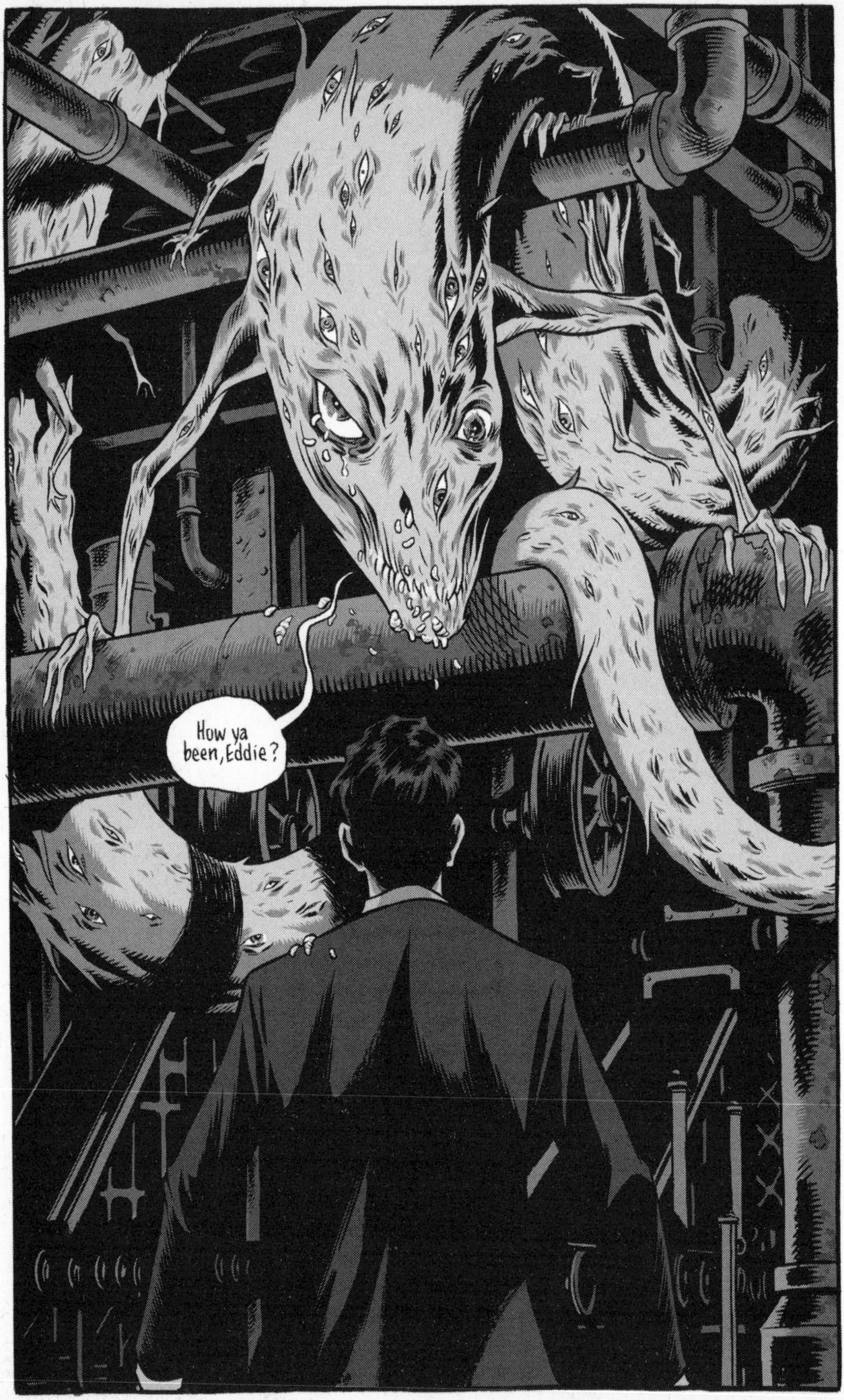
How ya been, Eddie?

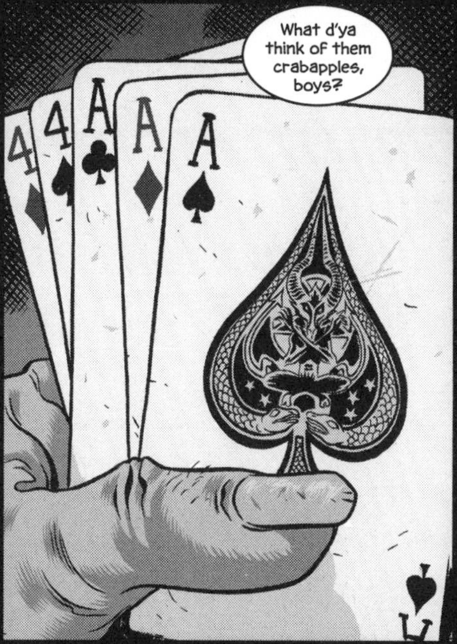
What d'ya think of them crabapples, boys?

CHAPTER 3

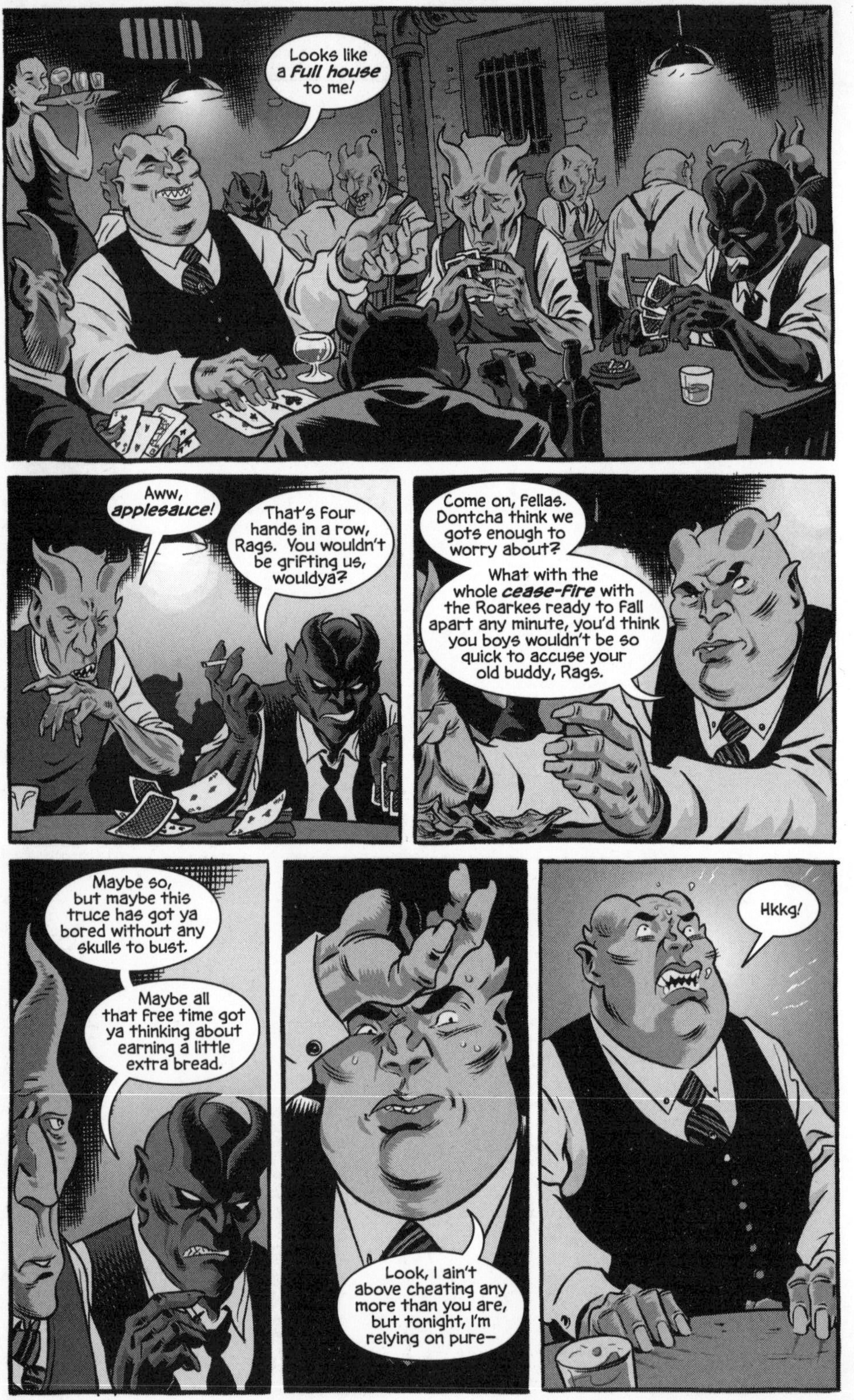
Looks like a full house to me!
Aww, applesauce!
That's four hands in a row, Rags. You wouldn't be grifting us, wouldya?
Come on, fellas. Dontcha think we gots enough to worry about?
What with the whole cease-fire with the Roarkes ready to fall apart any minute, you'd think you boys wouldn't be so quick to accuse your old buddy, Rags.
Maybe so, but maybe this truce has got ya bored without any skulls to bust.
Maybe all that free time got ya thinking about earning a little extra bread.
Look, I ain't above cheating any more than you are, but tonight, I'm relying on pure—
Hkkg!

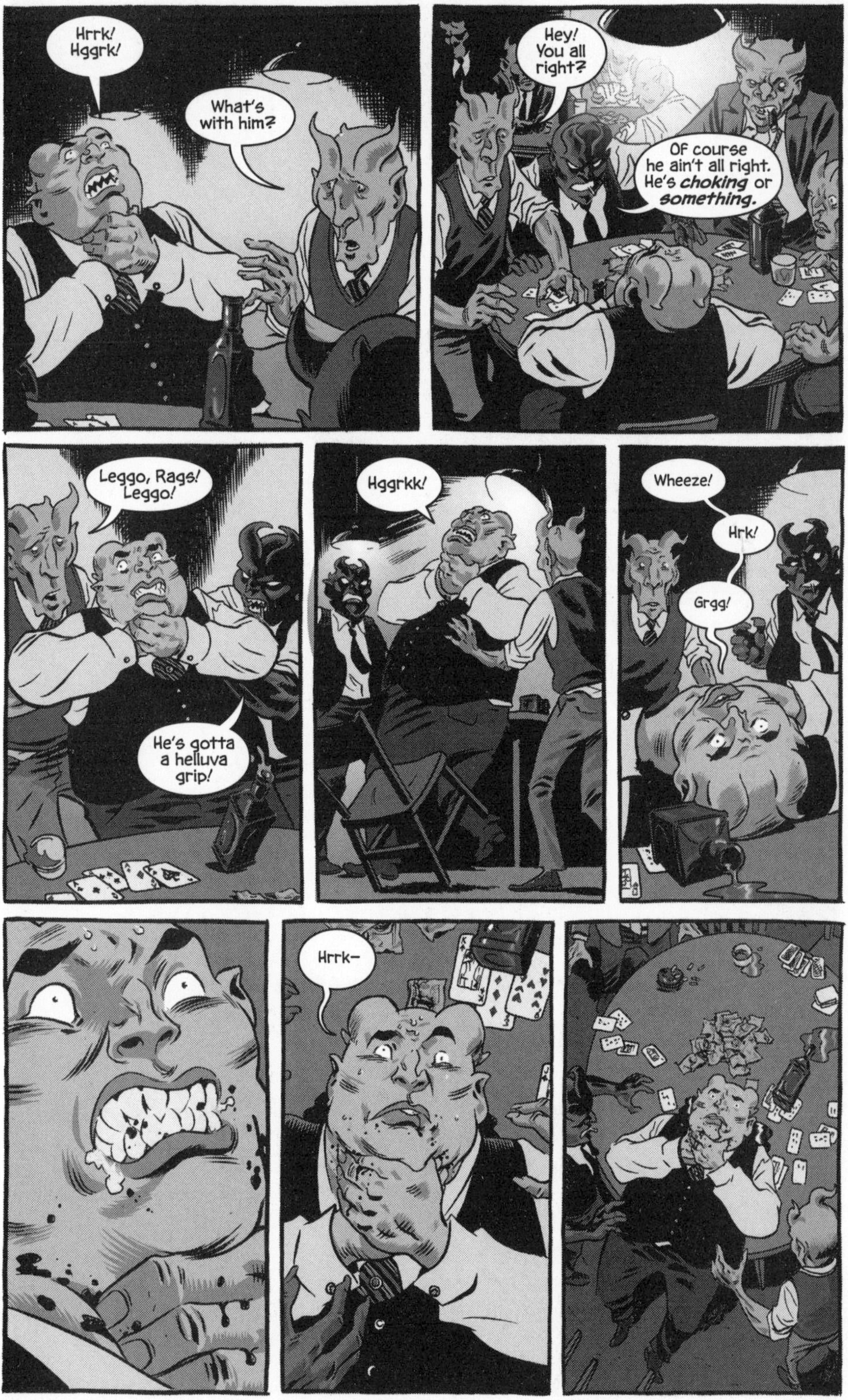
Hrrk!
Hggrk!
What's with him?
Hey! You all right?
Of course he ain't all right. He's *choking* or *something.*
Leggo, Rags! Leggo!
He's gotta a helluva grip!
Hggrkk!
Wheeze!
Hrk!
Grgg!
Hrrk-

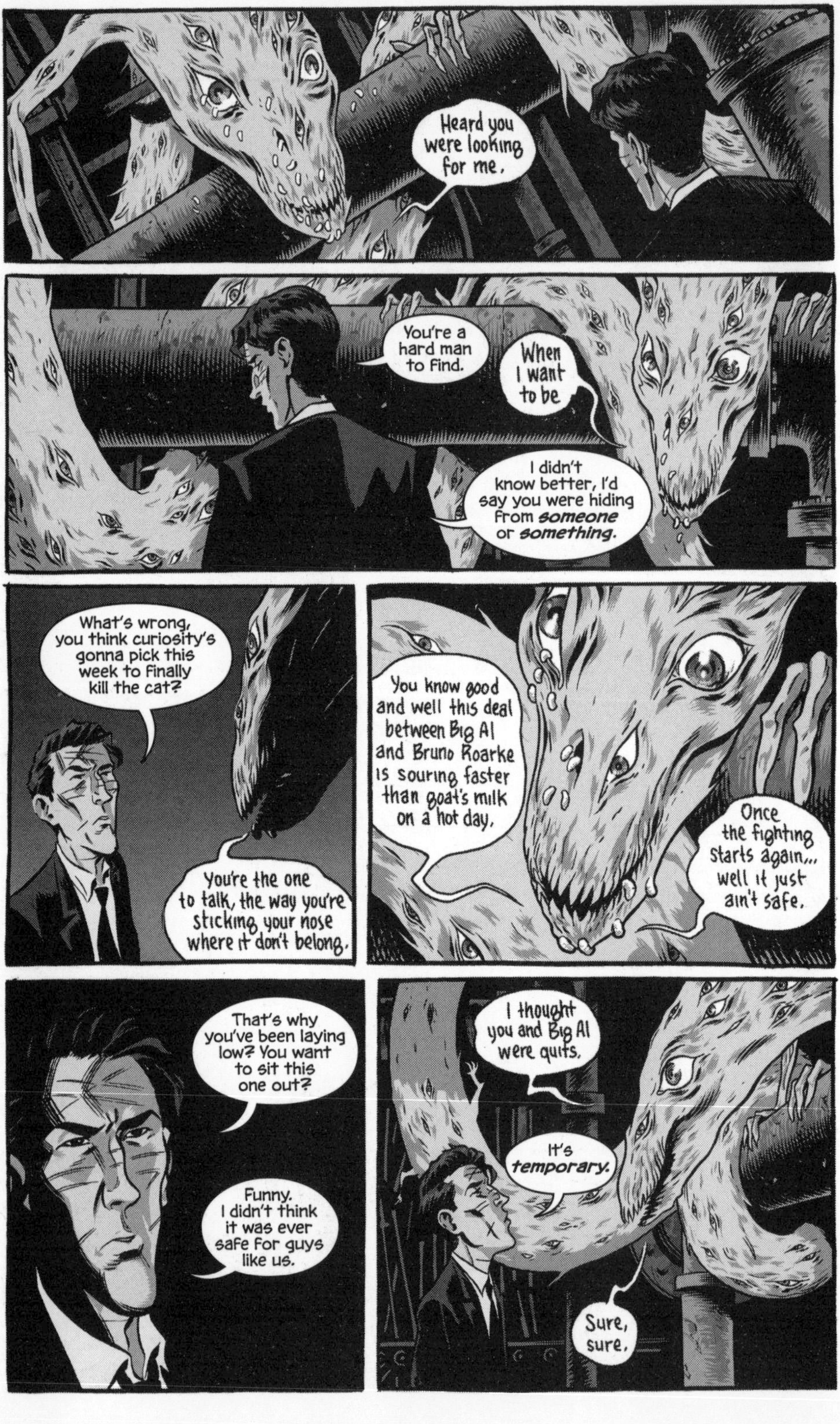
Heard you were looking for me.
You're a hard man to find.
When I want to be
I didn't know better, I'd say you were hiding from *someone* or *something*.
What's wrong, you think curiosity's gonna pick this week to finally kill the cat?
You're the one to talk, the way you're sticking your nose where it don't belong.
You know good and well this deal between Big Al and Bruno Roarke is souring faster than goat's milk on a hot day.
Once the fighting starts again... well it just ain't safe.
That's why you've been laying low? You want to sit this one out?
Funny. I didn't think it was ever safe for guys like us.
I thought you and Big Al were quits.
It's *temporary.*
Sure, sure.

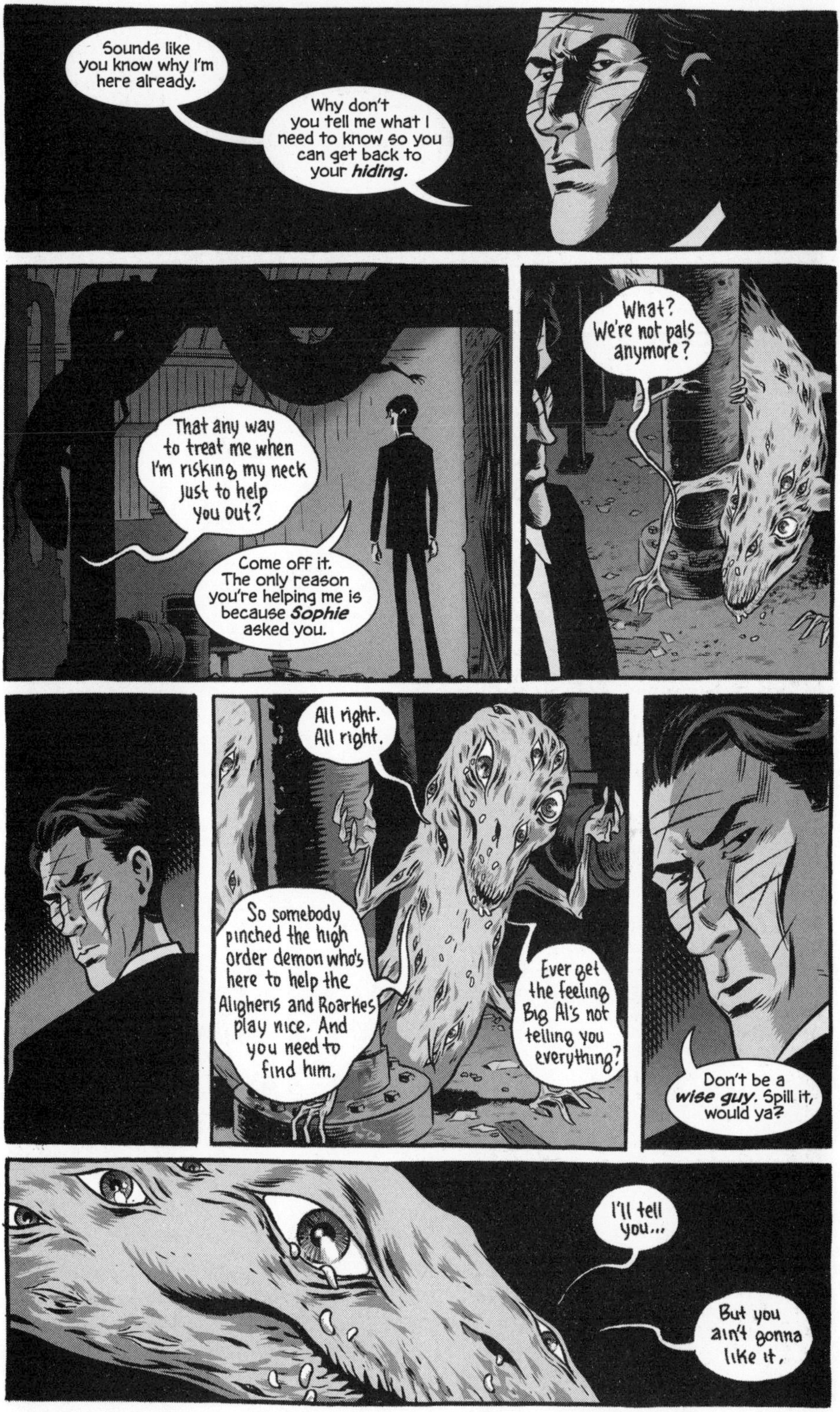
Sounds like you know why I'm here already.
Why don't you tell me what I need to know so you can get back to your *hiding*.
That any way to treat me when I'm risking my neck just to help you out?
Come off it. The only reason you're helping me is because *Sophie* asked you.
What? We're not pals anymore?
All right. All right.
So somebody pinched the high order demon who's here to help the Aligheris and Roarkes play nice. And you need to find him.
Ever get the feeling Big Al's not telling you everything?
Don't be a *wise guy*. Spill it, would ya?
I'll tell you...
But you ain't gonna like it.

Crowley's Creek.

Never a nice neighborhood, not even on the best of days. Now it's downright eerie.

Few years back, it was overrun with demons.

The *Verlochin*.

They're the family that makes the other demons afraid of the boogeyman.

I don't even like thinking about what went on in the cellars in these parts when the Verlochin were in charge.

Of course, the Aligheris and the Roarkes sent them packing, back when Big Al and Bruno had a common enemy to keep them occupied.

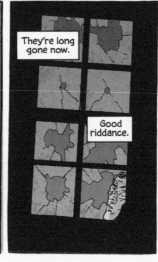

They're long gone now.

Good riddance.

Unless they're back.

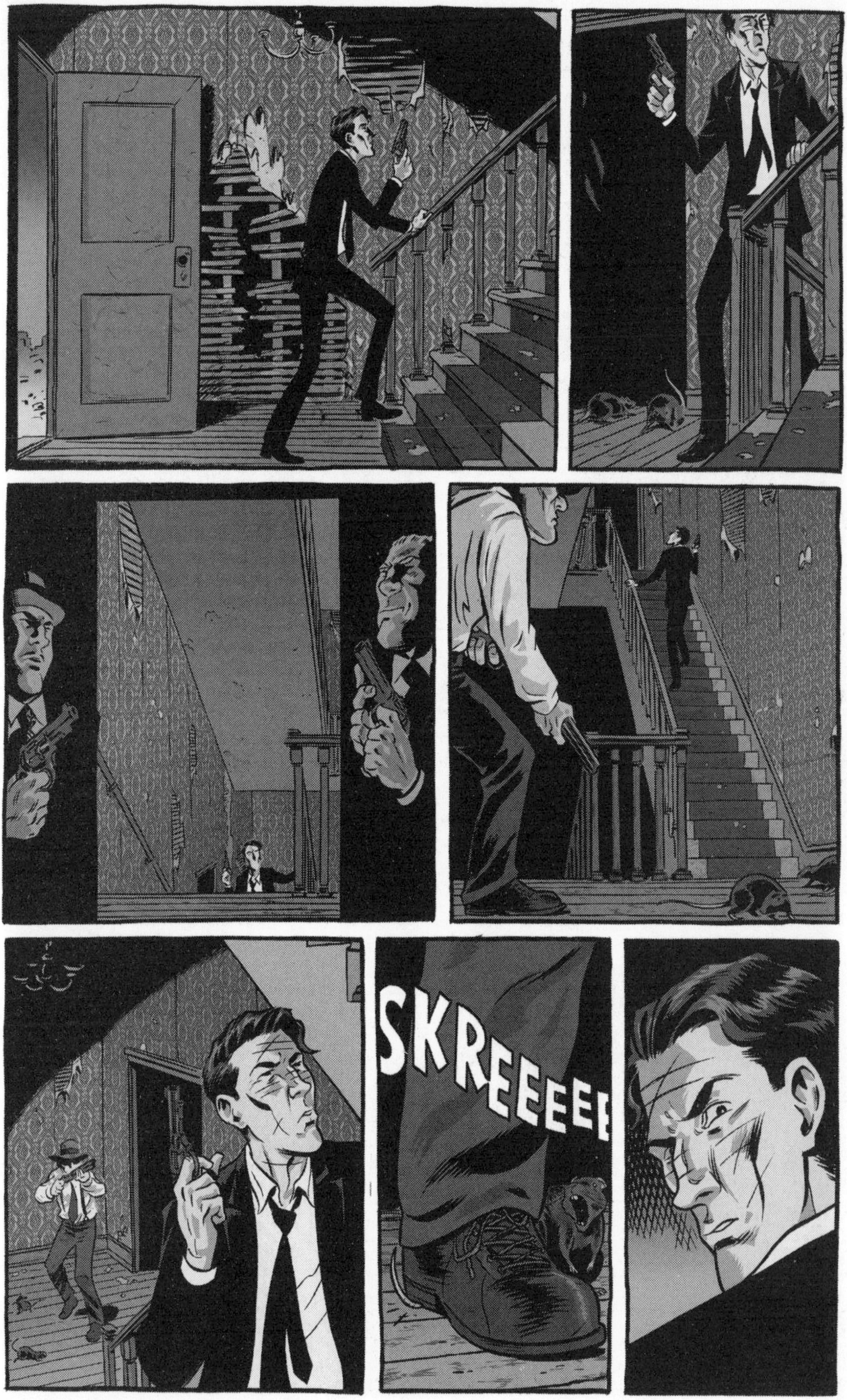
SKREEEEE

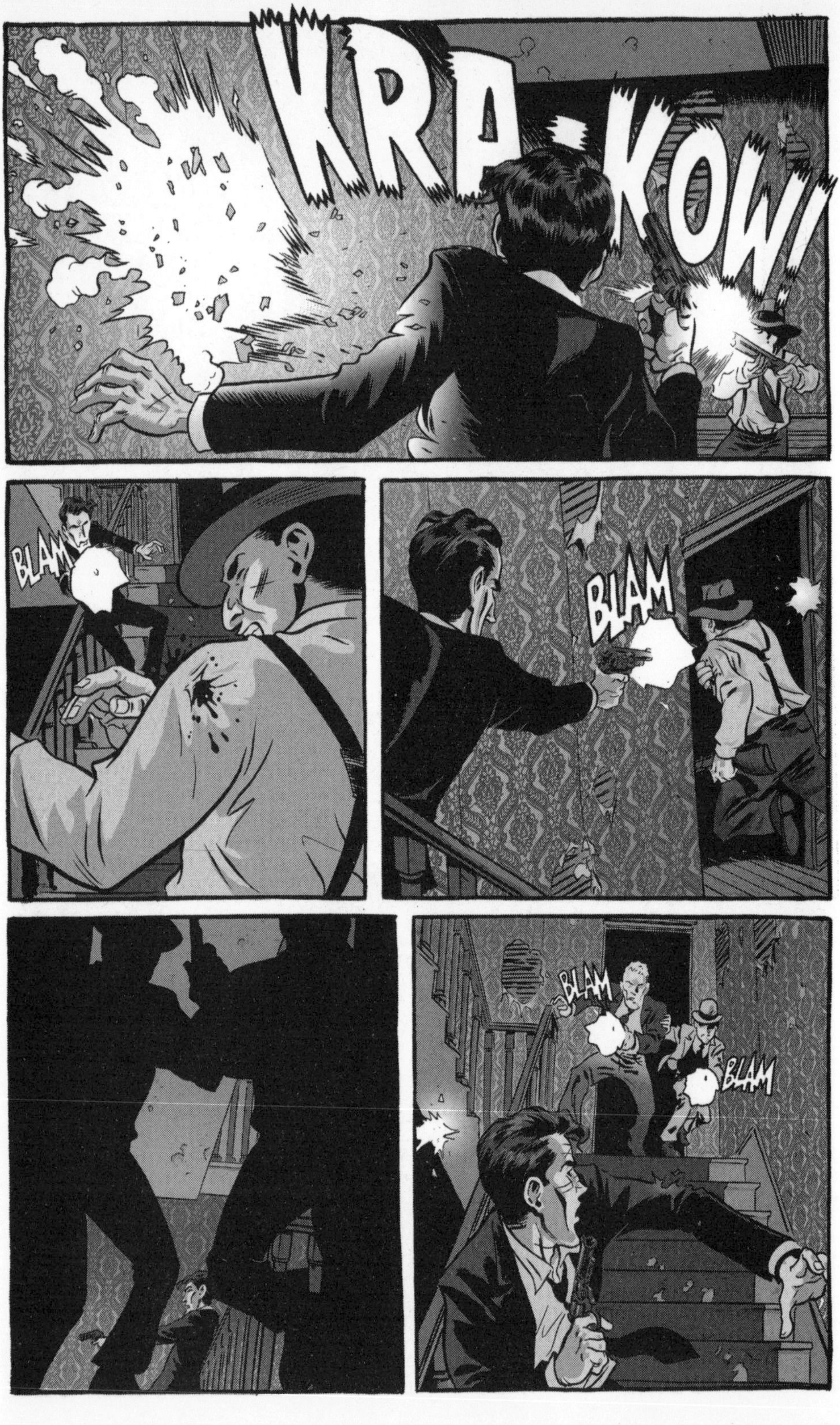
KRA-KOW!
BLAM
BLAM
BLAM
BLAM

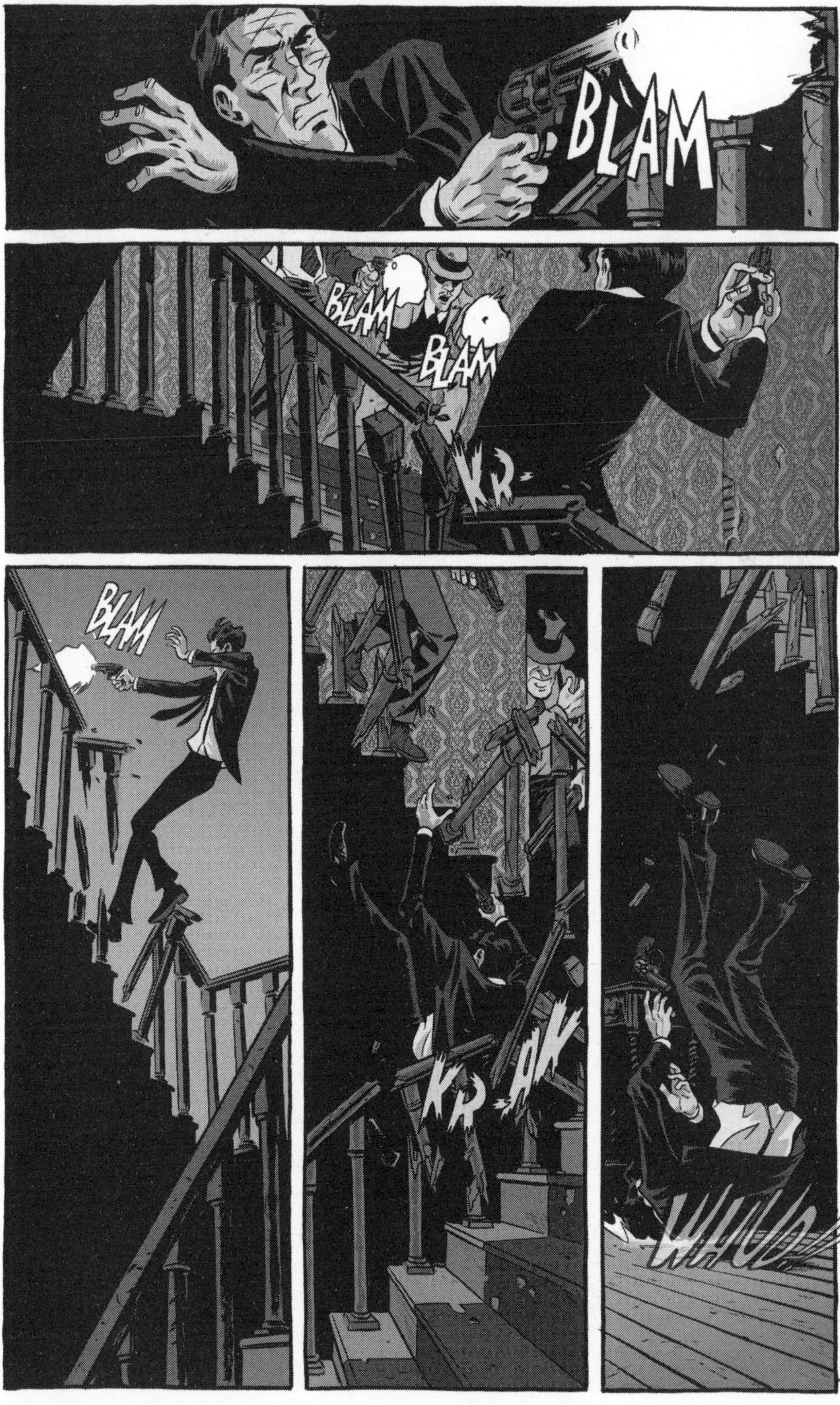
BLAM
BLAM
BLAM
KR
BLAM
KR
AK
WHUD!!

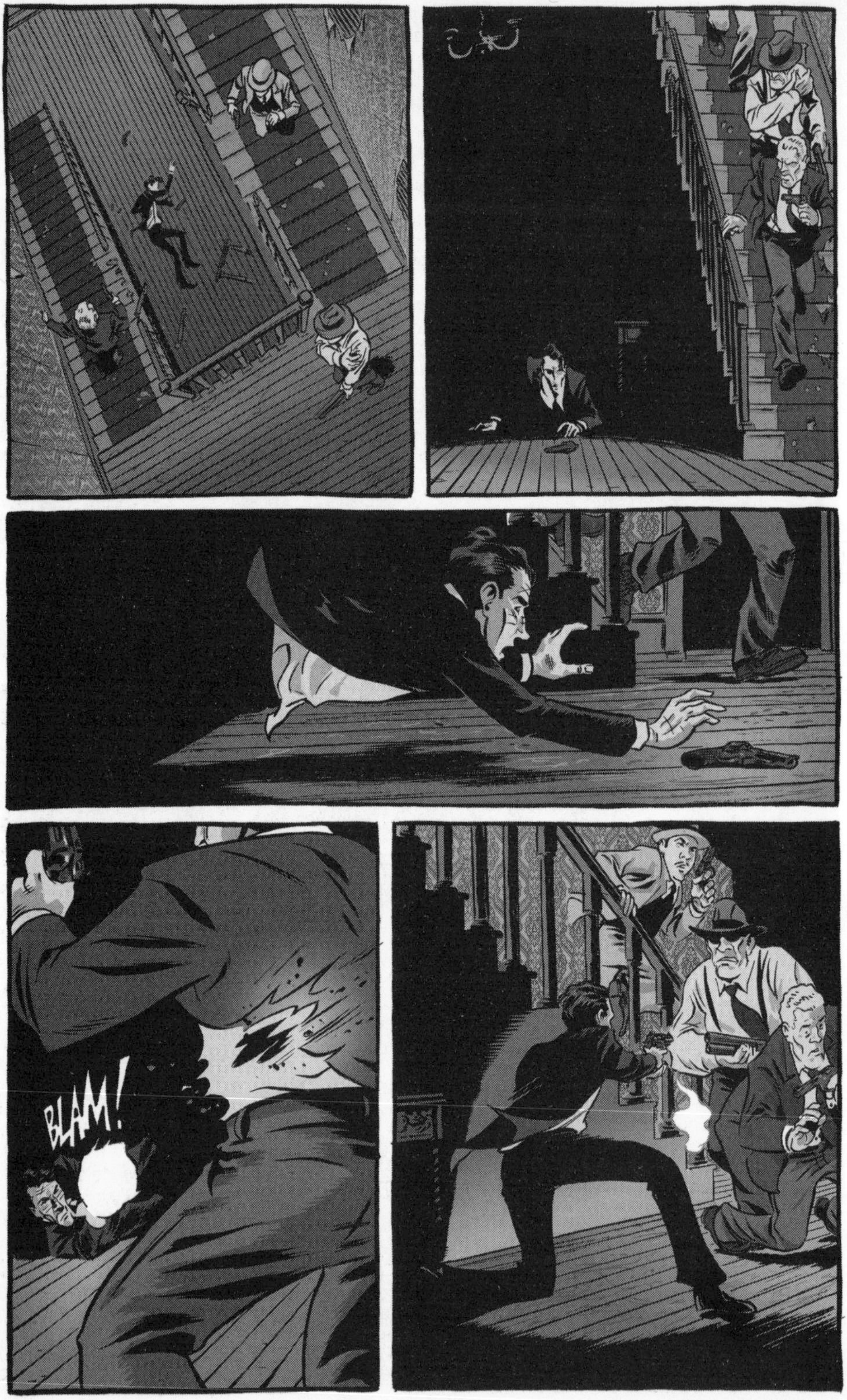
BLAM!

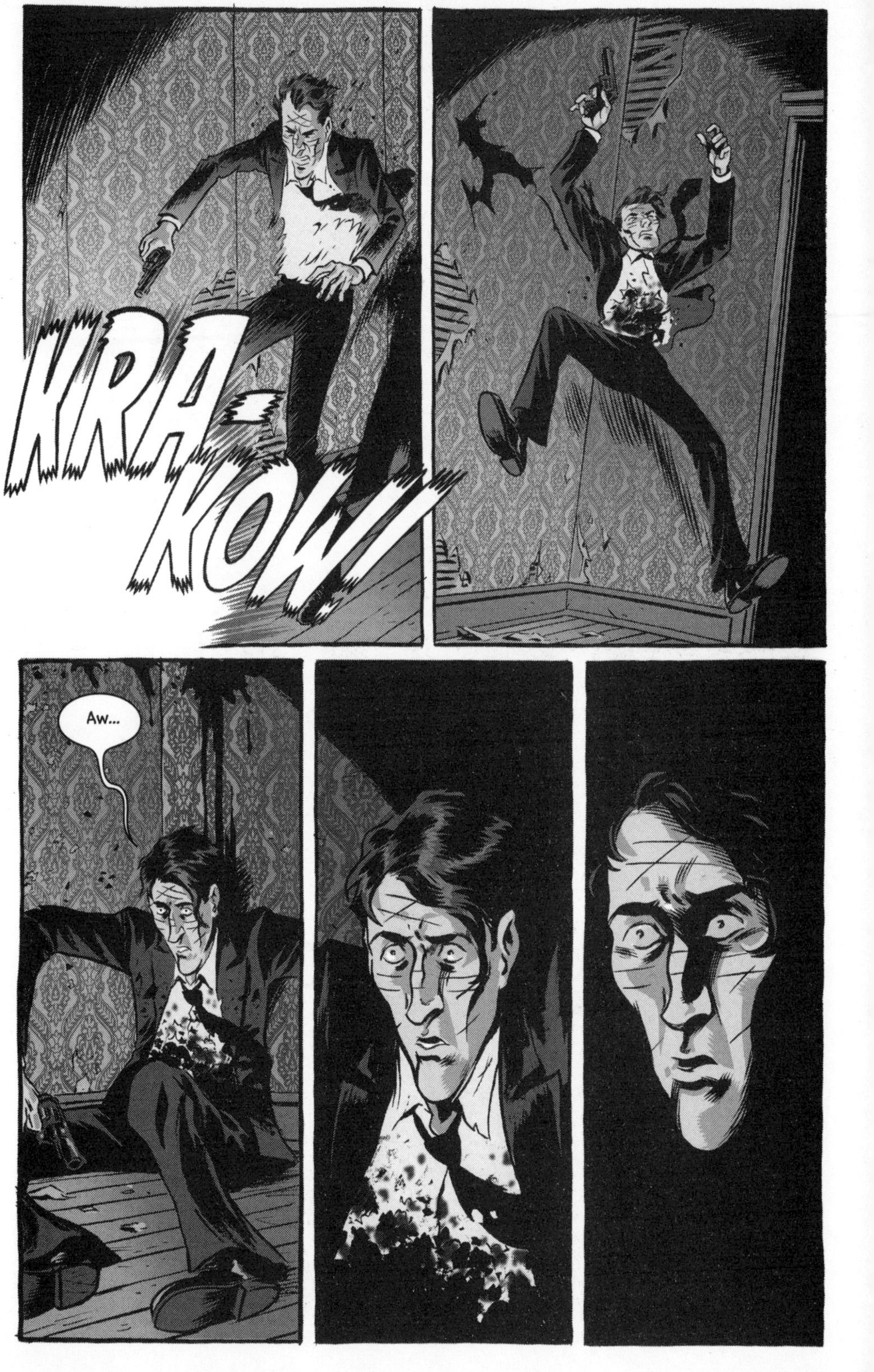
KRA-KOW!
Aw...

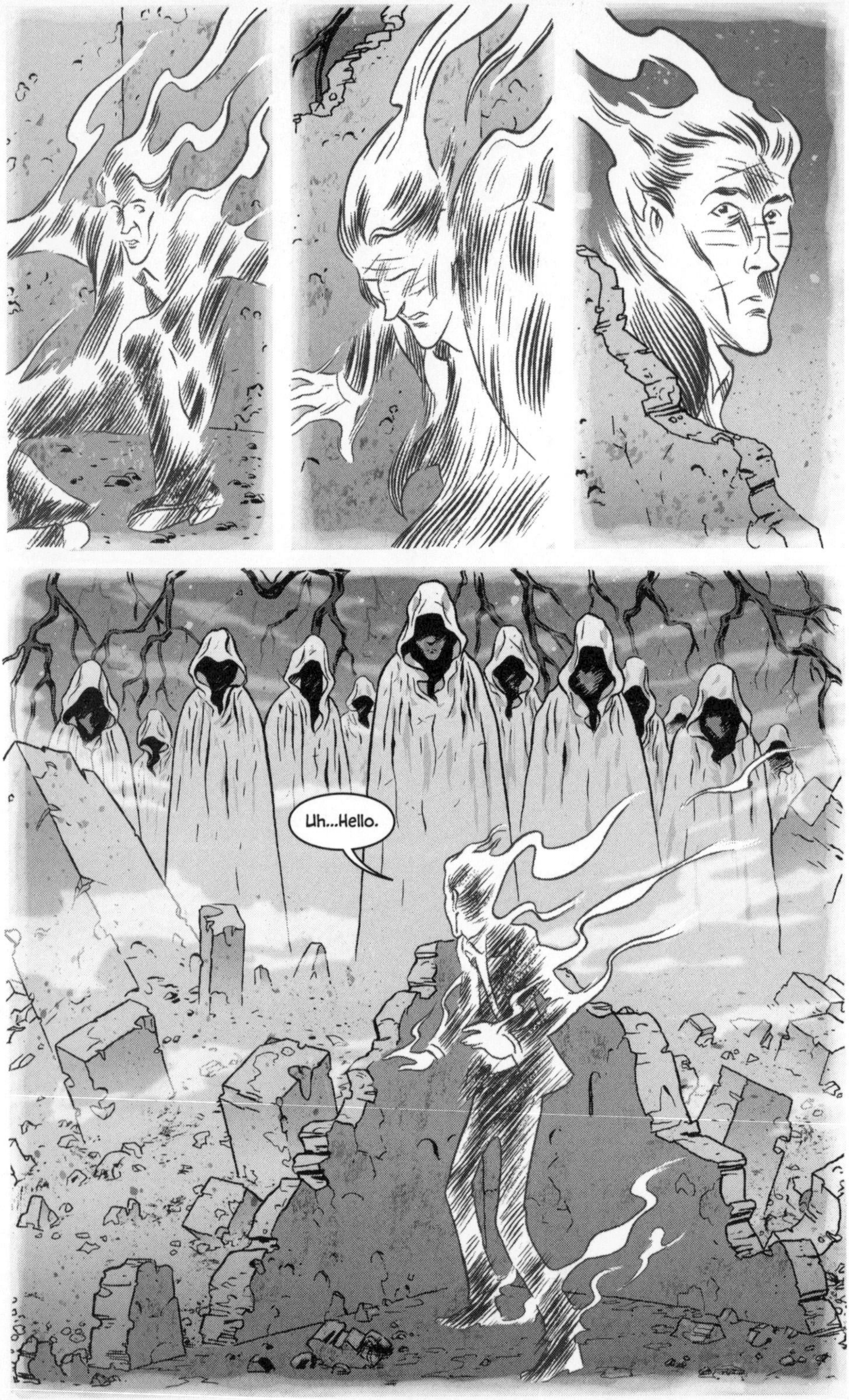
Uh...Hello.

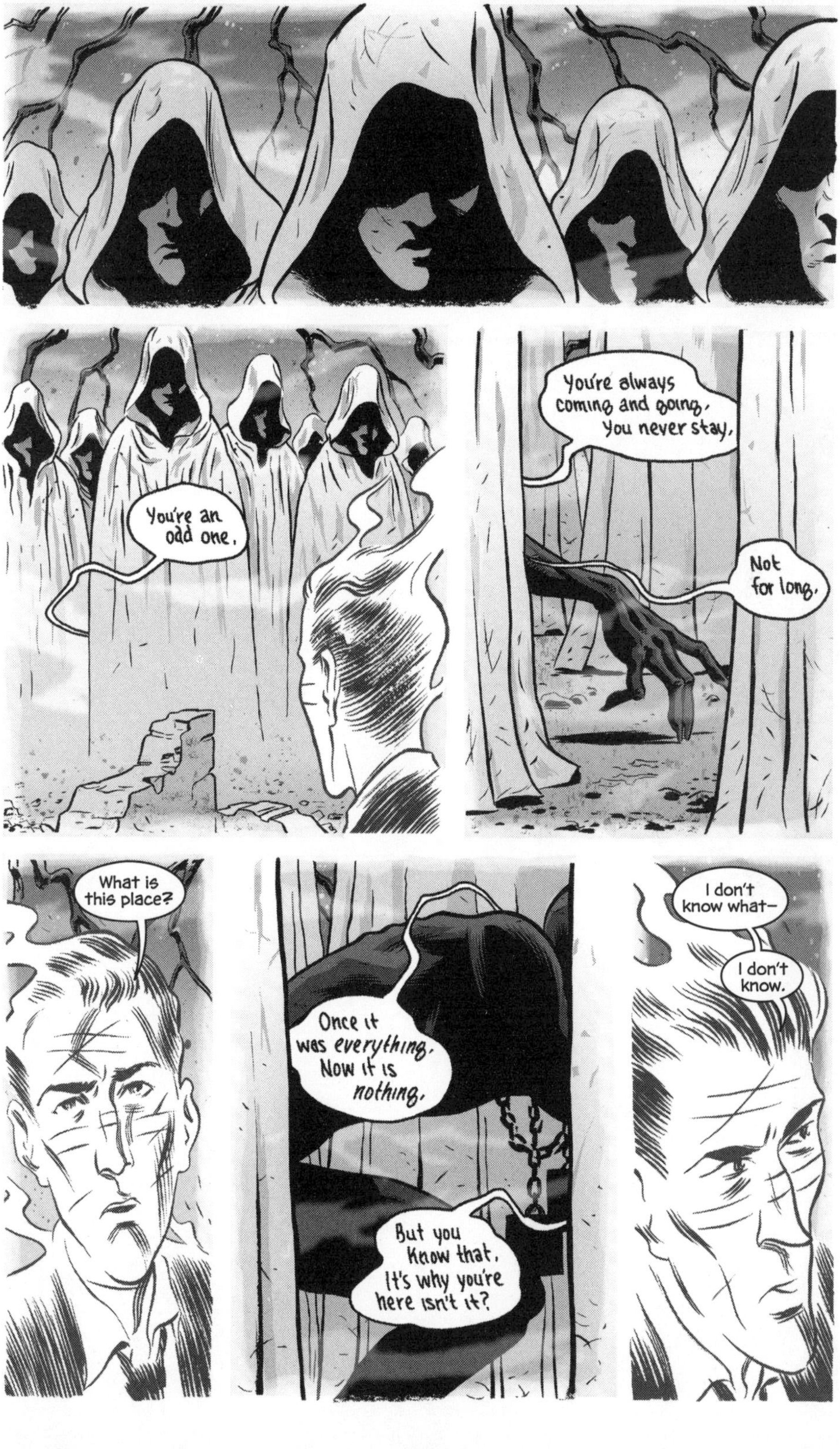
You're an odd one.
You're always coming and going, You never stay.
Not for long.
What is this place?
Once it was everything. Now it is nothing.
But you know that. It's why you're here isn't it?
I don't know what–
I don't know.

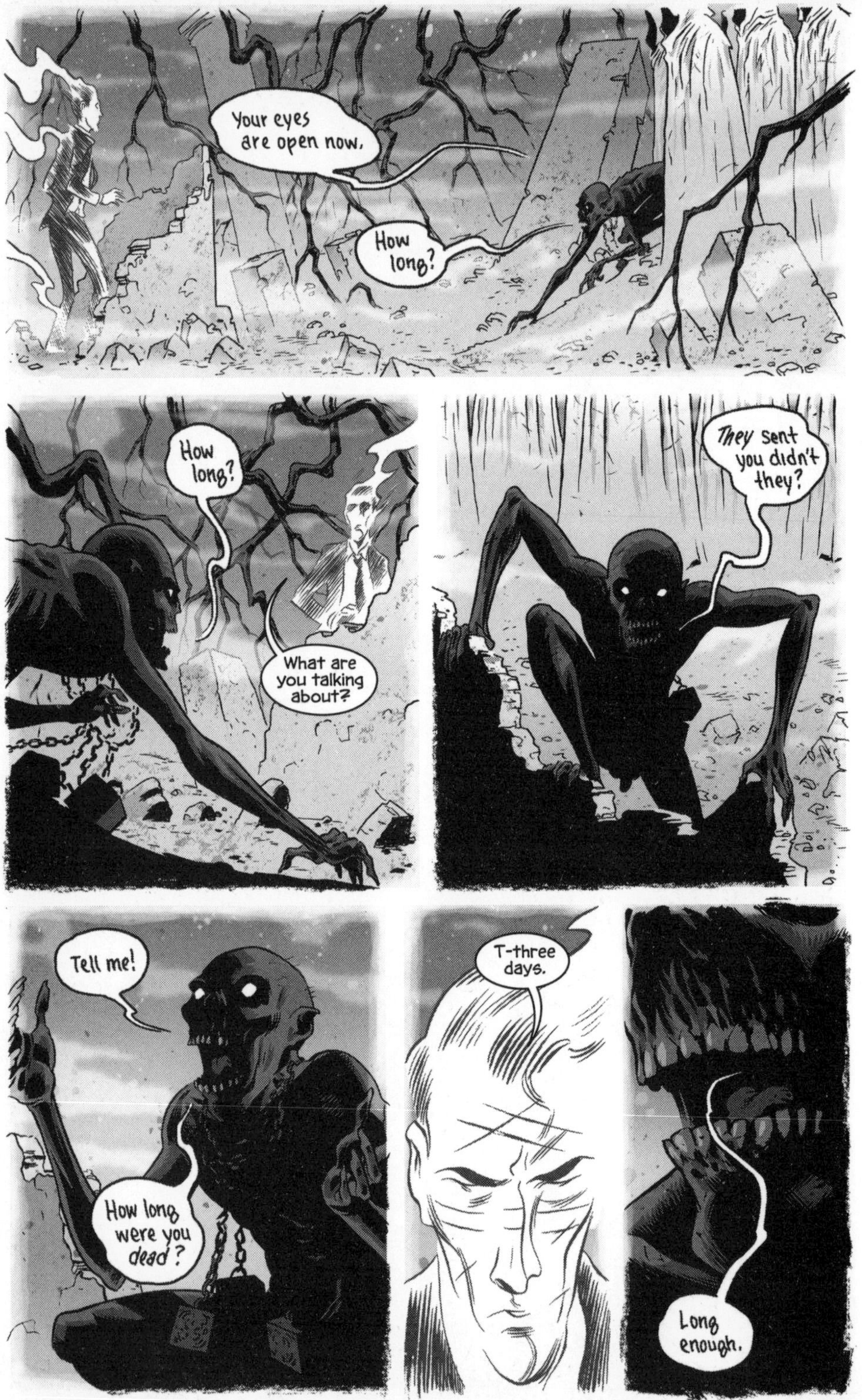
Your eyes are open now,
How long?
How long?
What are you talking about?
They sent you didn't they?
Tell me!
How long were you dead?
T-three days.
Long enough.

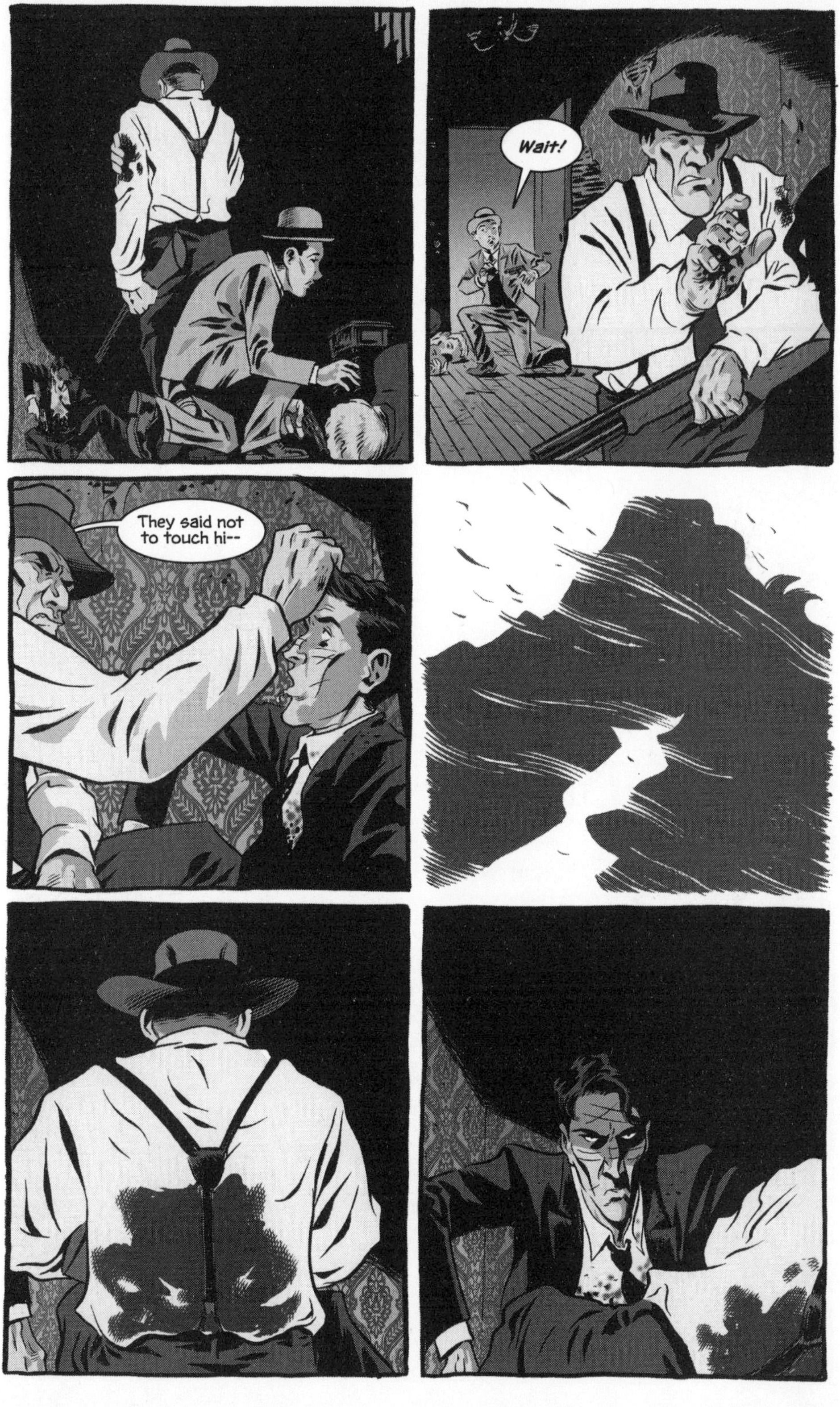
Wait!
They said not to touch hi--

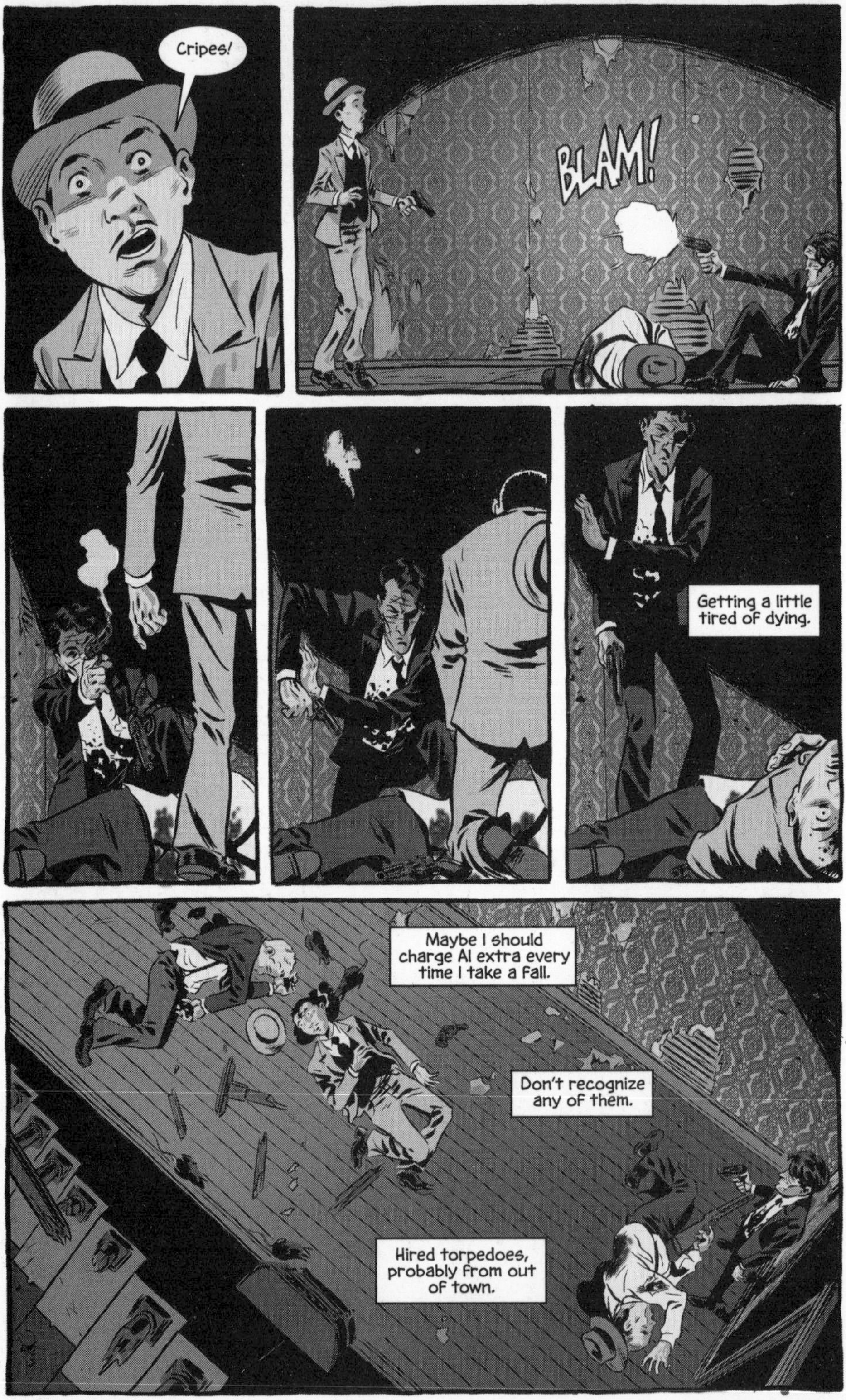
Cripes!
BLAM!
Getting a little tired of dying.
Maybe I should charge Al extra every time I take a fall.
Don't recognize any of them.
Hired torpedoes, probably from out of town.

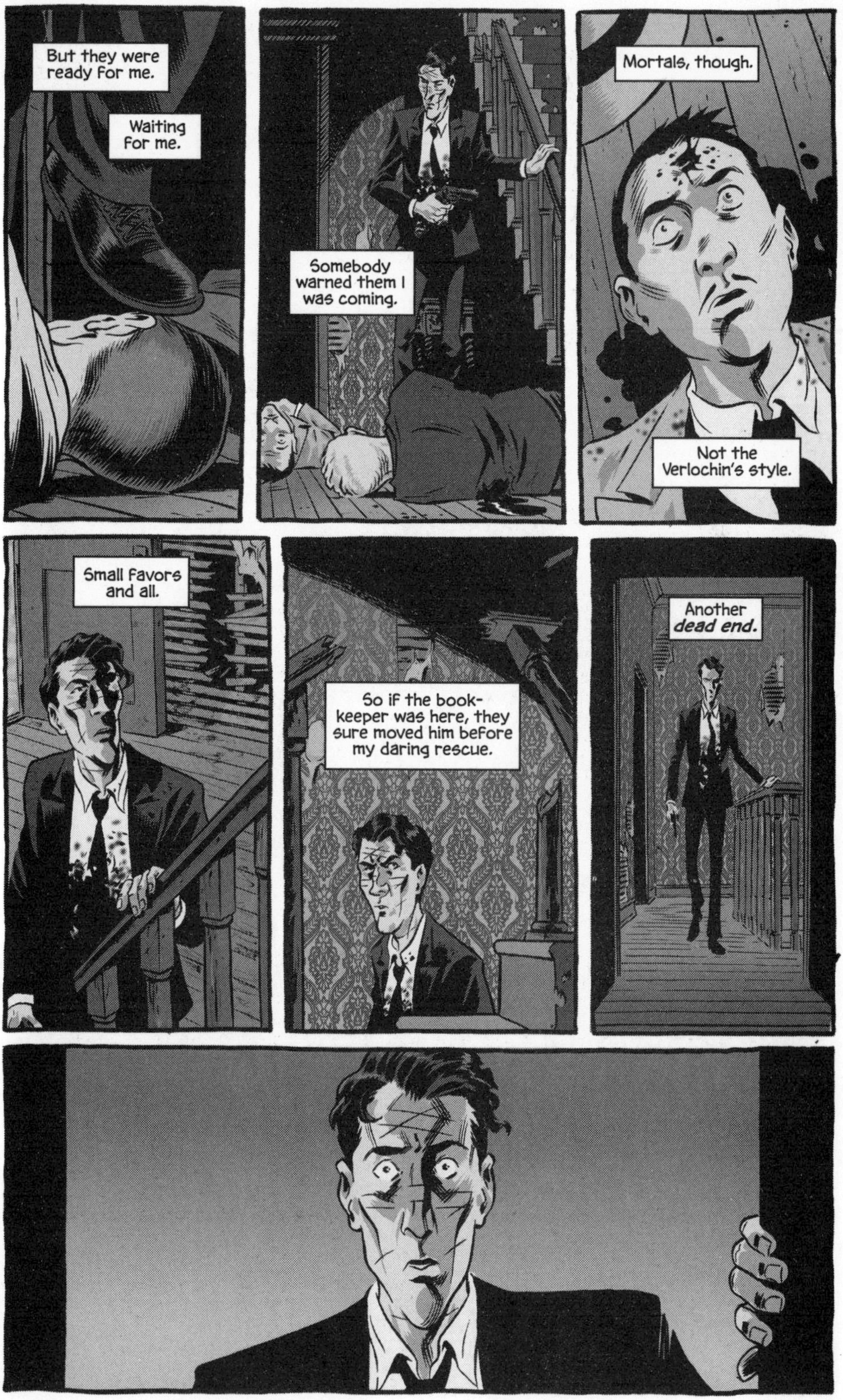

But they were ready for me.
Waiting for me.
Somebody warned them I was coming.
Mortals, though.
Not the Verlochin's style.
Small favors and all.
So if the book-keeper was here, they sure moved him before my daring rescue.
Another *dead end.*

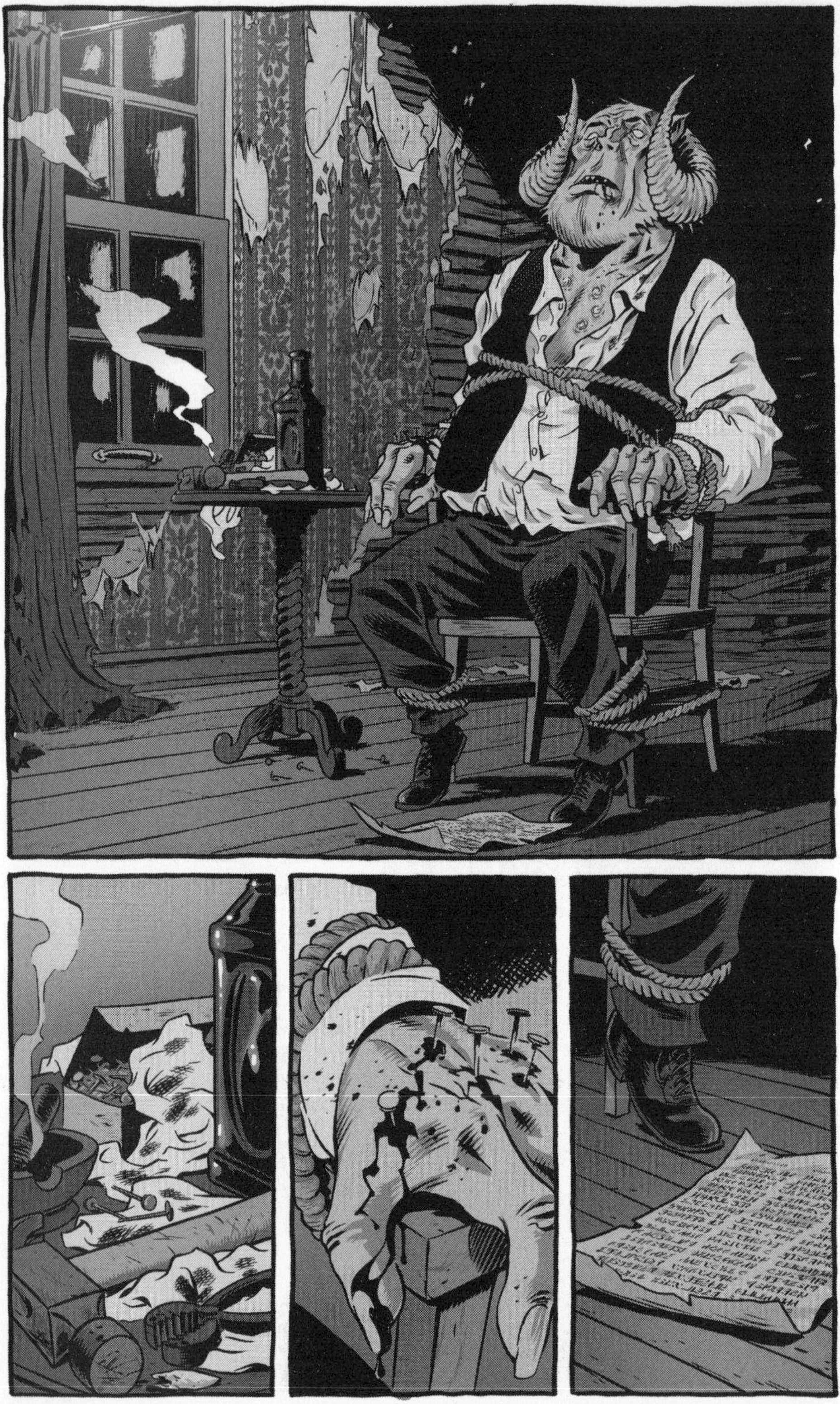

So much for *Lazlo.*

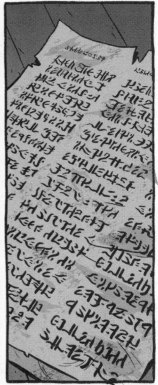

Tell me this isn't what I think it is...

What?

Got nothing to say?

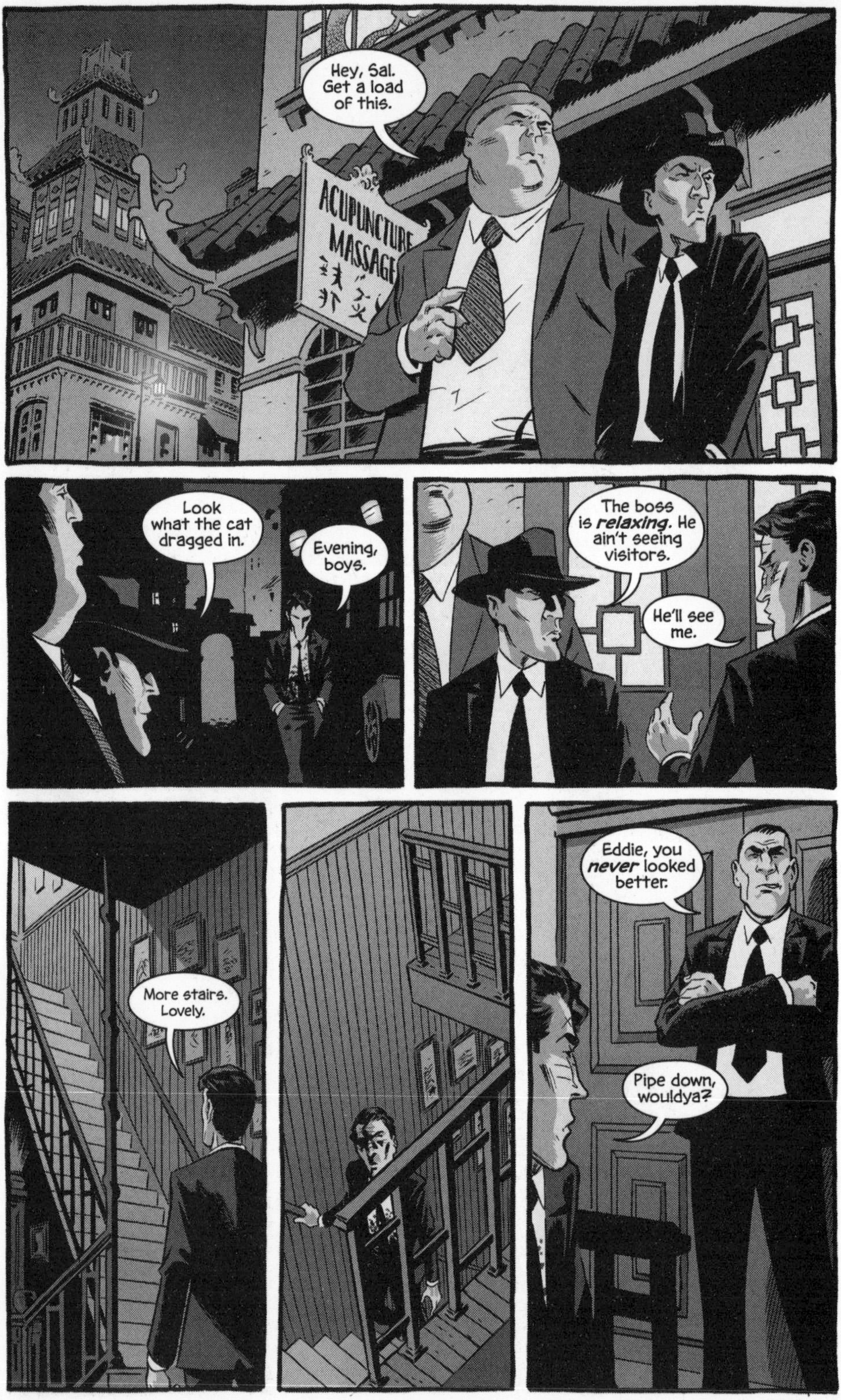
Hey, Sal. Get a load of this.
ACUPUNCTURE MASSAGE
Look what the cat dragged in.
Evening, boys.
The boss is *relaxing*. He ain't seeing visitors.
He'll see me.
More stairs. Lovely.
Eddie, you *never* looked better.
Pipe down, wouldya?

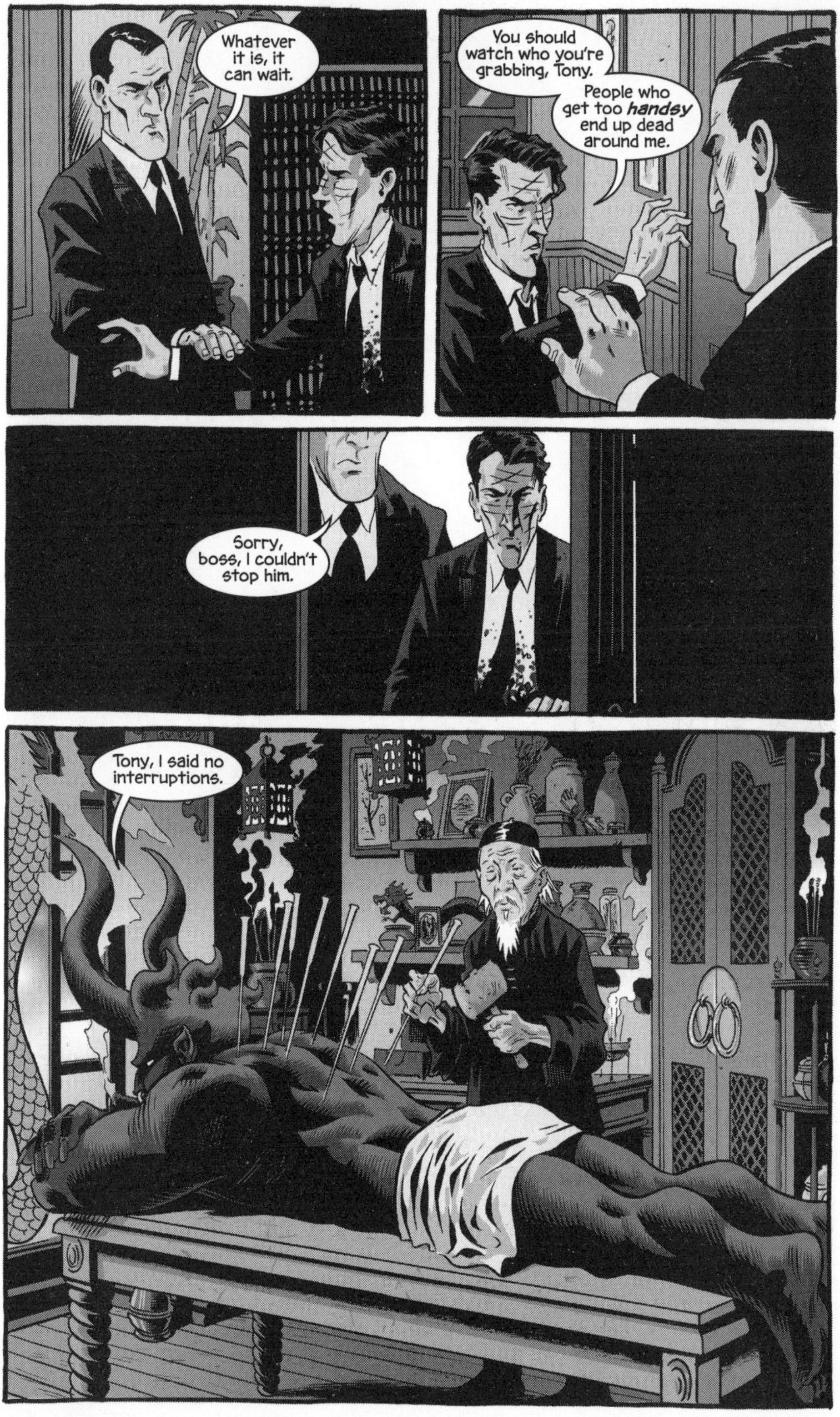
Whatever it is, it can wait.
You should watch who you're grabbing, Tony.
People who get too *handsy* end up dead around me.
Sorry, boss, I couldn't stop him.
Tony, I said no interruptions.

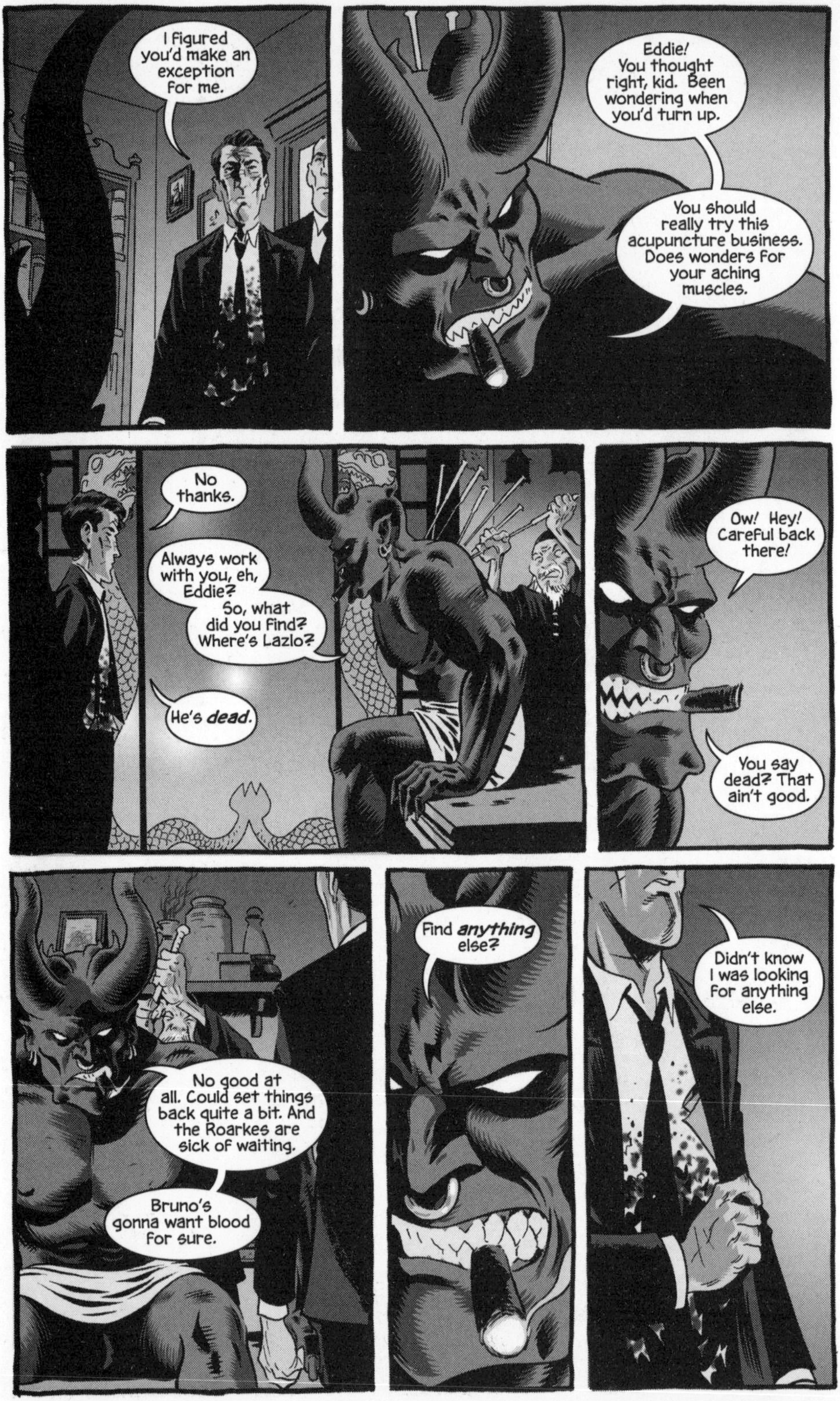
I figured you'd make an exception for me.
Eddie! You thought right, kid. Been wondering when you'd turn up.
You should really try this acupuncture business. Does wonders for your aching muscles.
No thanks.
Always work with you, eh, Eddie?
So, what did you find? Where's Lazlo?
He's *dead.*
Ow! Hey! Careful back there!
You say dead? That ain't good.
No good at all. Could set things back quite a bit. And the Roarkes are sick of waiting.
Bruno's gonna want blood for sure.
Find *anything* else?
Didn't know I was looking for anything else.

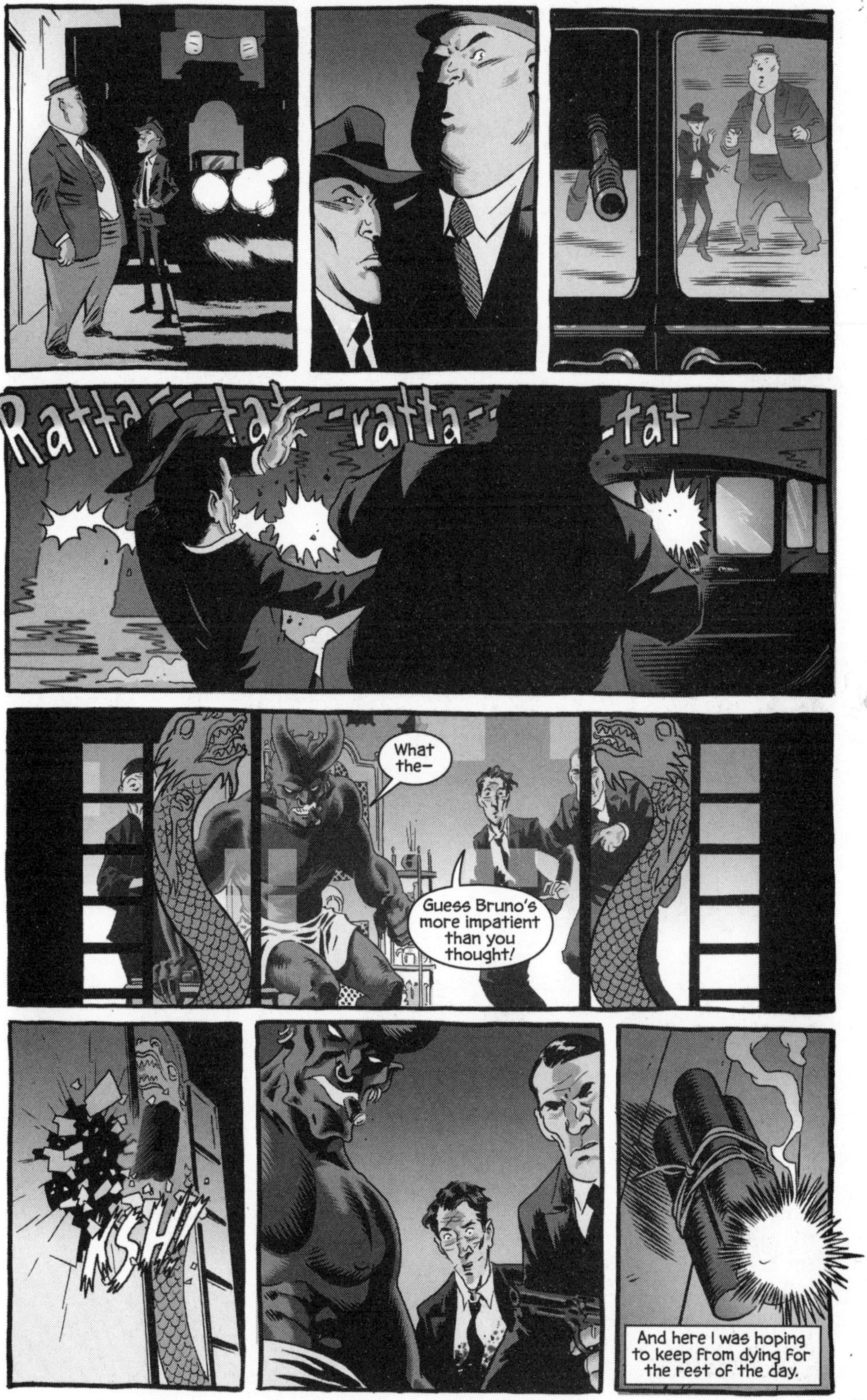
Ratta-tat-ratta-tat
What the-
Guess Bruno's more impatient than you thought!
KSH!
And here I was hoping to keep from dying for the rest of the day.

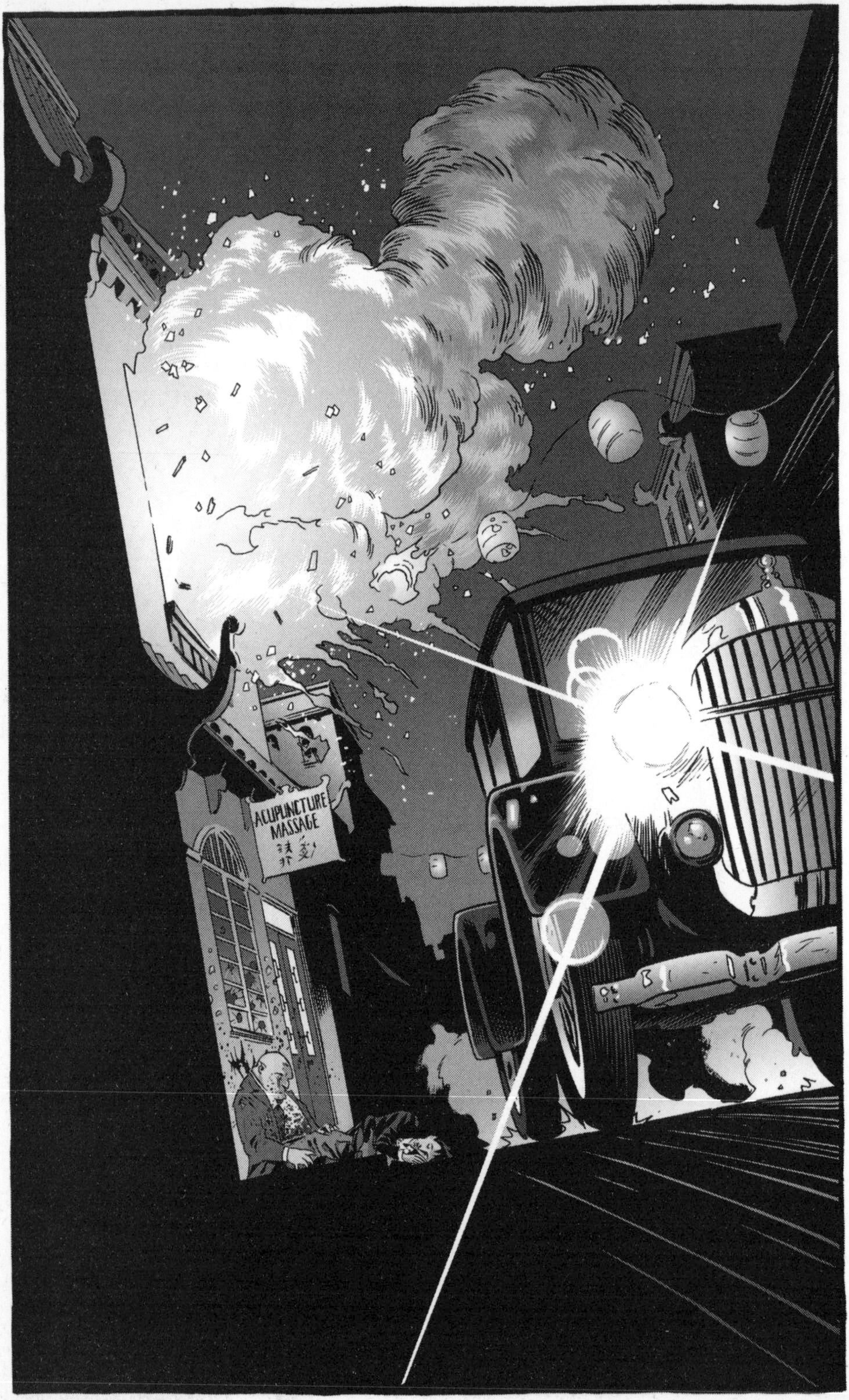
ACUPUNCTURE
MASSAGE

CHAPTER 4

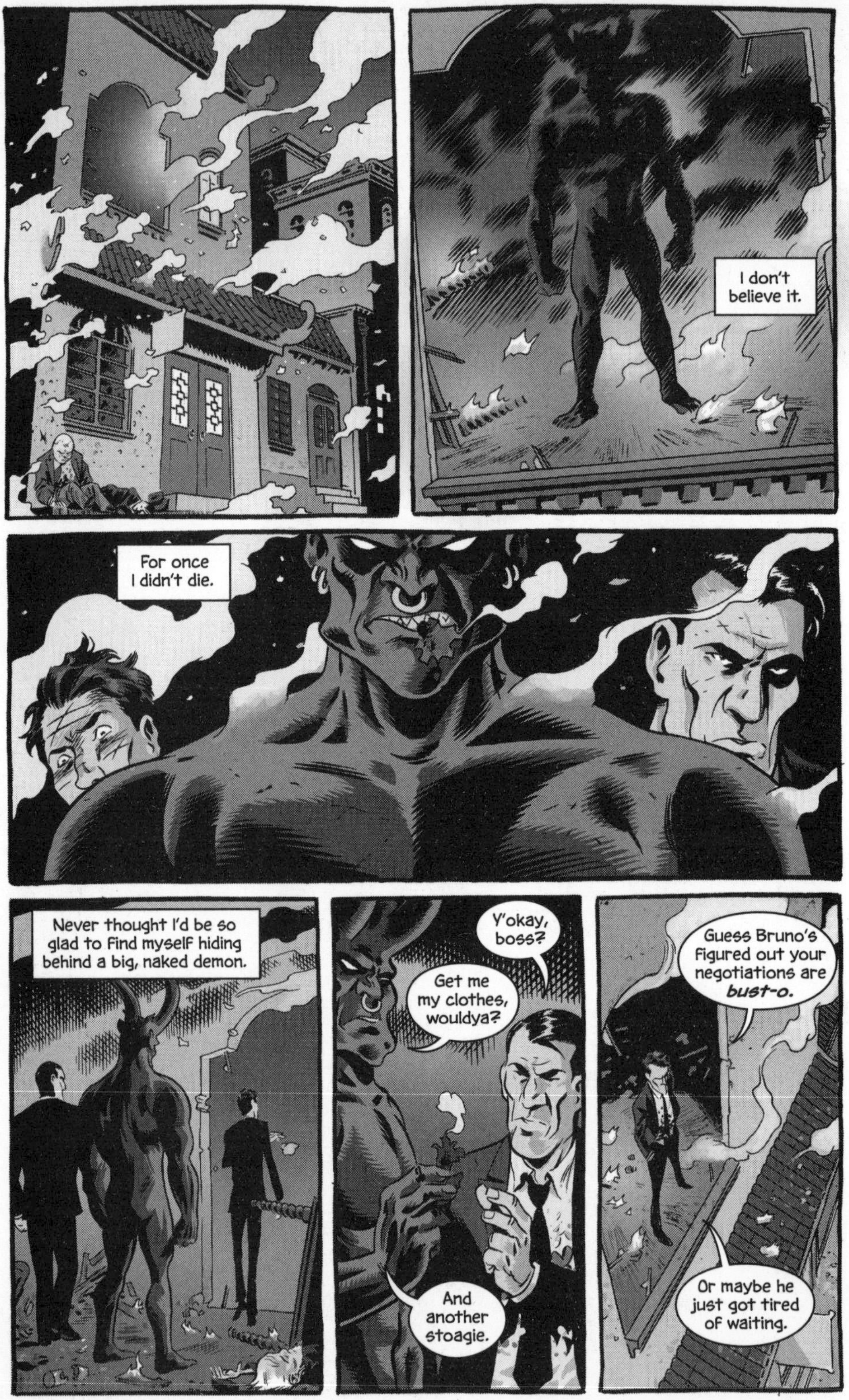
I don't believe it.
For once I didn't die.
Never thought I'd be so glad to find myself hiding behind a big, naked demon.
Y'okay, boss?
Get me my clothes, wouldya?
And another stoagie.
Guess Bruno's figured out your negotiations are *bust-o.*
Or maybe he just got tired of waiting.

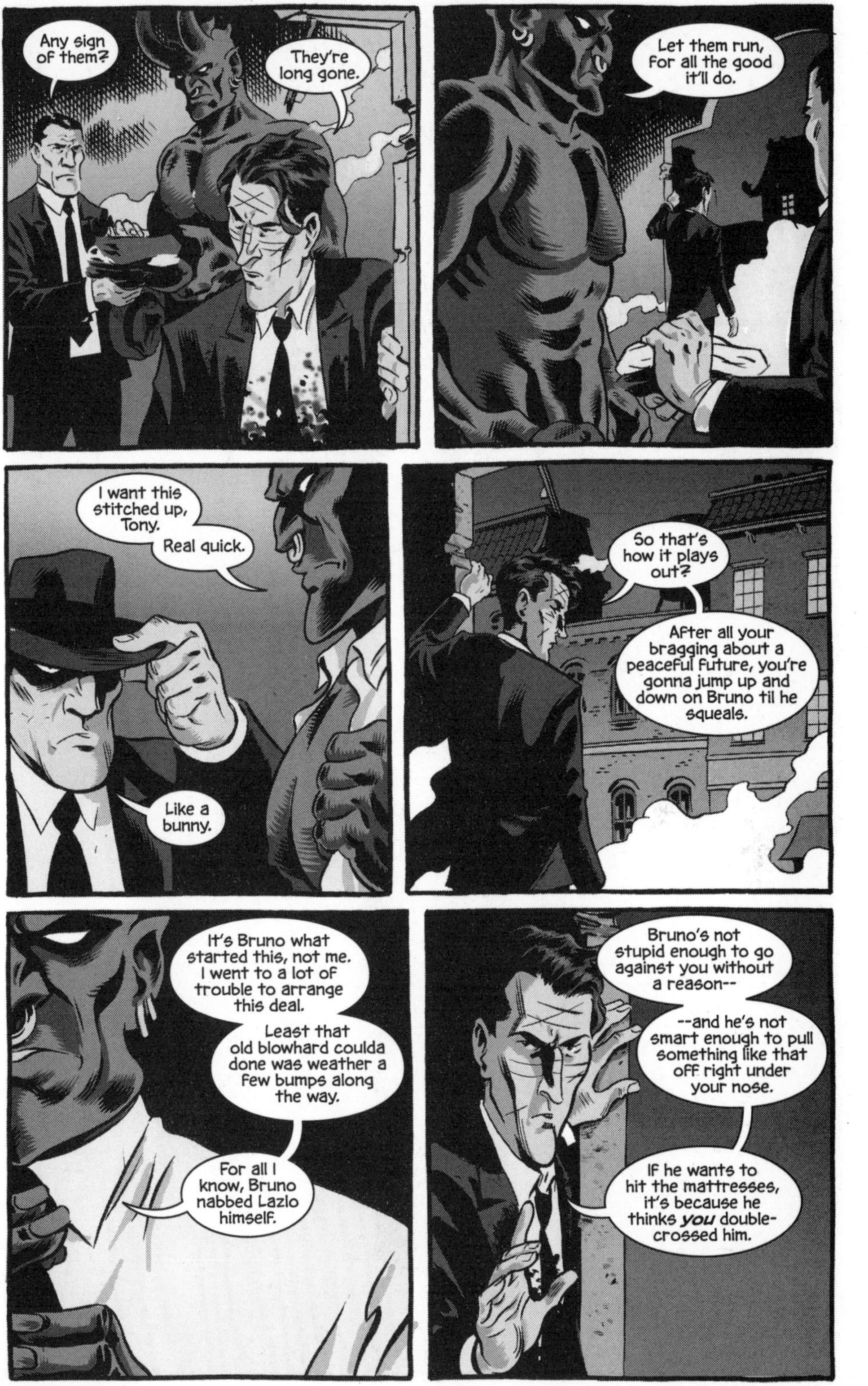
Any sign of them?
They're long gone.
Let them run, for all the good it'll do.
I want this stitched up, Tony.
Real quick.
Like a bunny.
So that's how it plays out?
After all your bragging about a peaceful future, you're gonna jump up and down on Bruno til he squeals.
It's Bruno what started this, not me. I went to a lot of trouble to arrange this deal.
Least that old blowhard coulda done was weather a few bumps along the way.
For all I know, Bruno nabbed Lazlo himself.
Bruno's not stupid enough to go against you without a reason--
--and he's not smart enough to pull something like that off right under your nose.
If he wants to hit the mattresses, it's because he thinks *you* double-crossed him.

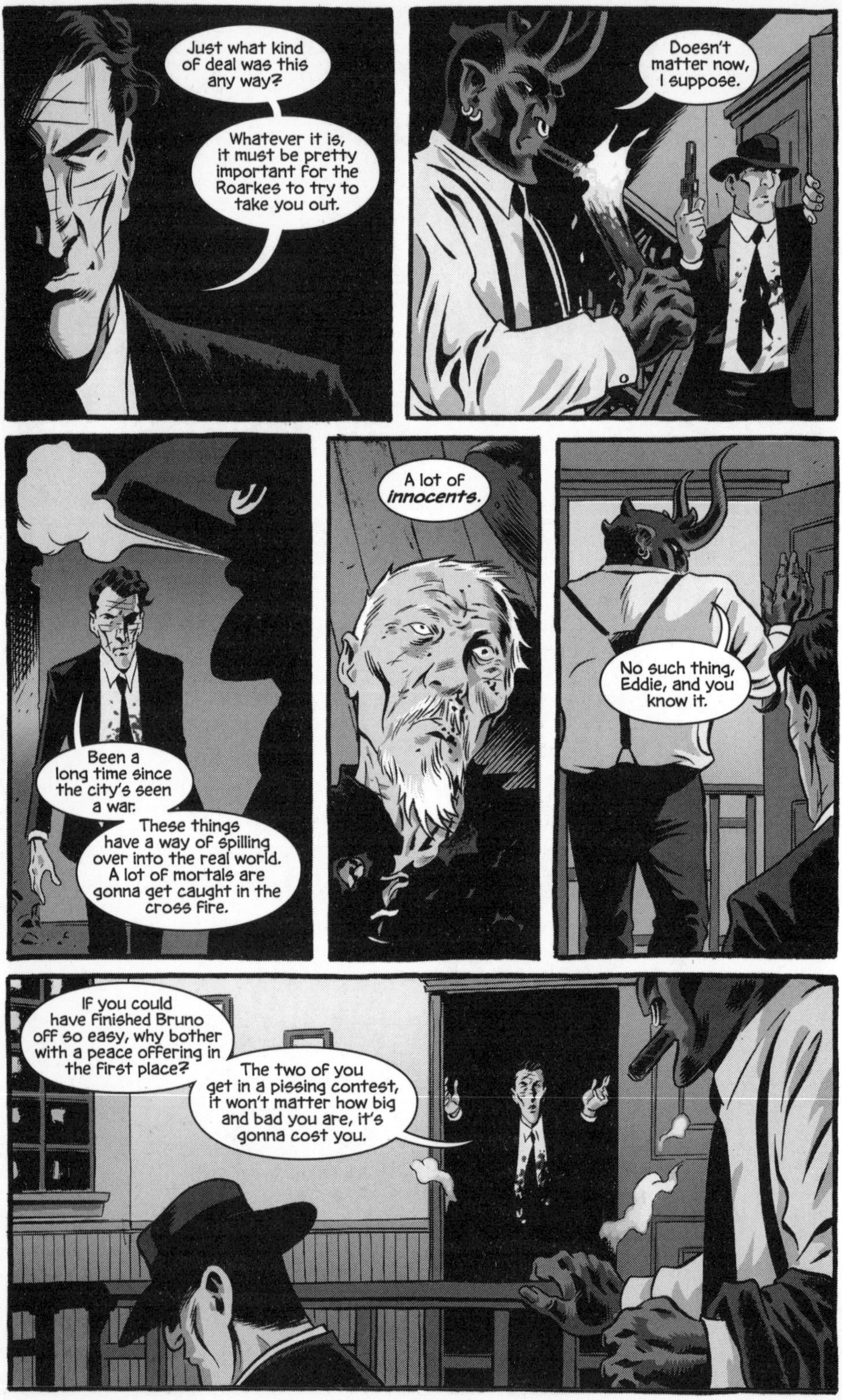
Just what kind of deal was this any way?
Whatever it is, it must be pretty important for the Roarkes to try to take you out.
Doesn't matter now, I suppose.
Been a long time since the city's seen a war.
These things have a way of spilling over into the real world. A lot of mortals are gonna get caught in the cross fire.
A lot of *innocents.*
No such thing, Eddie, and you know it.
If you could have finished Bruno off so easy, why bother with a peace offering in the first place?
The two of you get in a pissing contest, it won't matter how big and bad you are, it's gonna cost you.

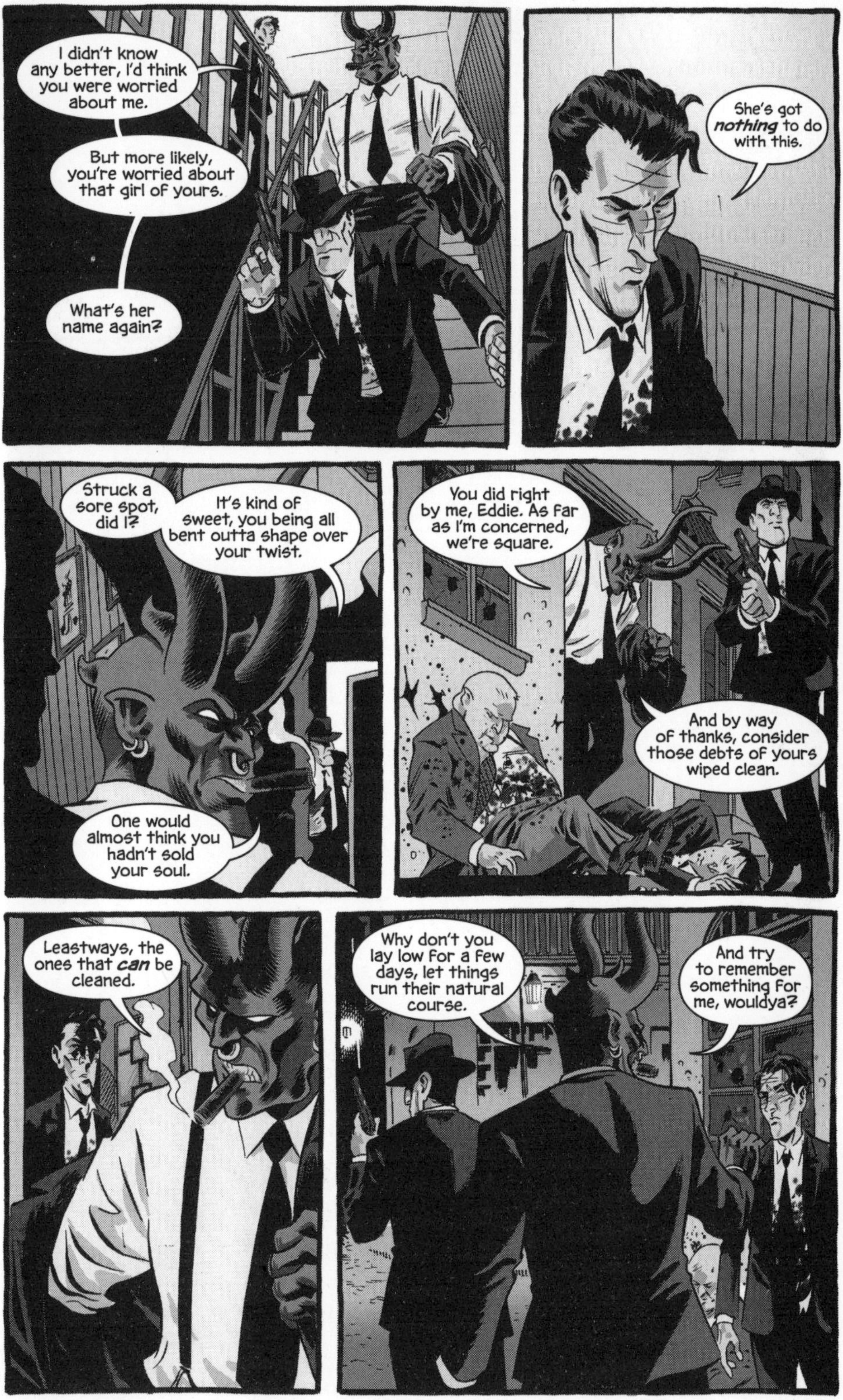

I didn't know any better, I'd think you were worried about me.
But more likely, you're worried about that girl of yours.
What's her name again?
She's got *nothing* to do with this.
Struck a sore spot, did I?
It's kind of sweet, you being all bent outta shape over your twist.
One would almost think you hadn't sold your soul.
You did right by me, Eddie. As far as I'm concerned, we're square.
And by way of thanks, consider those debts of yours wiped clean.
Leastways, the ones that *can* be cleaned.
Why don't you lay low for a few days, let things run their natural course.
And try to remember something for me, wouldya?

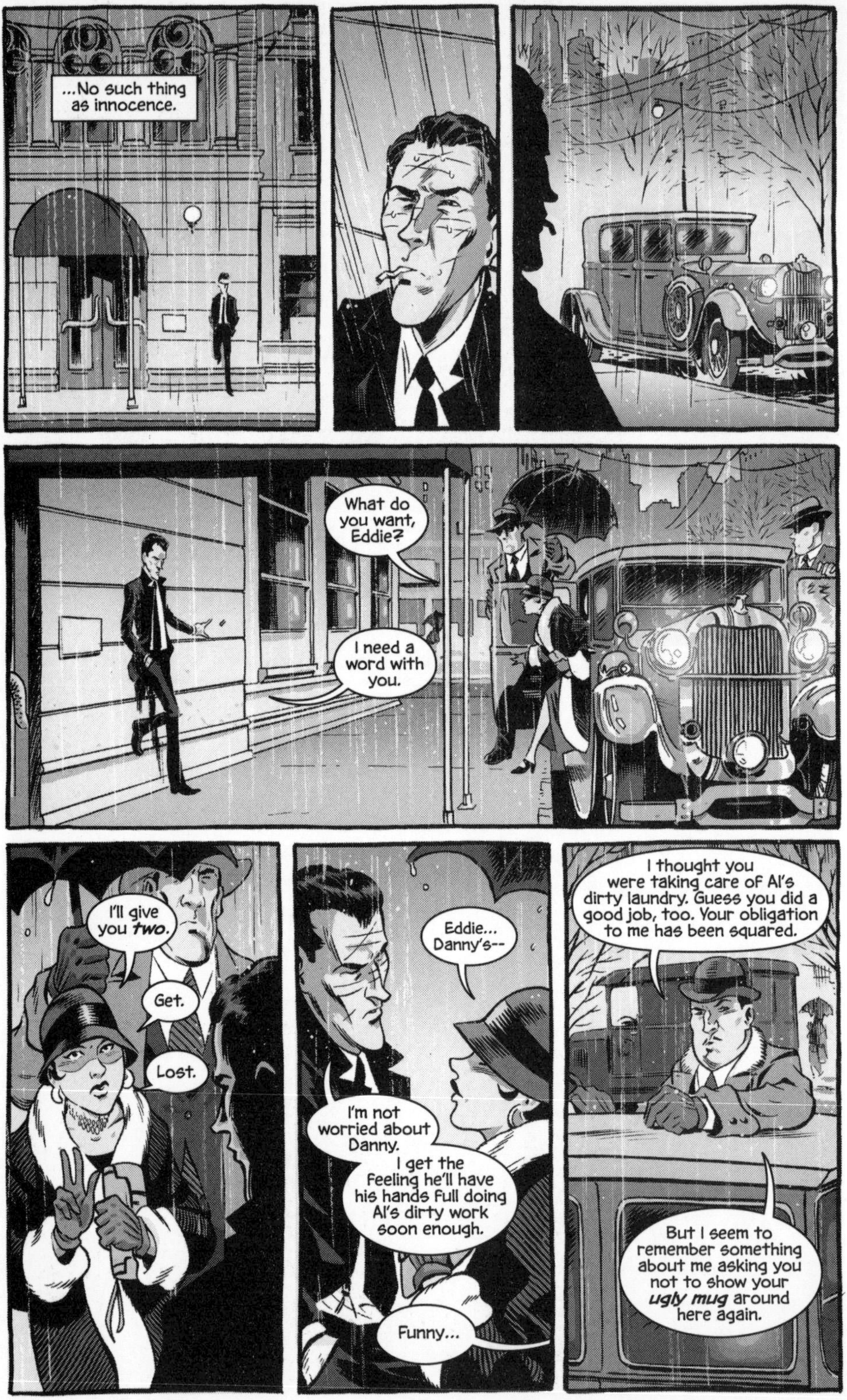

...No such thing as innocence.
What do you want, Eddie?
I need a word with you.
I'll give you *two*.
Get.
Lost.
Eddie... Danny's--
I'm not worried about Danny.
I get the feeling he'll have his hands full doing Al's dirty work soon enough.
Funny...
I thought you were taking care of Al's dirty laundry. Guess you did a good job, too. Your obligation to me has been squared.
But I seem to remember something about me asking you not to show your *ugly mug* around here again.

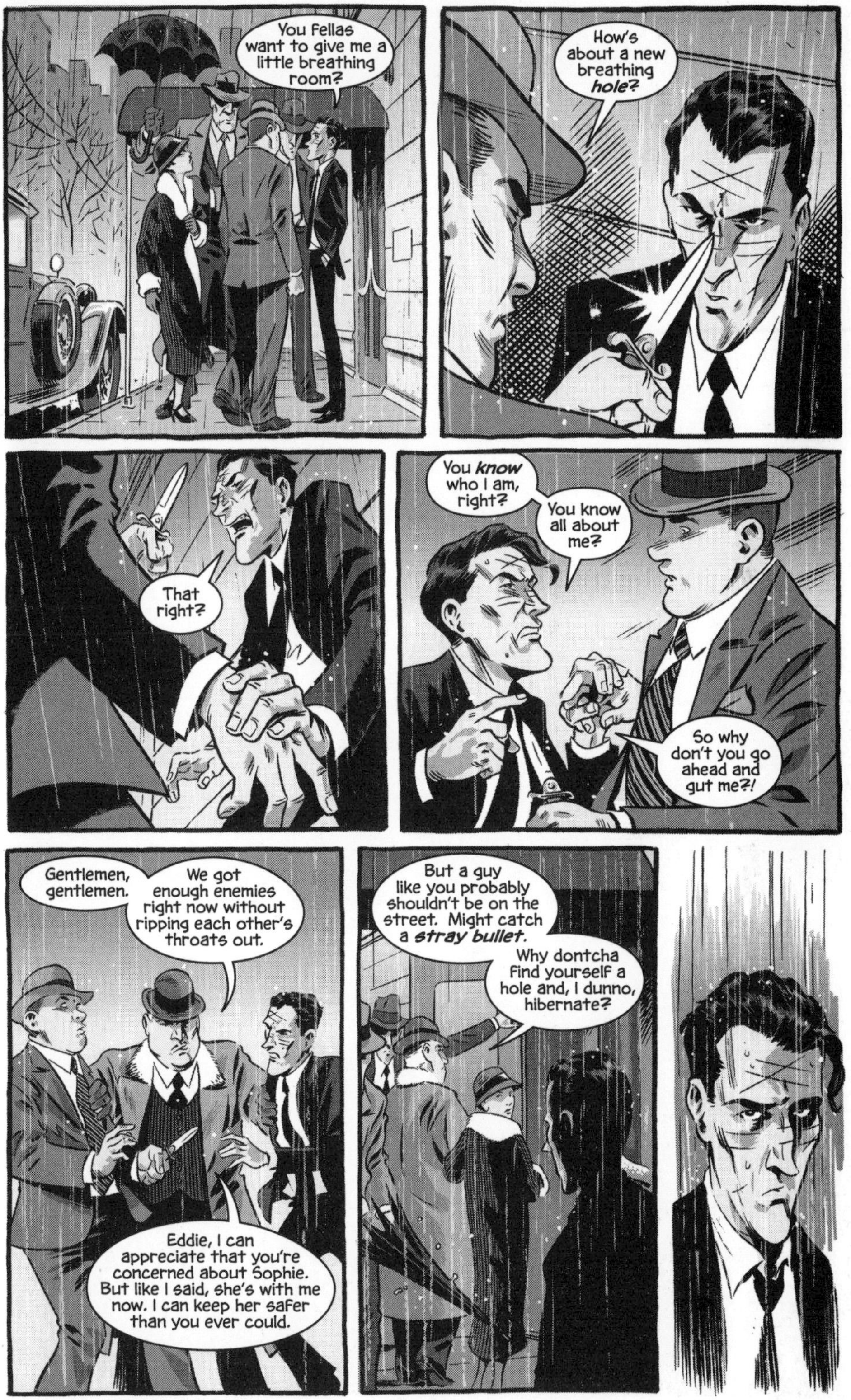
You Fellas want to give me a little breathing room?
How's about a new breathing hole?
That right?
You know who I am, right?
You know all about me?
So why don't you go ahead and gut me?!
Gentlemen, gentlemen.
We got enough enemies right now without ripping each other's throats out.
Eddie, I can appreciate that you're concerned about Sophie. But like I said, she's with me now. I can keep her safer than you ever could.
But a guy like you probably shouldn't be on the street. Might catch a stray bullet.
Why dontcha find yourself a hole and, I dunno, hibernate?

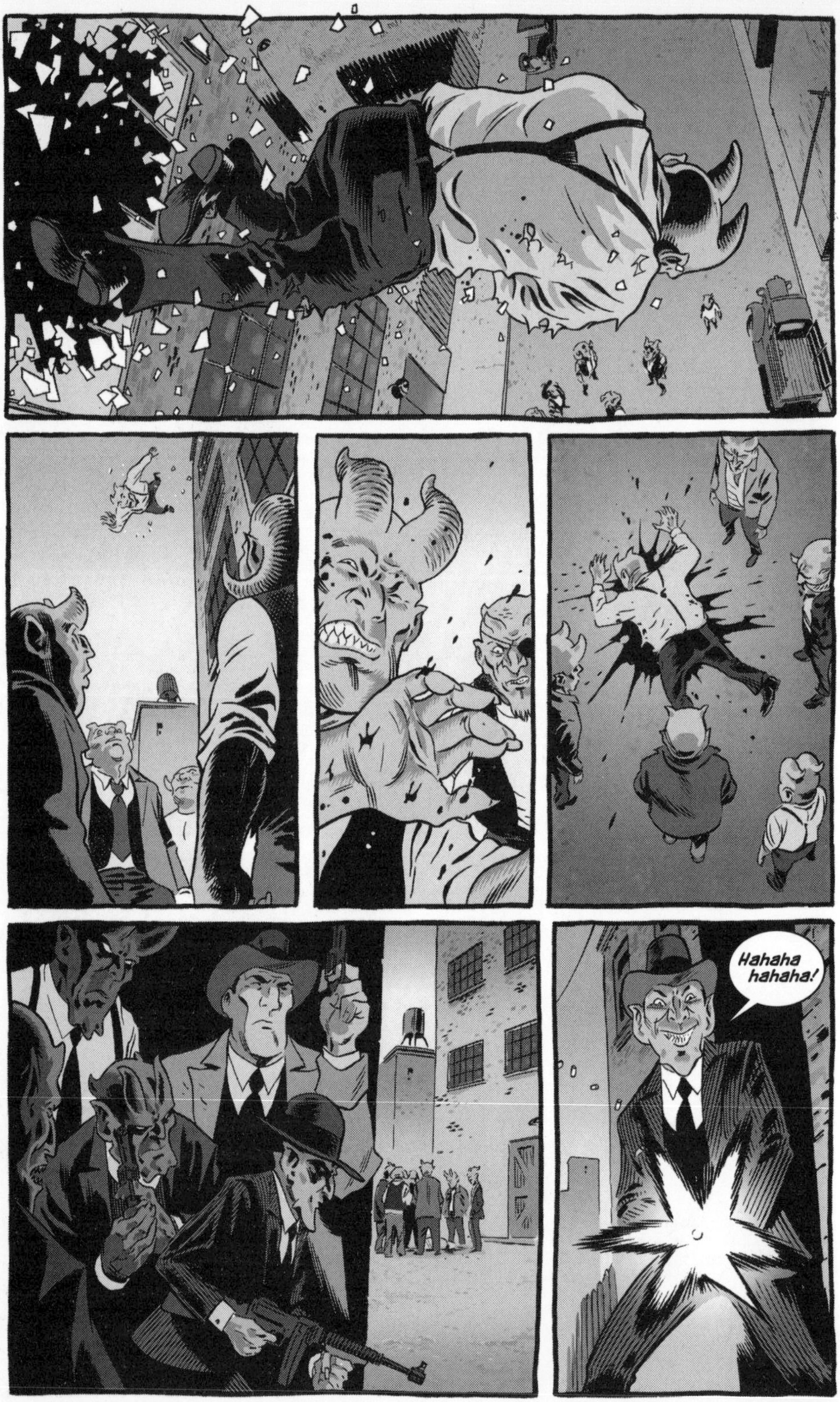
Hahaha
hahaha!

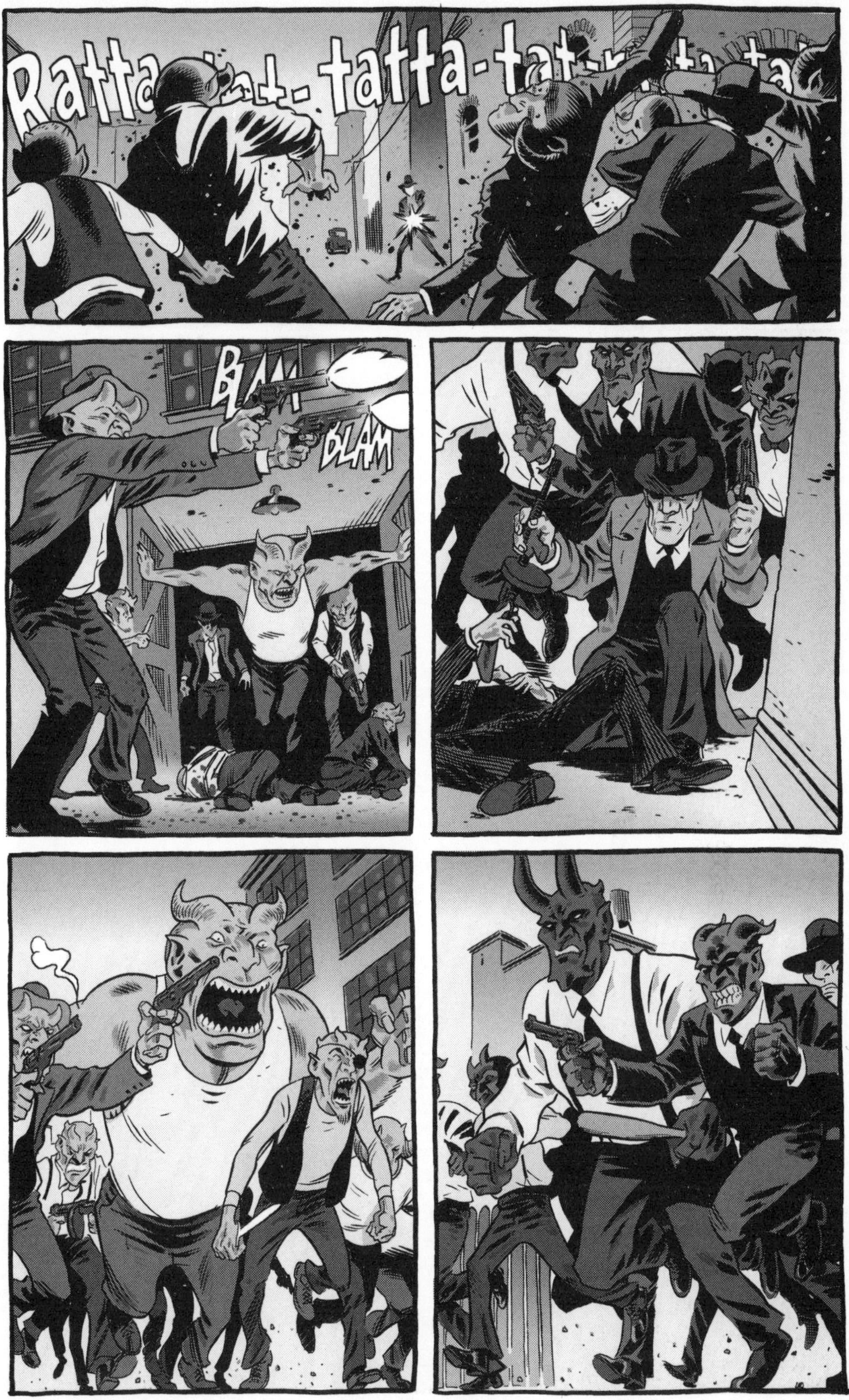
Ratta
tatta-tat
BLAM
BLAM

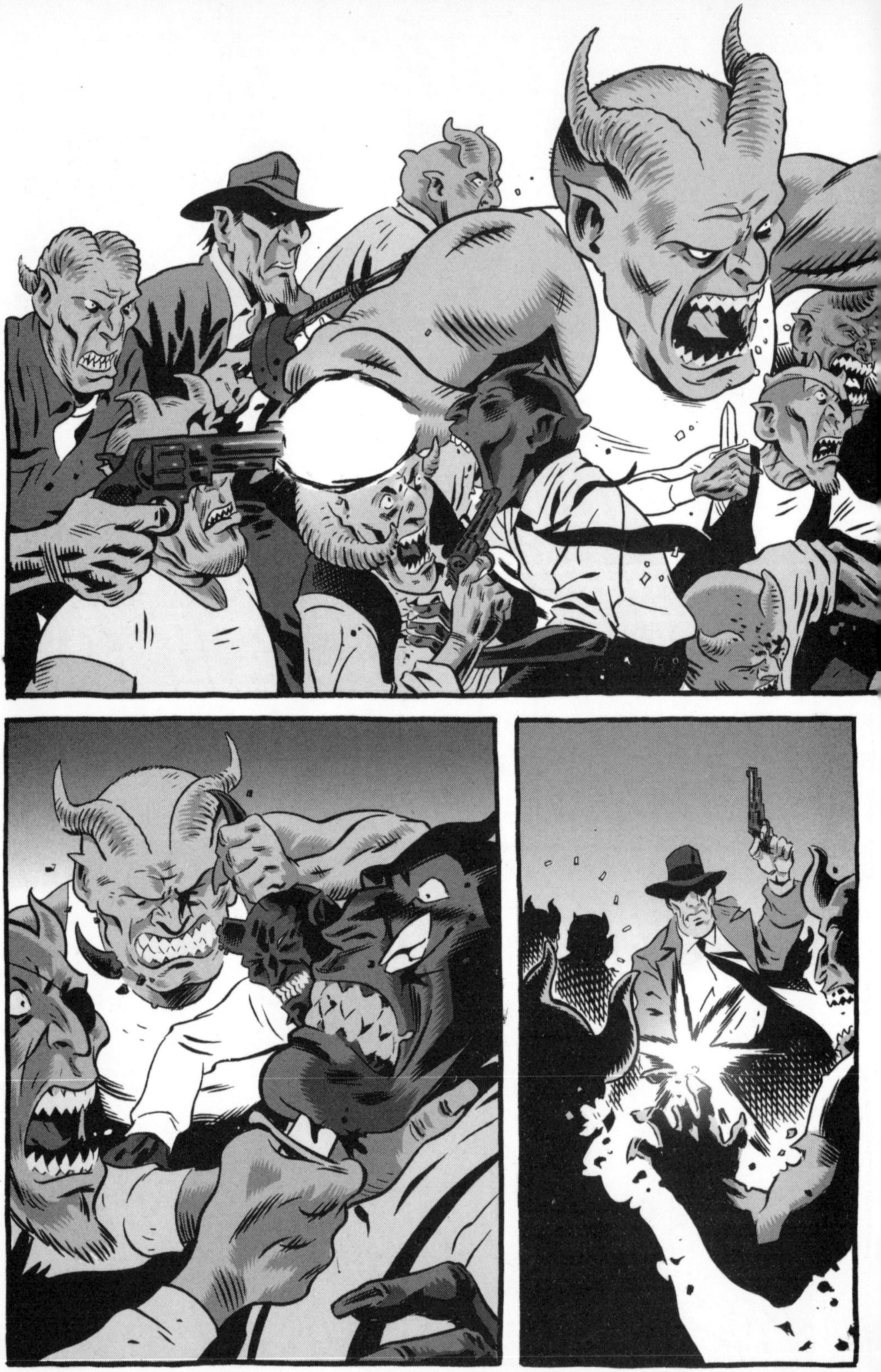

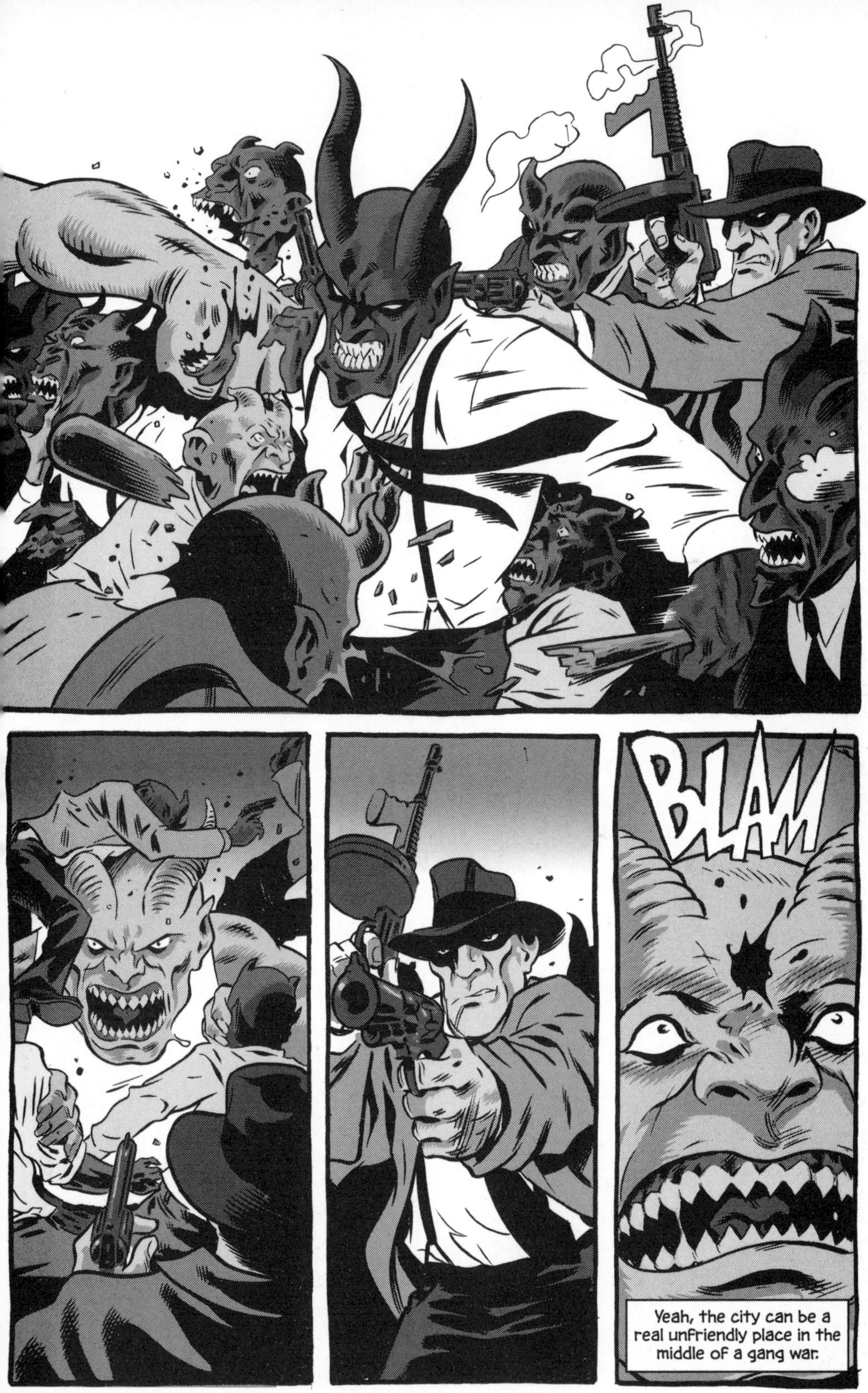
BLAM
Yeah, the city can be a real unfriendly place in the middle of a gang war.

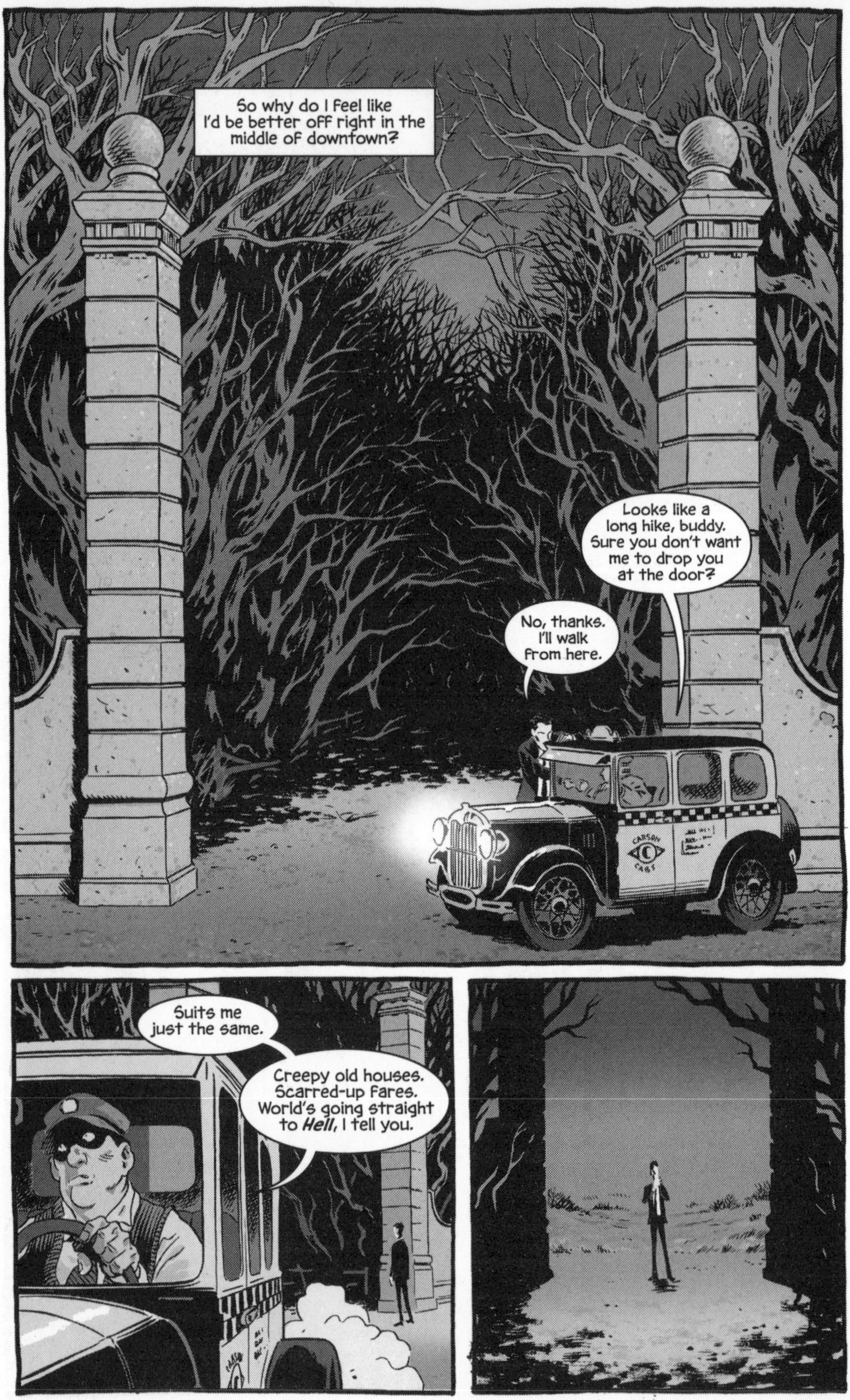
So why do I feel like I'd be better off right in the middle of downtown?
Looks like a long hike, buddy. Sure you don't want me to drop you at the door?
No, thanks. I'll walk from here.
CARSON CABS
Suits me just the same.
Creepy old houses. Scarred-up fares. World's going straight to *Hell*, I tell you.

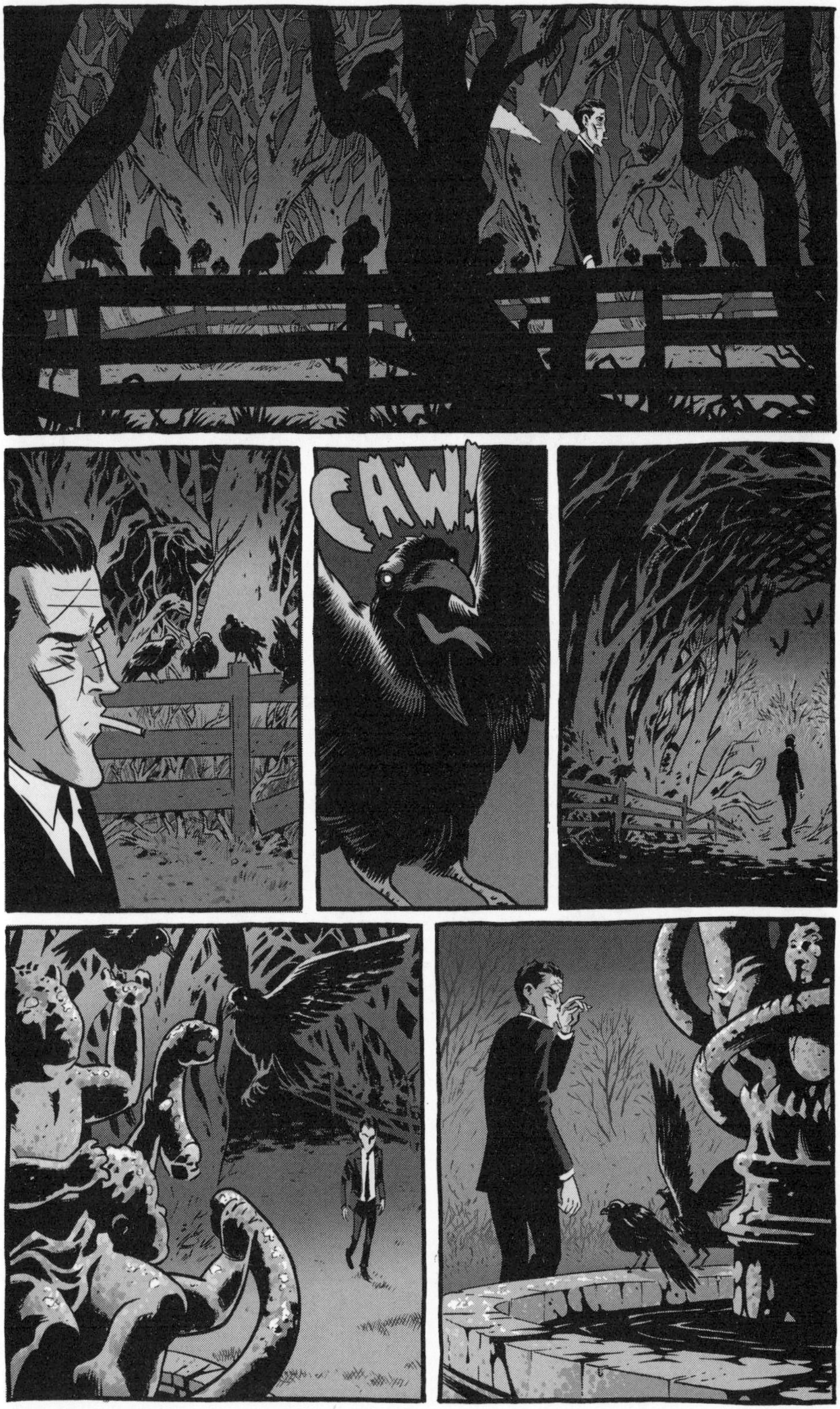
CAW!

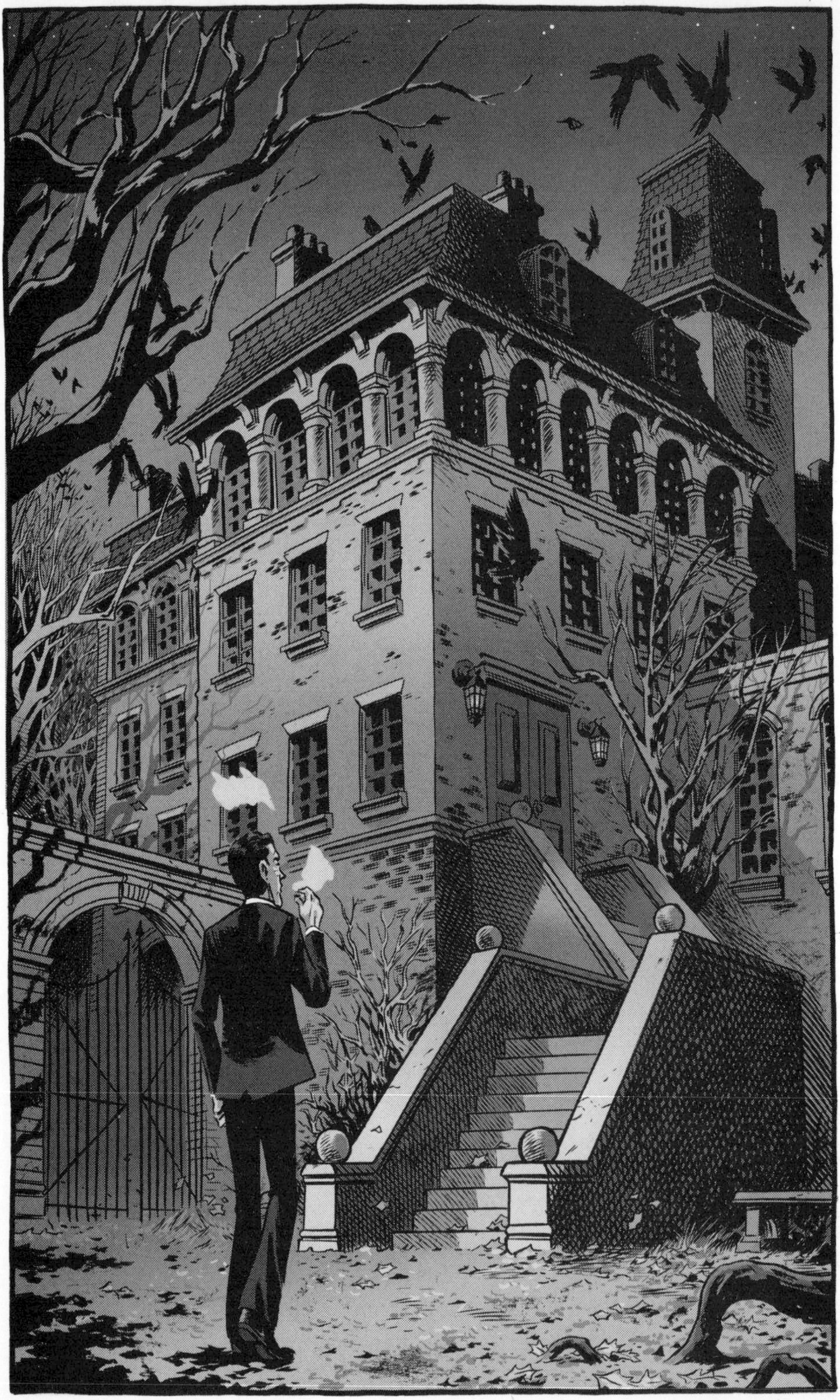

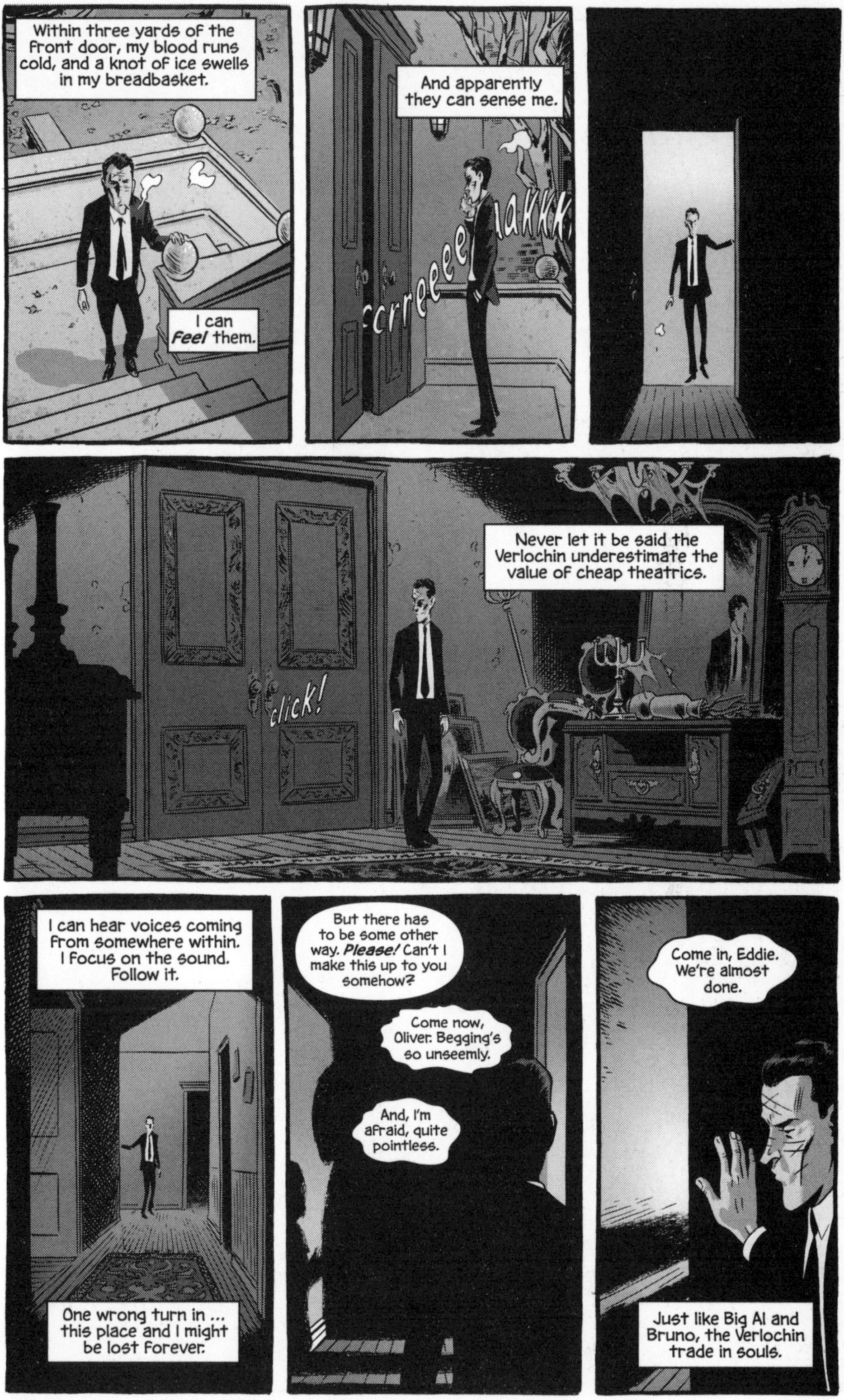

Within three yards of the front door, my blood runs cold, and a knot of ice swells in my breadbasket.
I can *Feel* them.
And apparently they can sense me.
ccrreeeeeaakkkk
Never let it be said the Verlochin underestimate the value of cheap theatrics.
click!
I can hear voices coming from somewhere within. I focus on the sound. Follow it.
One wrong turn in ... this place and I might be lost forever.
But there has to be some other way. *Please!* Can't I make this up to you somehow?
Come now, Oliver. Begging's so unseemly.
And, I'm afraid, quite pointless.
Come in, Eddie. We're almost done.
Just like Big Al and Bruno, the Verlochin trade in souls.

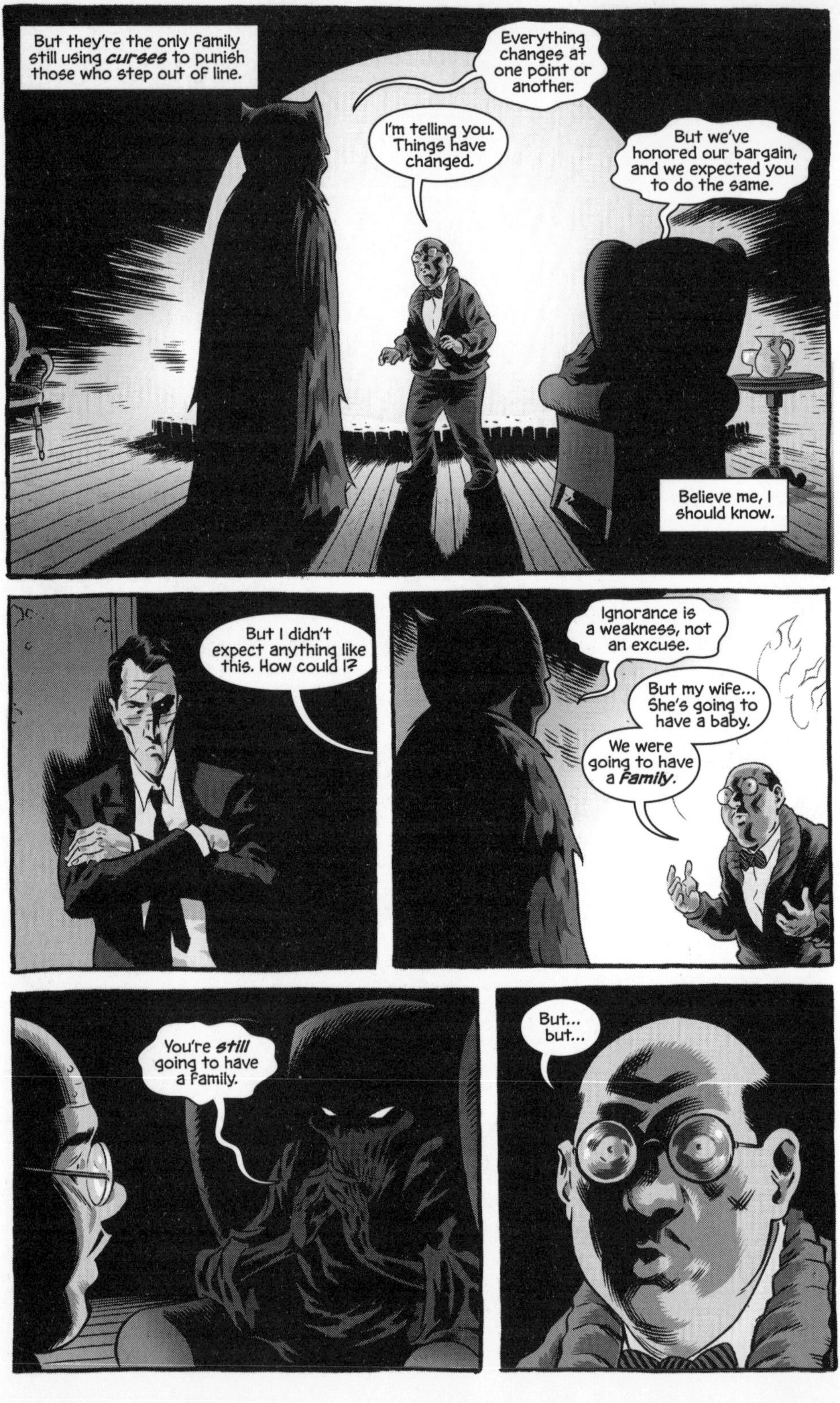
But they're the only family still using *curses* to punish those who step out of line.
Everything changes at one point or another.
I'm telling you. Things have changed.
But we've honored our bargain, and we expected you to do the same.
Believe me, I should know.
But I didn't expect anything like this. How could I?
Ignorance is a weakness, not an excuse.
But my wife... She's going to have a baby.
We were going to have a *family*.
You're *still* going to have a family.
But... but...

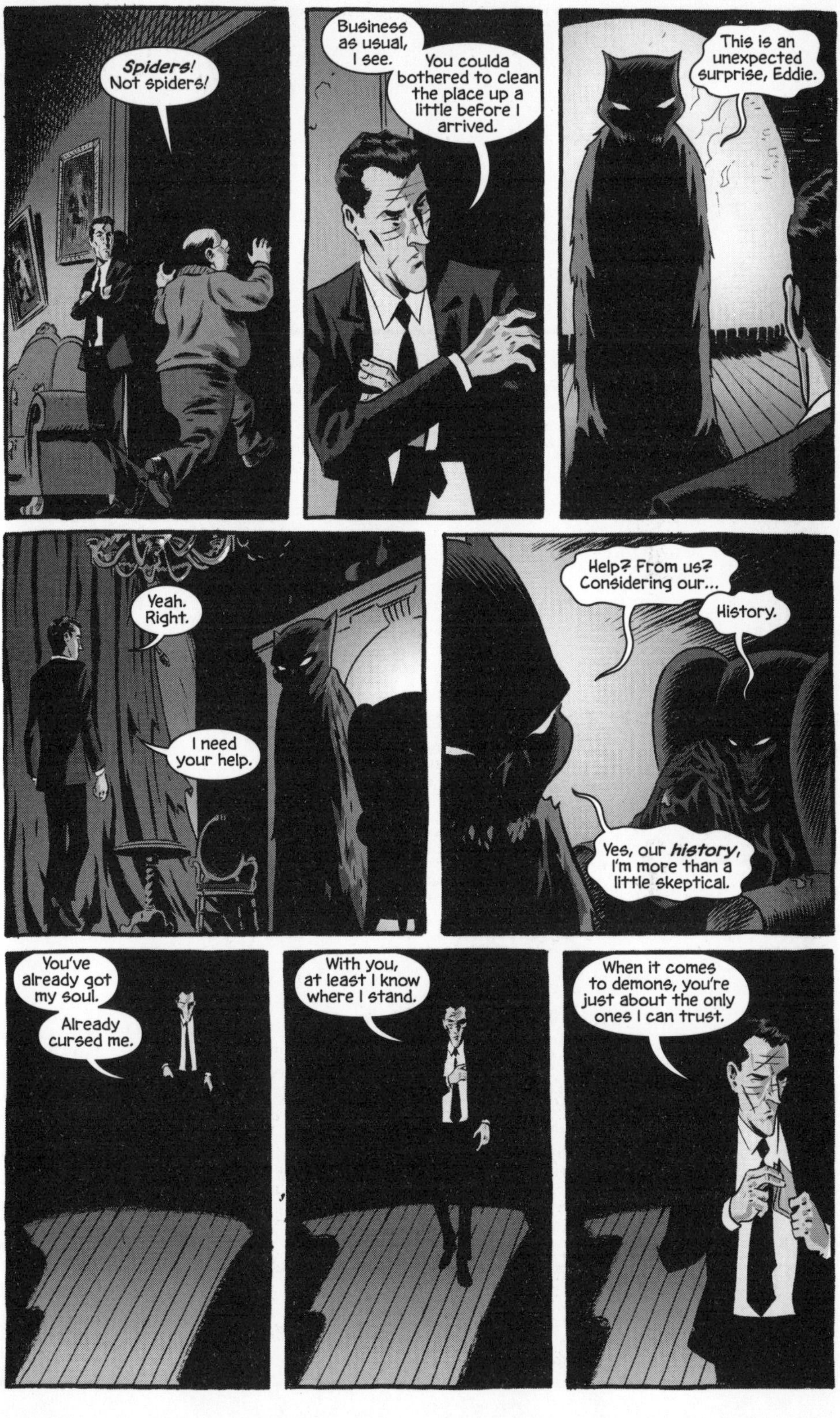
Spiders! Not spiders!
Business as usual, I see.
You coulda bothered to clean the place up a little before I arrived.
This is an unexpected surprise, Eddie.
Yeah. Right.
I need your help.
Help? From us? Considering our...
History.
Yes, our history, I'm more than a little skeptical.
You've already got my soul.
Already cursed me.
With you, at least I know where I stand.
When it comes to demons, you're just about the only ones I can trust.

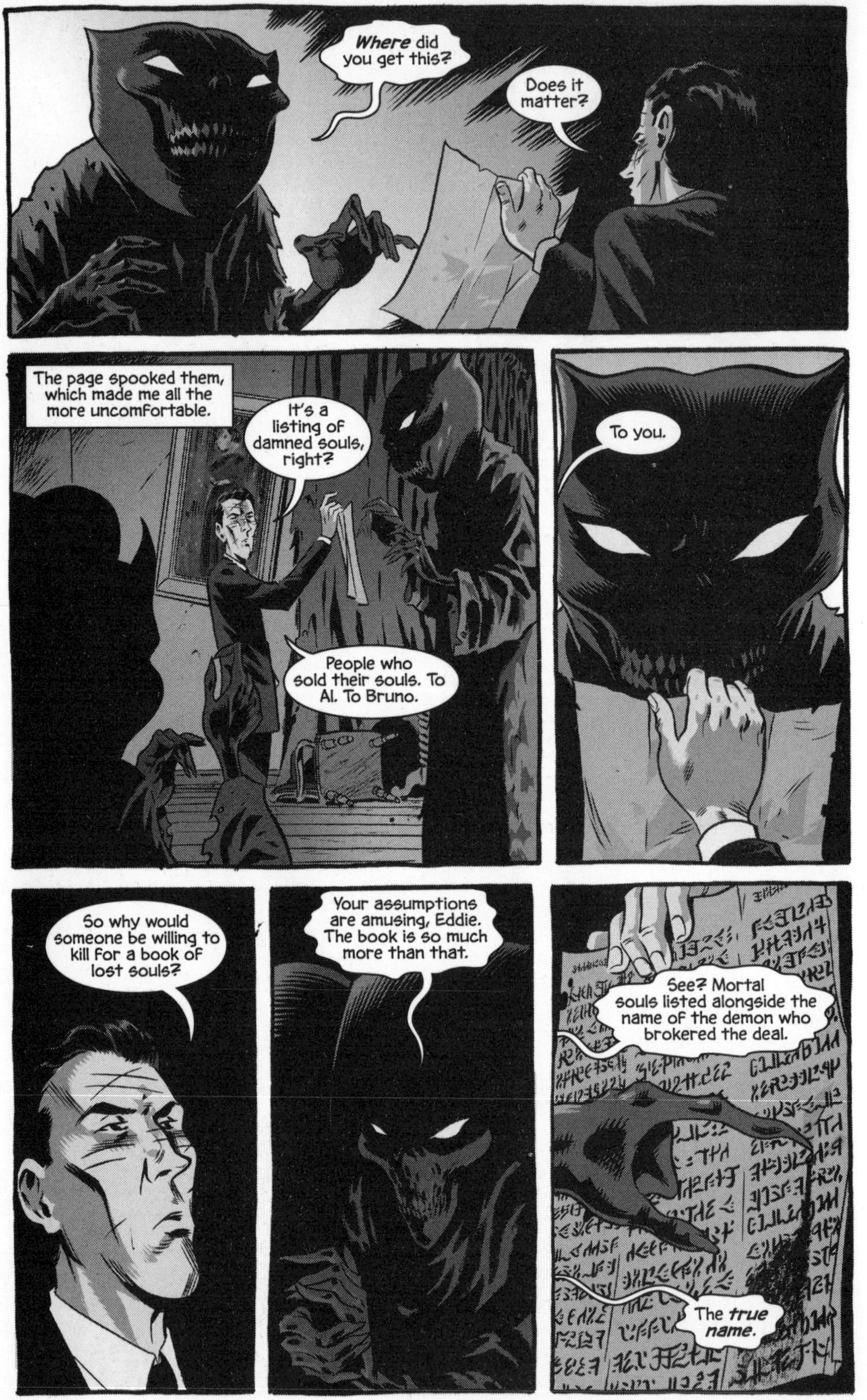
Where did you get this?
Does it matter?
The page spooked them, which made me all the more uncomfortable.
It's a listing of damned souls, right?
People who sold their souls. To Al. To Bruno.
To you.
So why would someone be willing to kill for a book of lost souls?
Your assumptions are amusing, Eddie. The book is so much more than that.
See? Mortal souls listed alongside the name of the demon who brokered the deal.
The *true name*.

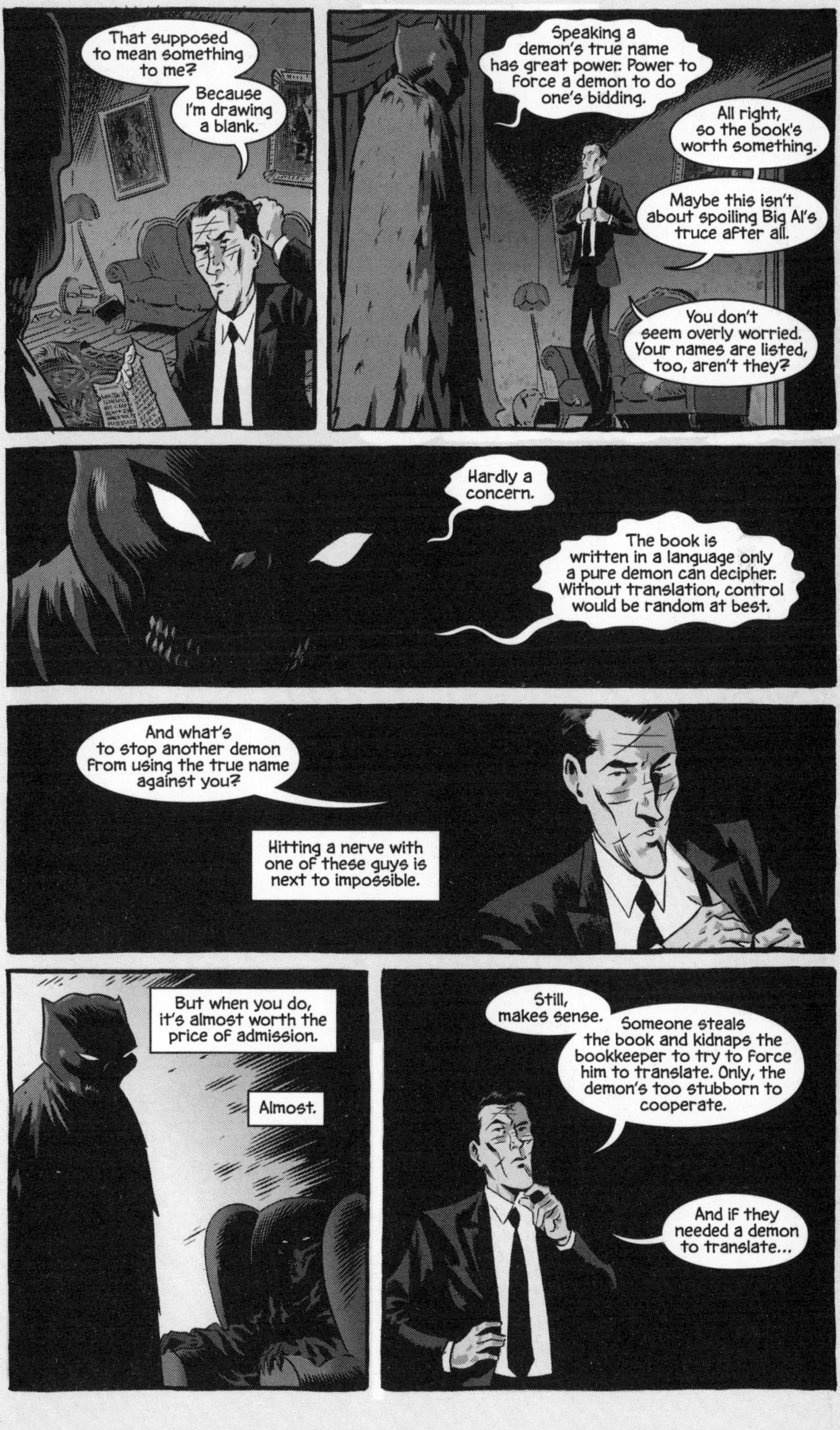
That supposed to mean something to me?
Because I'm drawing a blank.
Speaking a demon's true name has great power. Power to force a demon to do one's bidding.
All right, so the book's worth something.
Maybe this isn't about spoiling Big Al's truce after all.
You don't seem overly worried. Your names are listed, too, aren't they?
Hardly a concern.
The book is written in a language only a pure demon can decipher. Without translation, control would be random at best.
And what's to stop another demon from using the true name against you?
Hitting a nerve with one of these guys is next to impossible.
But when you do, it's almost worth the price of admission.
Almost.
Still, makes sense.
Someone steals the book and kidnaps the bookkeeper to try to force him to translate. Only, the demon's too stubborn to cooperate.
And if they needed a demon to translate...

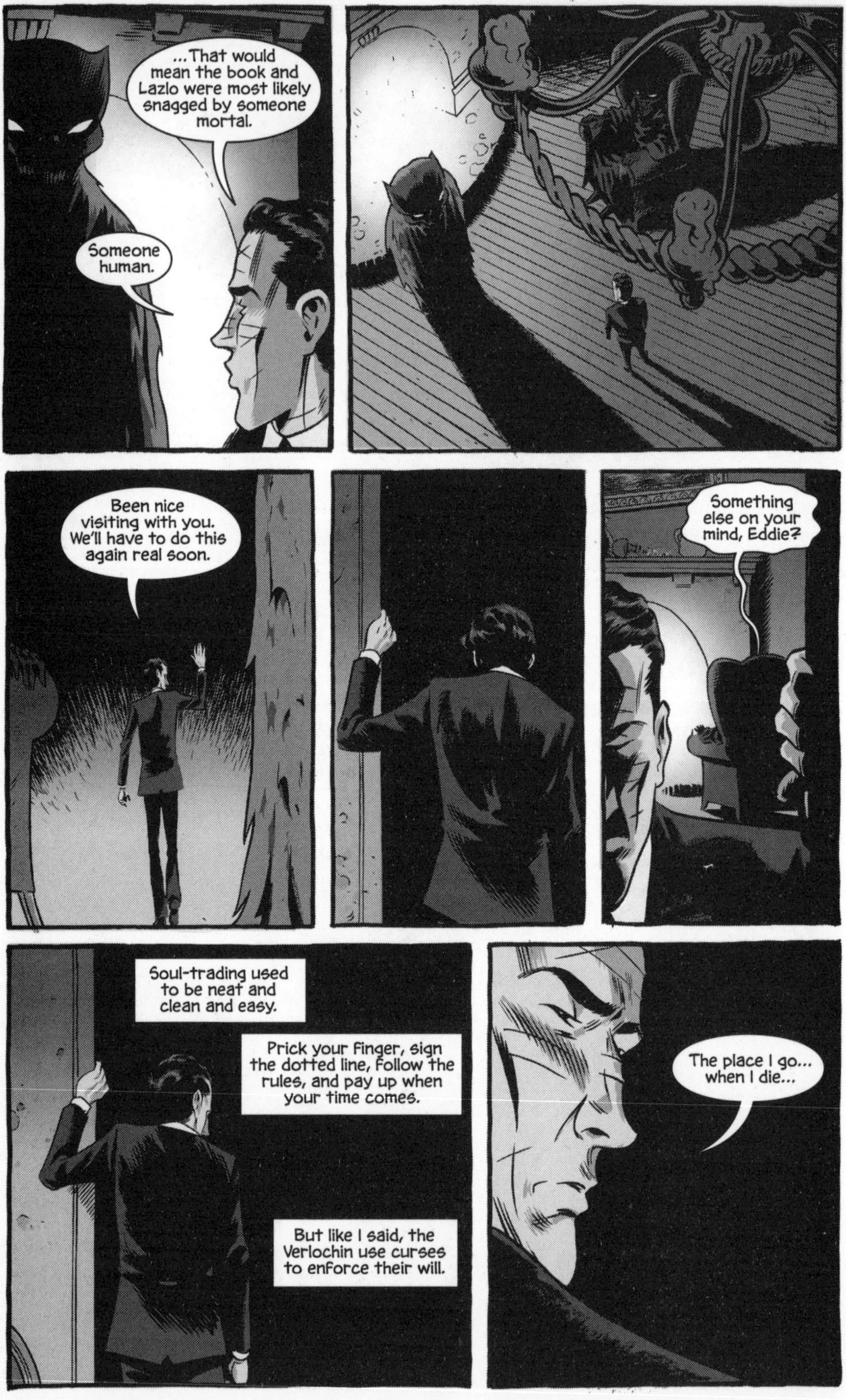
...That would mean the book and Lazlo were most likely snagged by someone mortal.
Someone human.
Been nice visiting with you. We'll have to do this again real soon.
Something else on your mind, Eddie?
Soul-trading used to be neat and clean and easy.
Prick your finger, sign the dotted line, follow the rules, and pay up when your time comes.
But like I said, the Verlochin use curses to enforce their will.
The place I go... when I die...

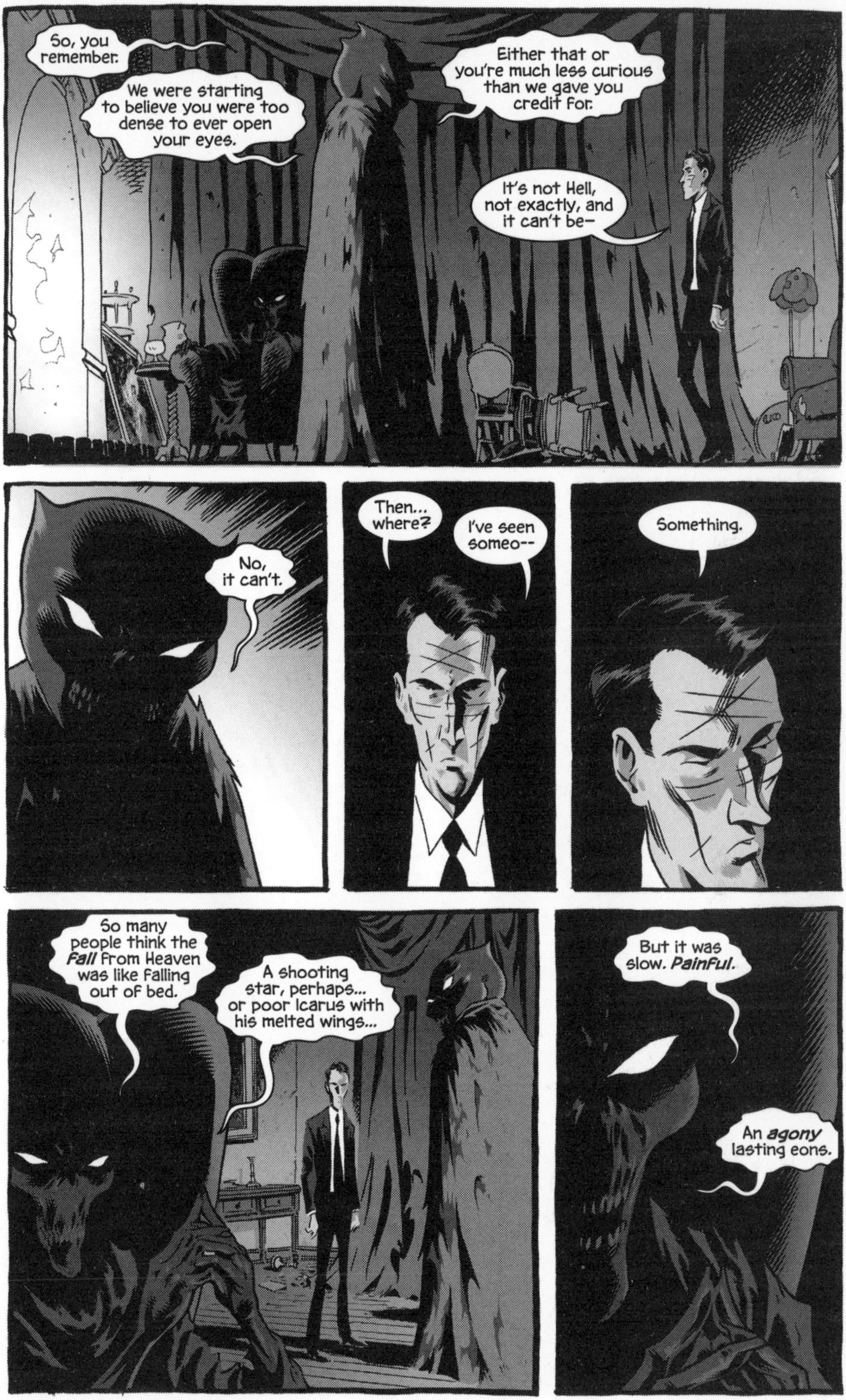

So, you remember.
We were starting to believe you were too dense to ever open your eyes.
Either that or you're much less curious than we gave you credit for.
It's not Hell, not exactly, and it can't be–
No, it can't.
Then... where?
I've seen someo--
Something.
So many people think the *Fall* from Heaven was like falling out of bed.
A shooting star, perhaps... or poor Icarus with his melted wings...
But it was slow. *Painful.*
An *agony* lasting eons.

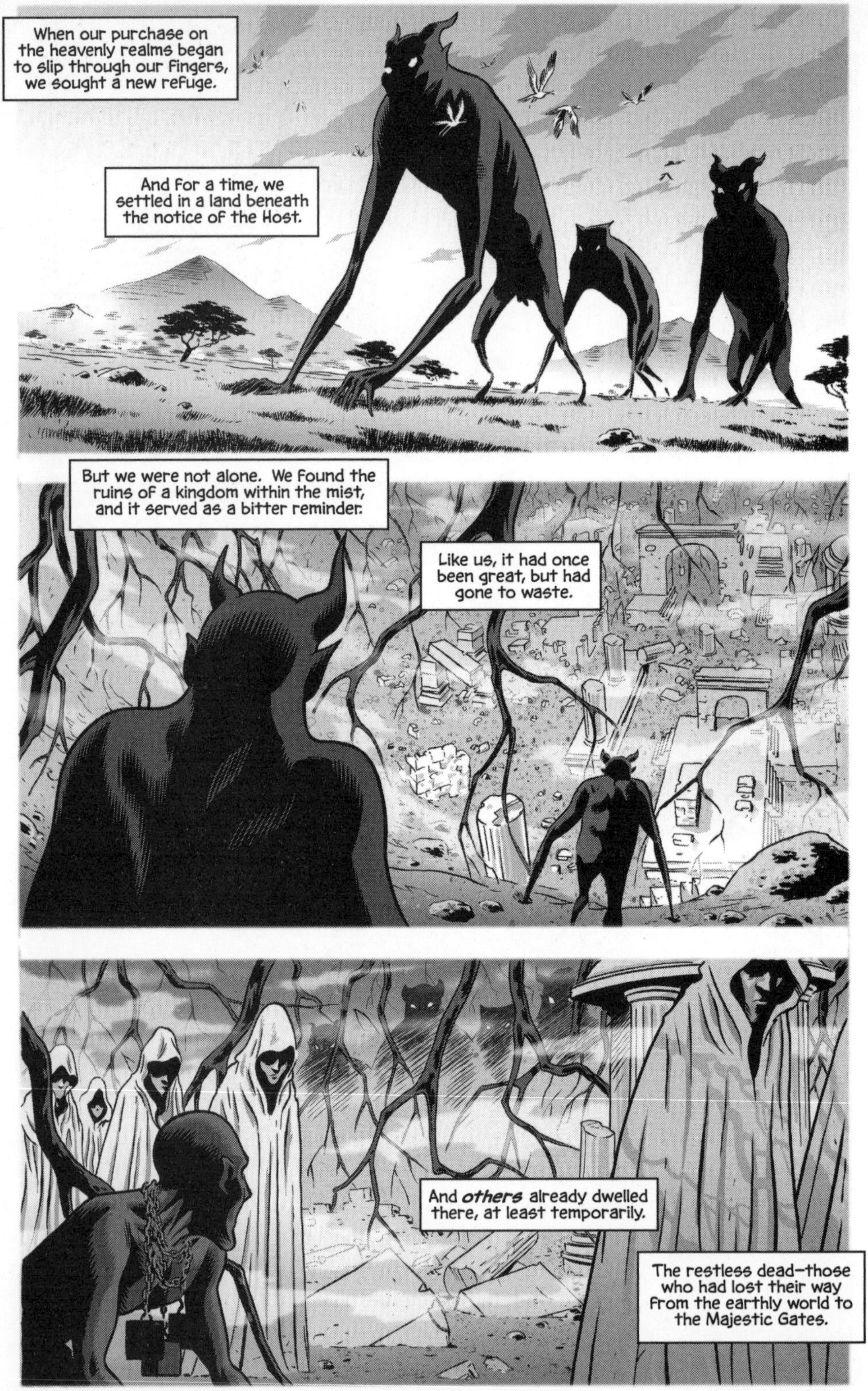
When our purchase on the heavenly realms began to slip through our fingers, we sought a new refuge.
And for a time, we settled in a land beneath the notice of the Host.
But we were not alone. We found the ruins of a kingdom within the mist, and it served as a bitter reminder.
Like us, it had once been great, but had gone to waste.
And *others* already dwelled there, at least temporarily.
The restless dead—those who had lost their way from the earthly world to the Majestic Gates.

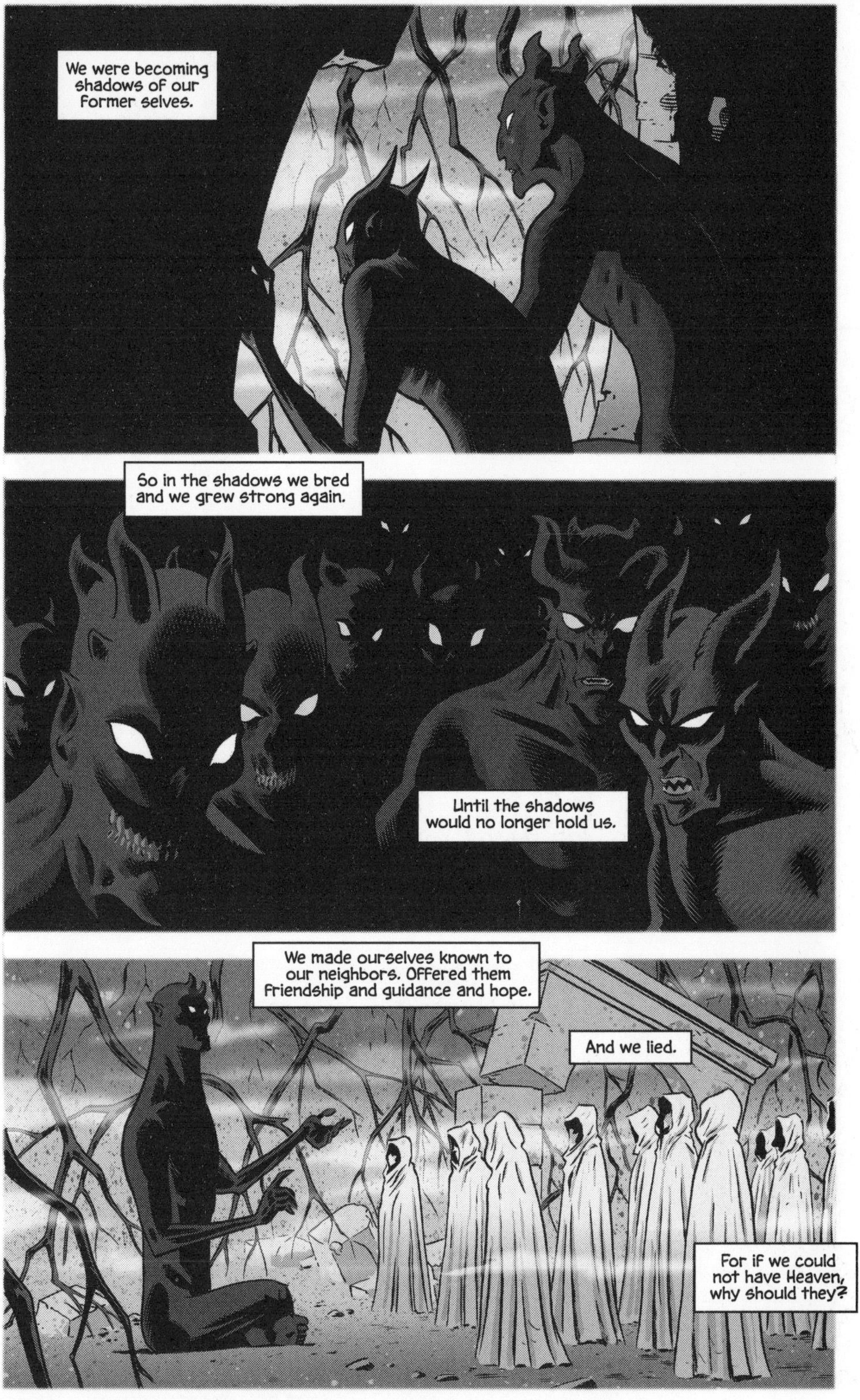
We were becoming shadows of our former selves.
So in the shadows we bred and we grew strong again.
Until the shadows would no longer hold us.
We made ourselves known to our neighbors. Offered them friendship and guidance and hope.
And we lied.
For if we could not have Heaven, why should they?

Once again, we felt strong and proud, and we instructed our students to rebuild the kingdom in our image.

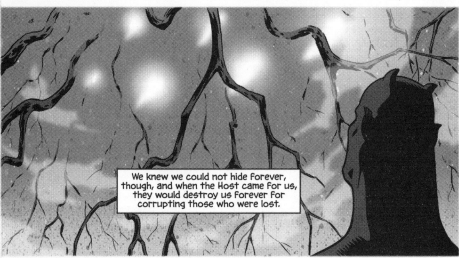

We knew we could not hide forever, though, and when the Host came for us, they would destroy us forever for corrupting those who were lost.

So we found even deeper places, and there we built ourselves a new home.

When the Host finally arrived, they found only our leavings. And they worked their wardings to bar us from that realm forever.

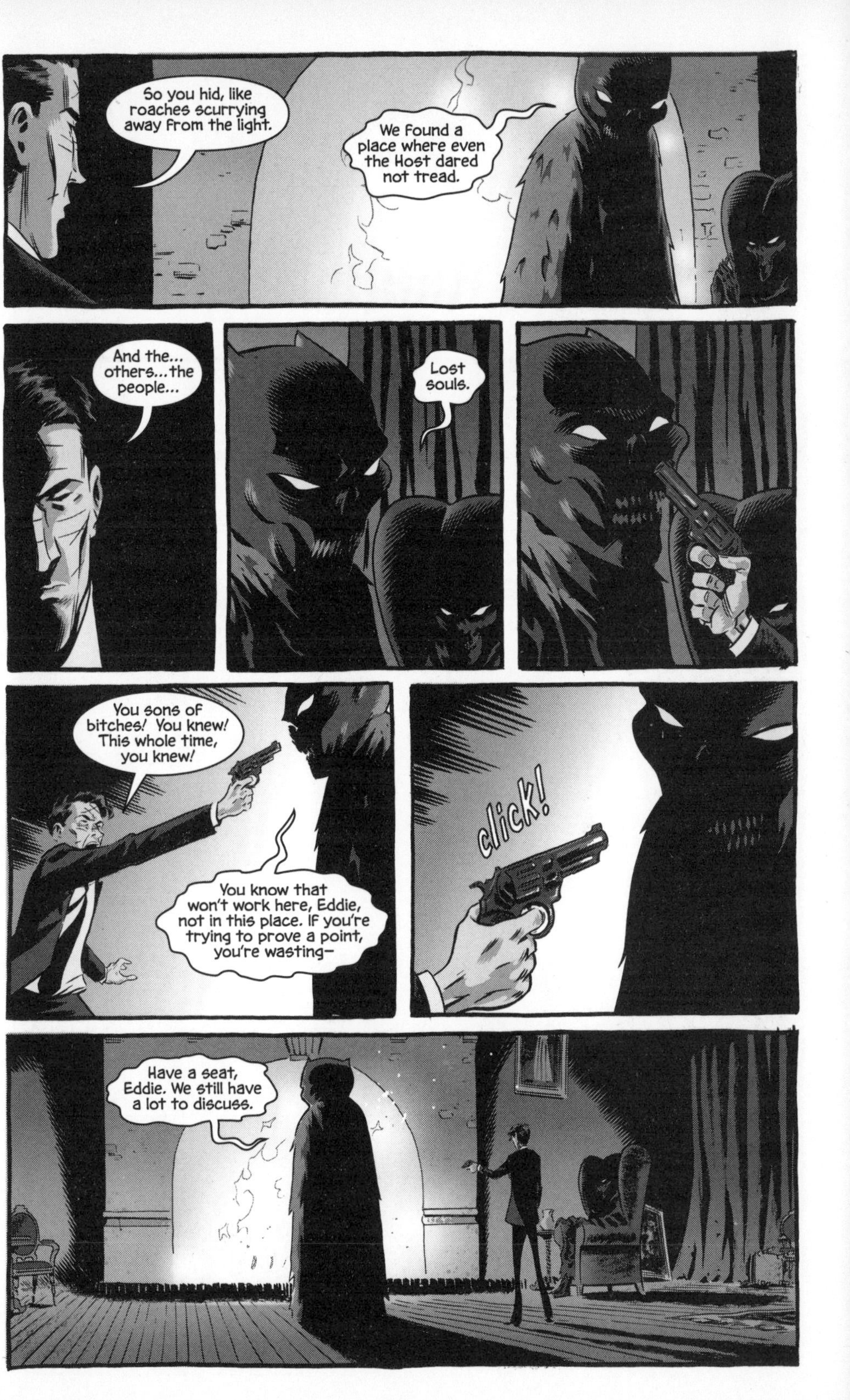
So you hid, like roaches scurrying away from the light.
We found a place where even the Host dared not tread.
And the... others...the people...
Lost souls.
You sons of bitches! You knew! This whole time, you knew!
You know that won't work here, Eddie, not in this place. If you're trying to prove a point, you're wasting—
click!
Have a seat, Eddie. We still have a lot to discuss.

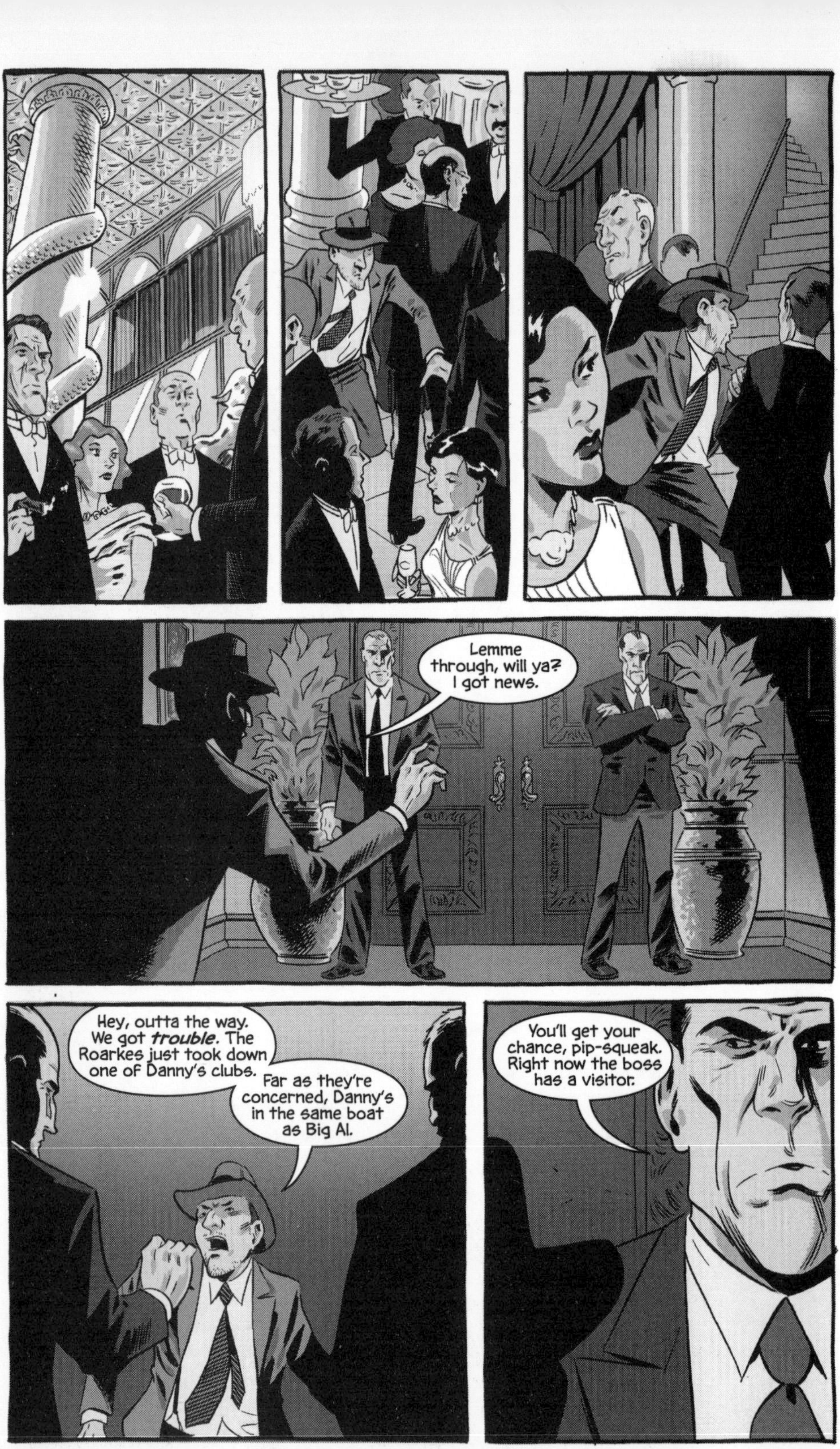
Lemme through, will ya? I got news.
Hey, outta the way. We got *trouble*. The Roarkes just took down one of Danny's clubs.
Far as they're concerned, Danny's in the same boat as Big Al.
You'll get your chance, pip-squeak. Right now the boss has a visitor.

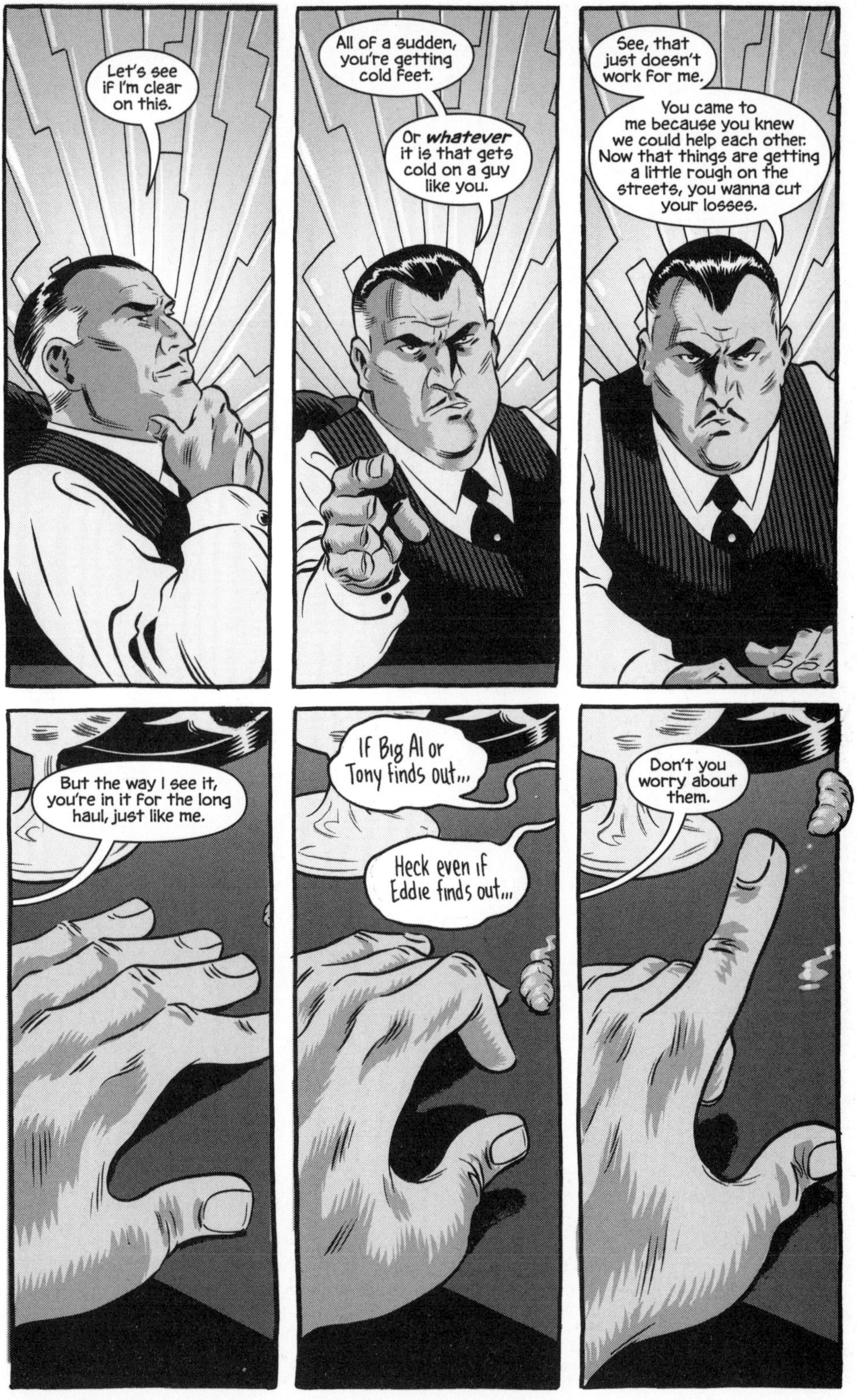
Let's see if I'm clear on this.
All of a sudden, you're getting cold feet.
Or *whatever* it is that gets cold on a guy like you.
See, that just doesn't work for me.
You came to me because you knew we could help each other. Now that things are getting a little rough on the streets, you wanna cut your losses.
But the way I see it, you're in it for the long haul, just like me.
If Big Al or Tony finds out...
Heck even if Eddie finds out...
Don't you worry about them.

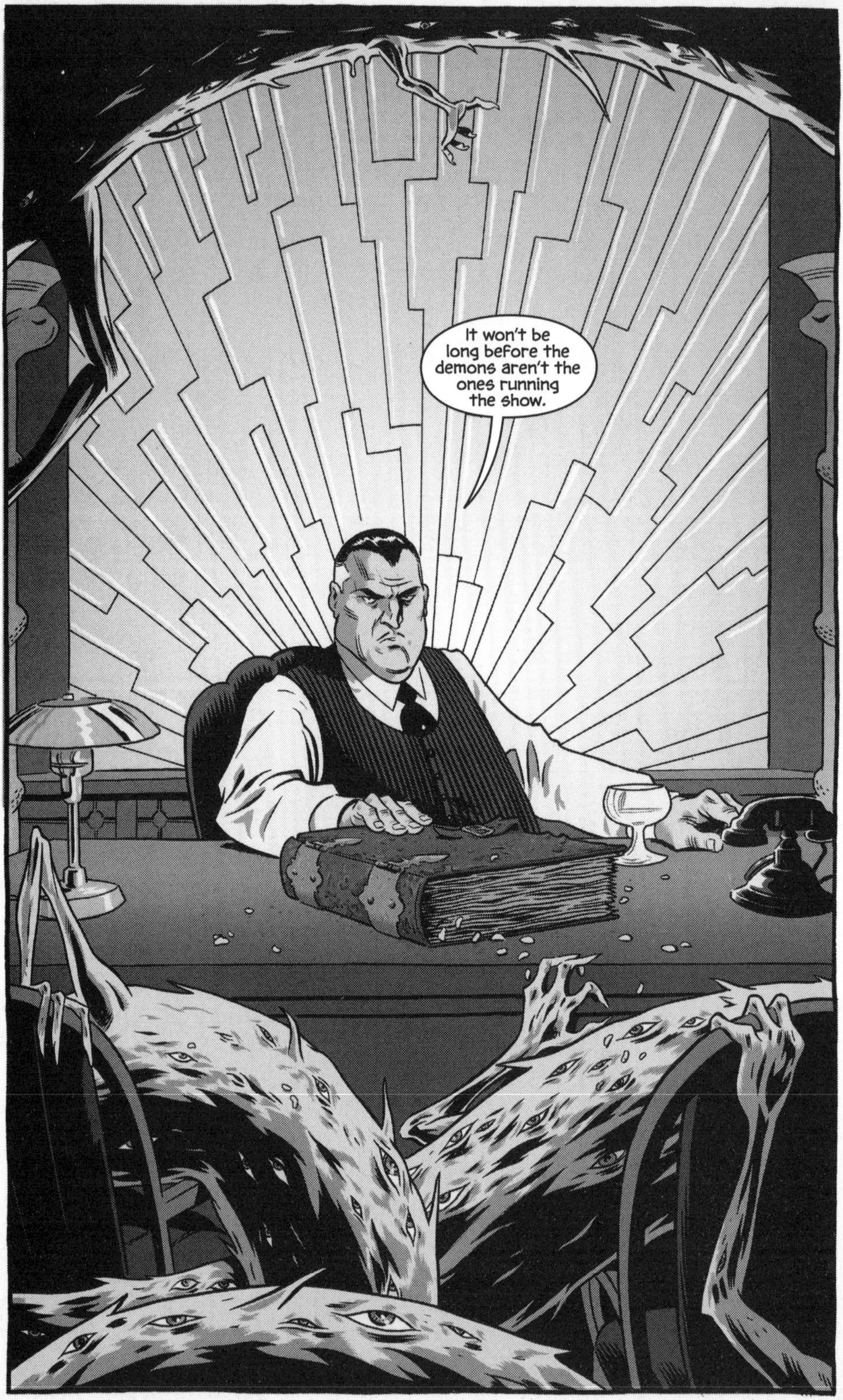
It won't be long before the demons aren't the ones running the show.

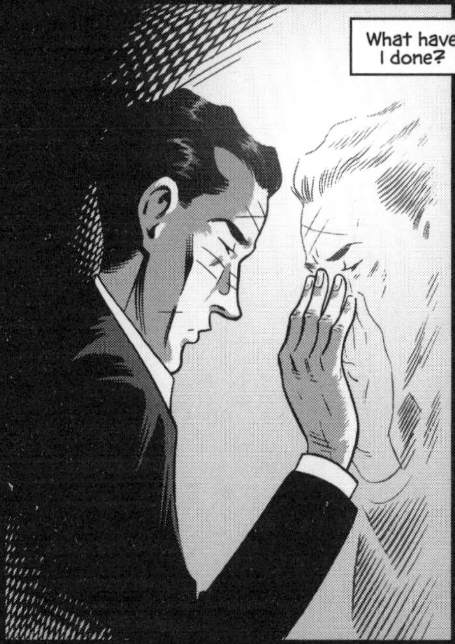
What have I done?

CHAPTER 5

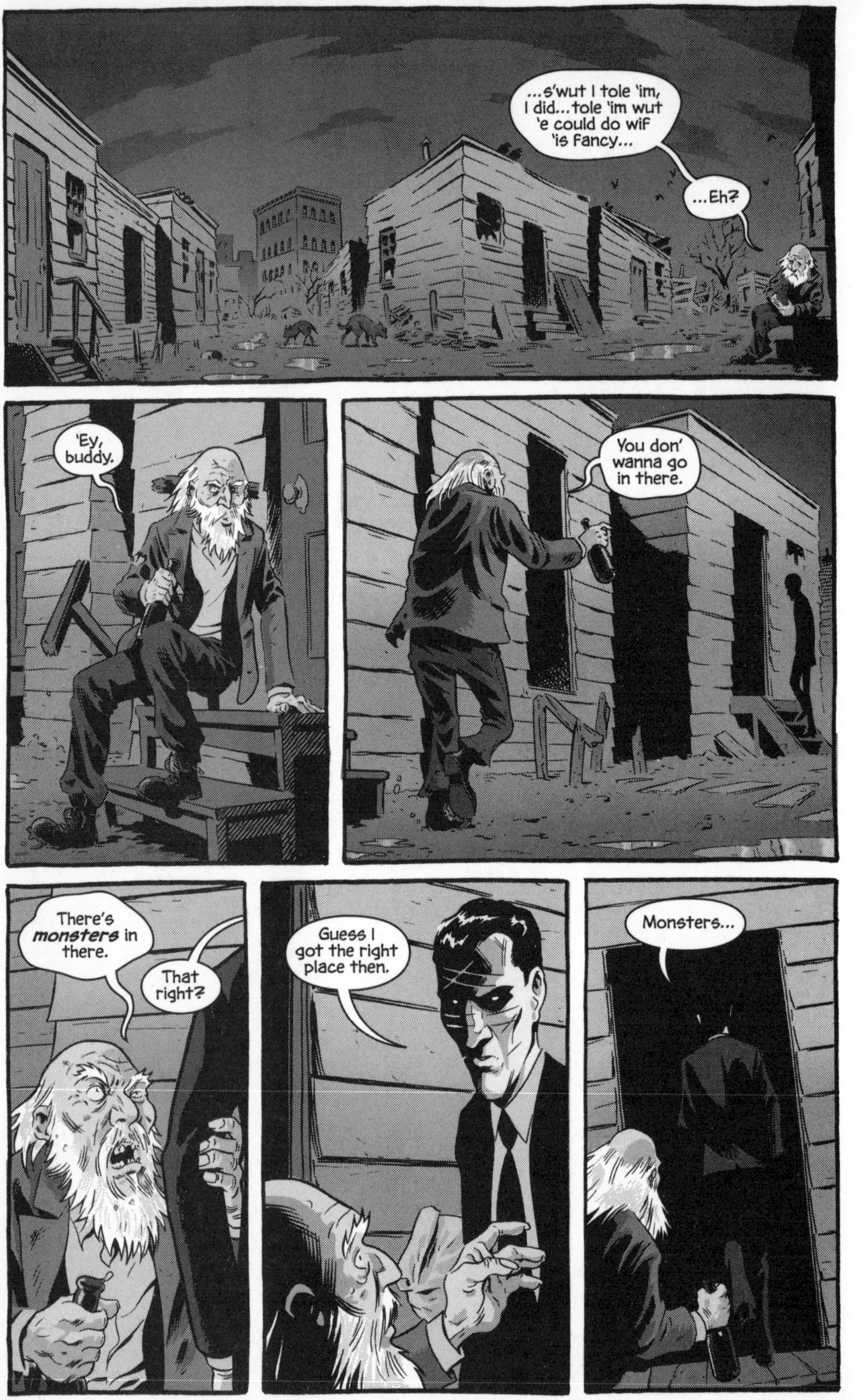
...s'wut I tole 'im, I did...tole 'im wut 'e could do wif 'is fancy...
...Eh?
'Ey, buddy.
You don' wanna go in there.
There's *monsters* in there.
That right?
Guess I got the right place then.
Monsters...

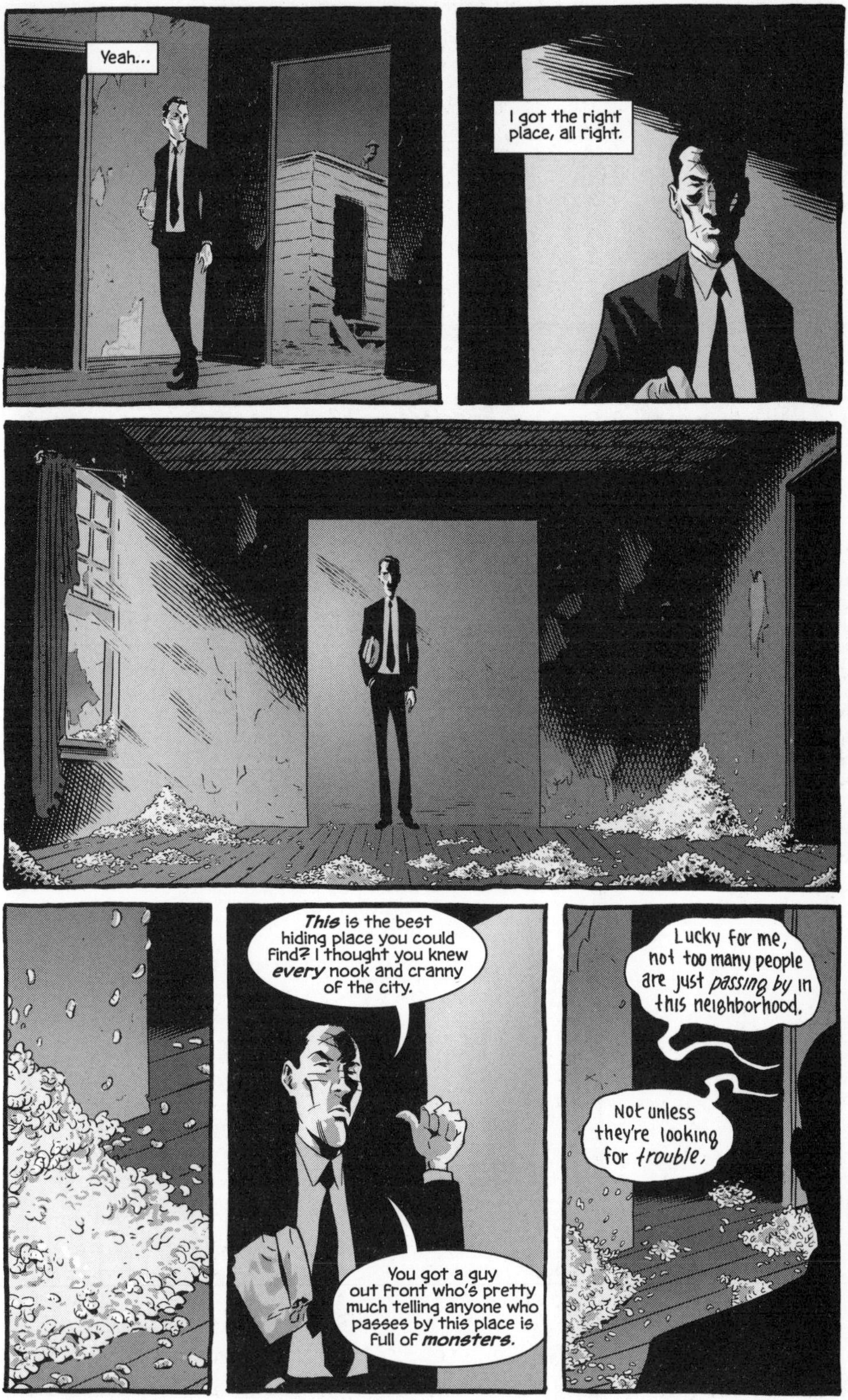
Yeah...
I got the right place, all right.
This is the best hiding place you could find? I thought you knew every nook and cranny of the city.
You got a guy out front who's pretty much telling anyone who passes by this place is full of monsters.
Lucky for me, not too many people are just passing by in this neighborhood.
Not unless they're looking for trouble.

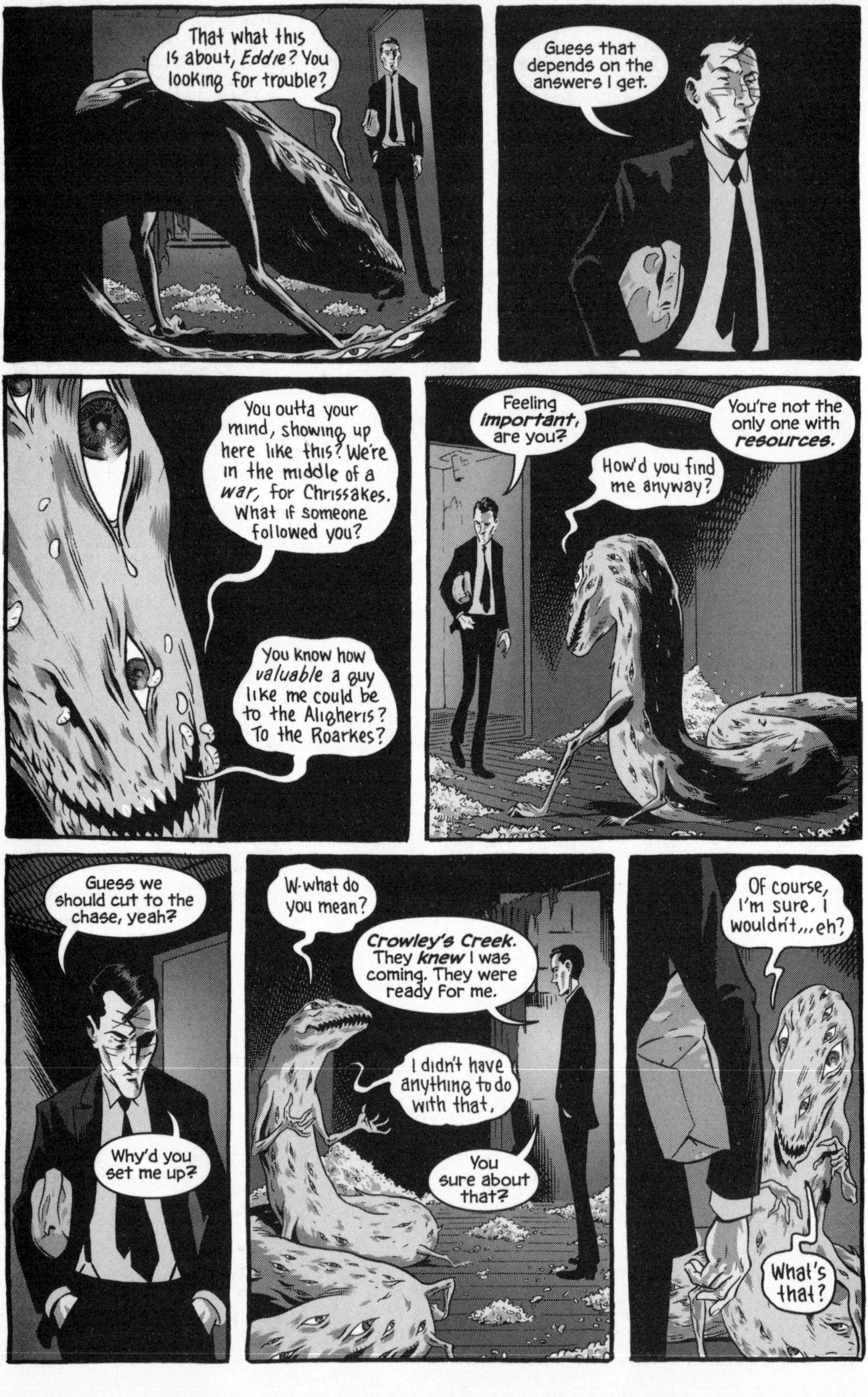
That what this is about, *Eddie?* You looking for trouble?
Guess that depends on the answers I get.
You outta your mind, showing up here like this? We're in the middle of a *war,* for Chrissakes. What if someone followed you?
You know how *valuable* a guy like me could be to the Aligheris? To the Roarkes?
Feeling ***important,*** are you?
You're not the only one with ***resources.***
How'd you find me anyway?
Guess we should cut to the chase, yeah?
Why'd you set me up?
W-what do you mean?
Crowley's Creek. They ***knew*** I was coming. They were ready for me.
I didn't have anything to do with that,
You sure about that?
Of course, I'm sure. I wouldn't... eh?
What's that?

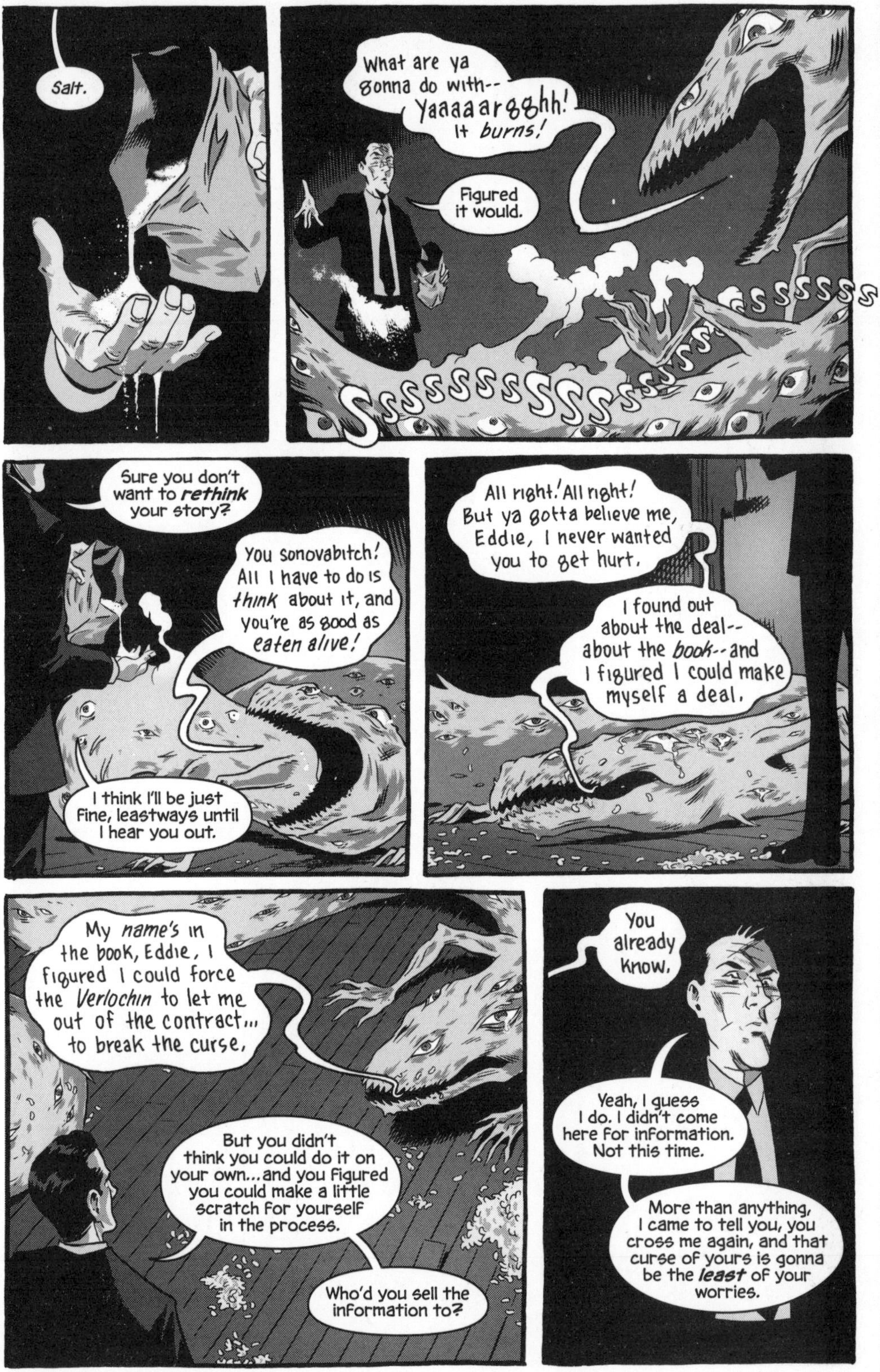
Salt.
What are ya gonna do with-- Yaaaaargghh! It burns!
Figured it would.
SSSSSSSSSSSSSSSSSSSS
Sure you don't want to rethink your story?
You sonovabitch! All I have to do is think about it, and you're as good as eaten alive!
I think I'll be just fine, leastways until I hear you out.
All right! All right! But ya gotta believe me, Eddie, I never wanted you to get hurt.
I found out about the deal-- about the book--and I figured I could make myself a deal.
My name's in the book, Eddie, I figured I could force the Verlochin to let me out of the contract... to break the curse.
But you didn't think you could do it on your own...and you figured you could make a little scratch for yourself in the process.
Who'd you sell the information to?
You already know.
Yeah, I guess I do. I didn't come here for information. Not this time.
More than anything, I came to tell you, you cross me again, and that curse of yours is gonna be the least of your worries.

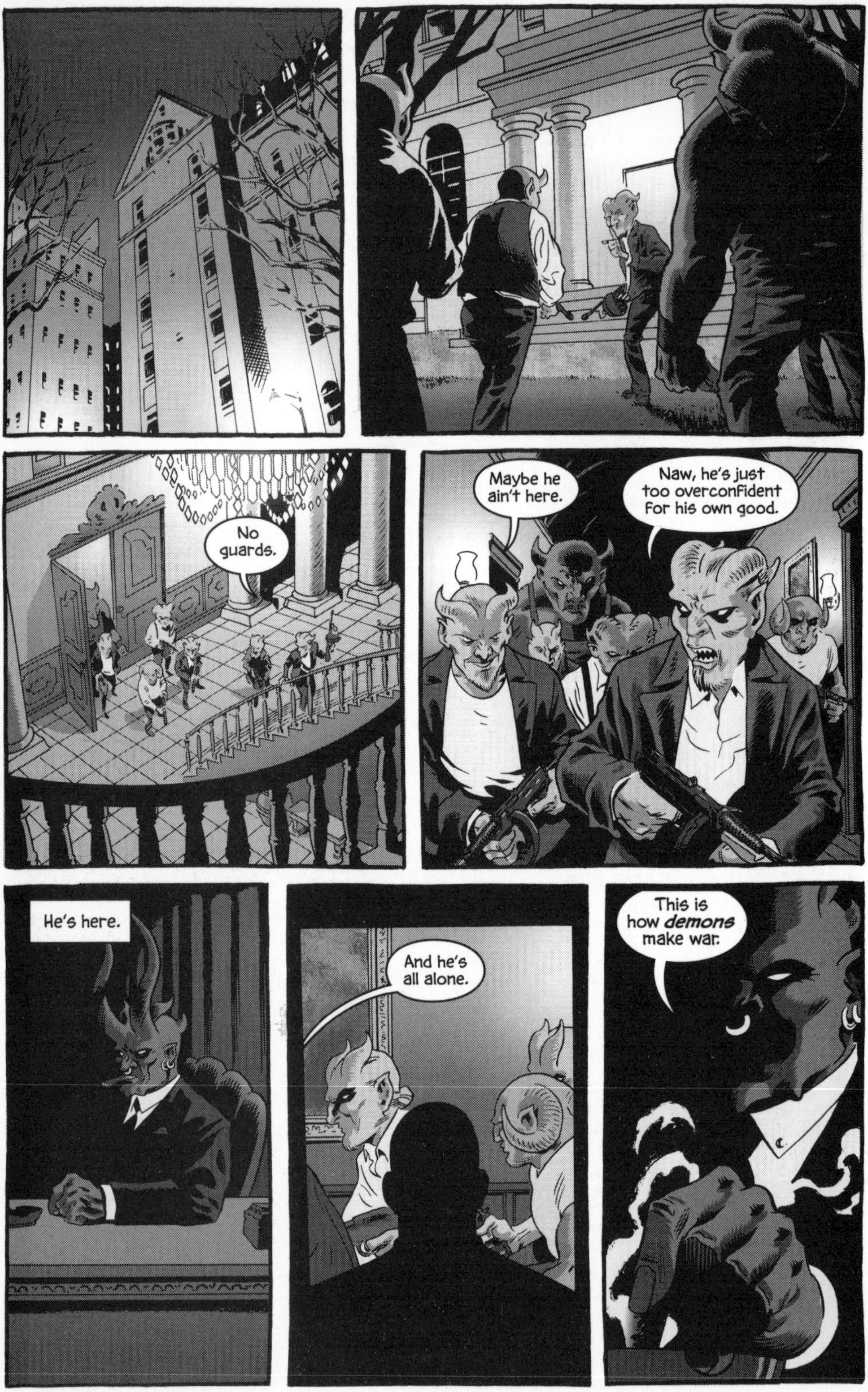
No guards.
Maybe he ain't here.
Naw, he's just too overconfident for his own good.
He's here.
And he's all alone.
This is how *demons* make war.

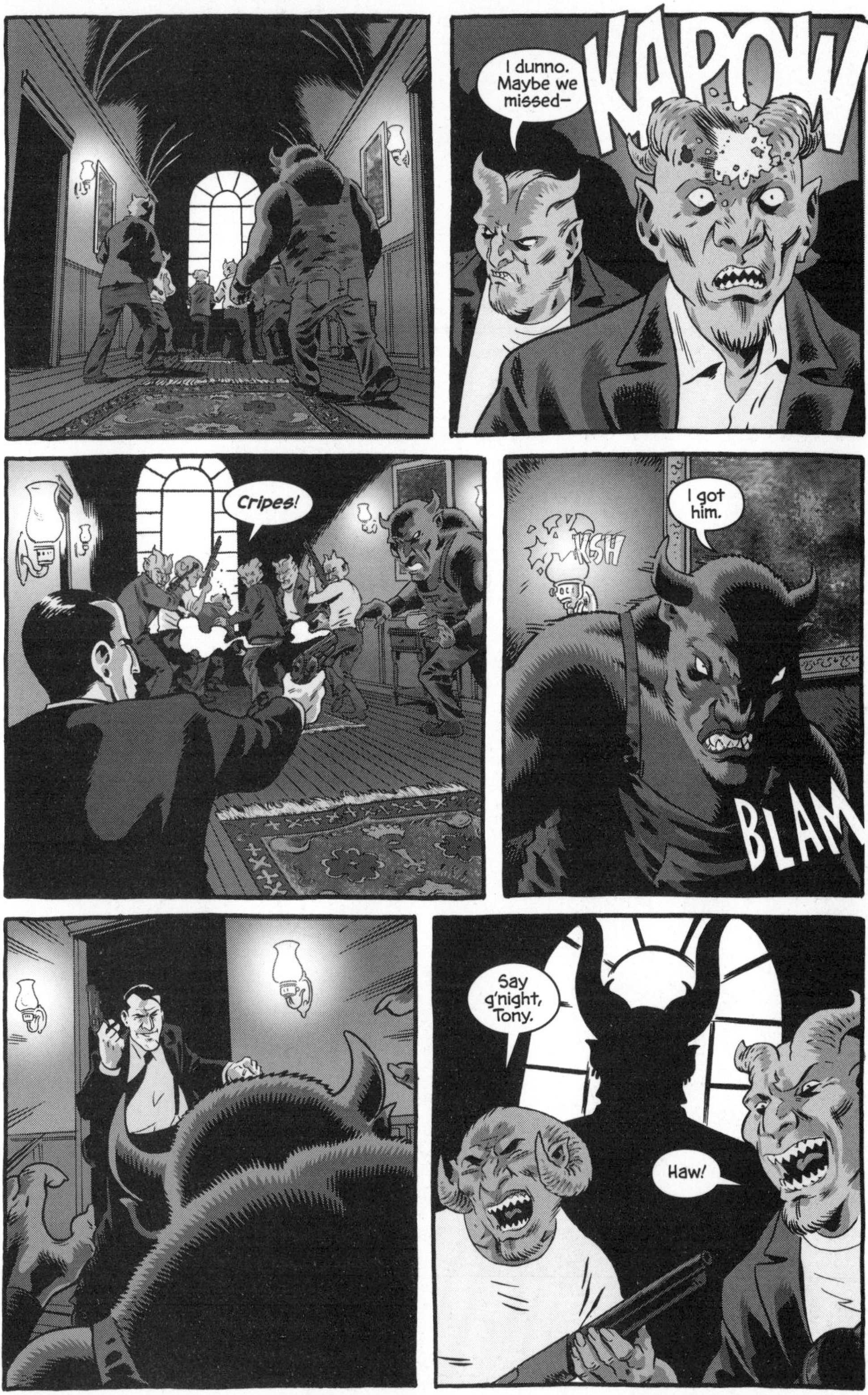
I dunno. Maybe we missed–
KAPOW
Cripes!
I got him.
KSH
BLAM
Say g'night, Tony.
Haw!

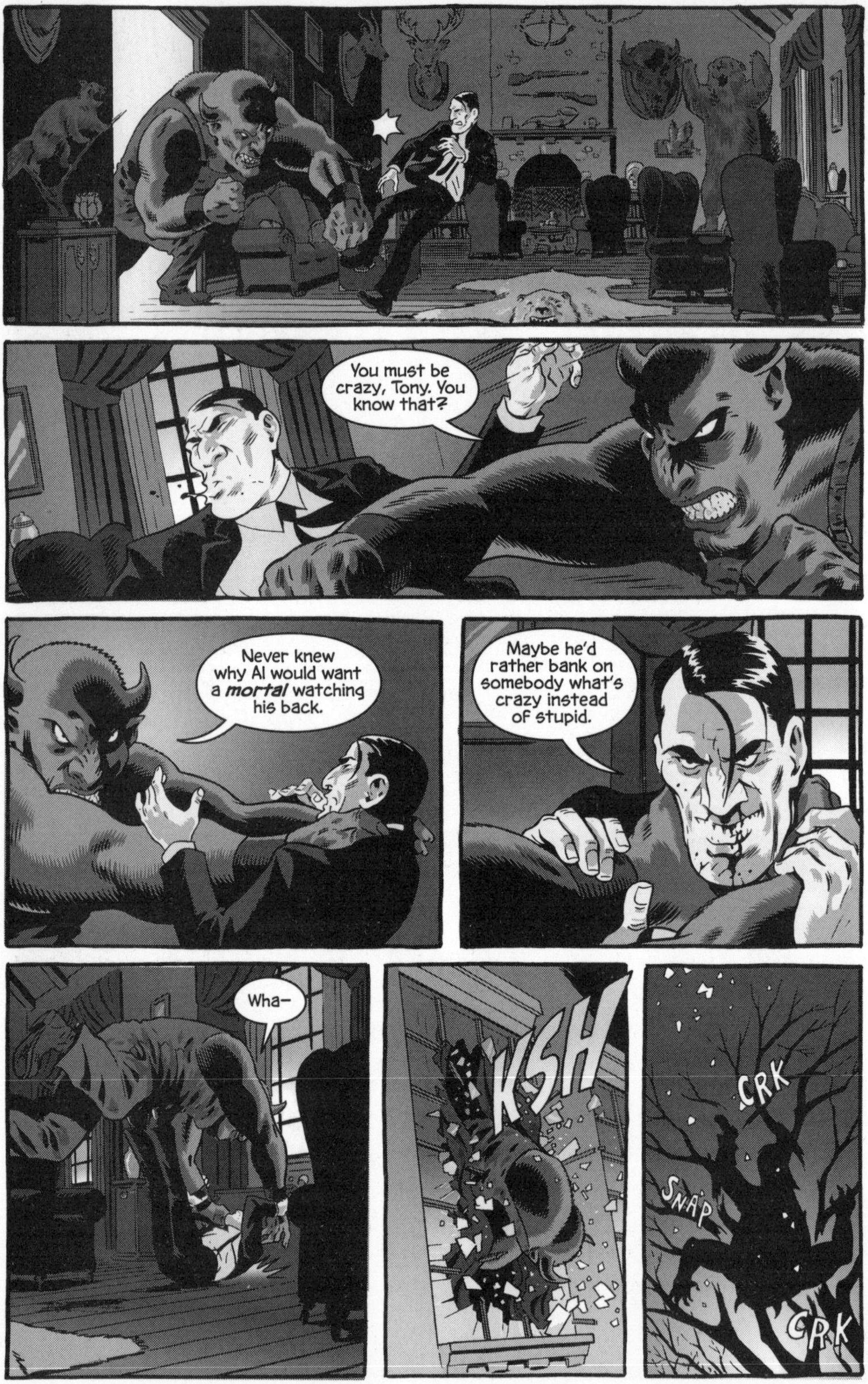
You must be crazy, Tony. You know that?
Never knew why Al would want a *mortal* watching his back.
Maybe he'd rather bank on somebody what's crazy instead of stupid.
Wha-
KSH
CRK
SNAP
CRK

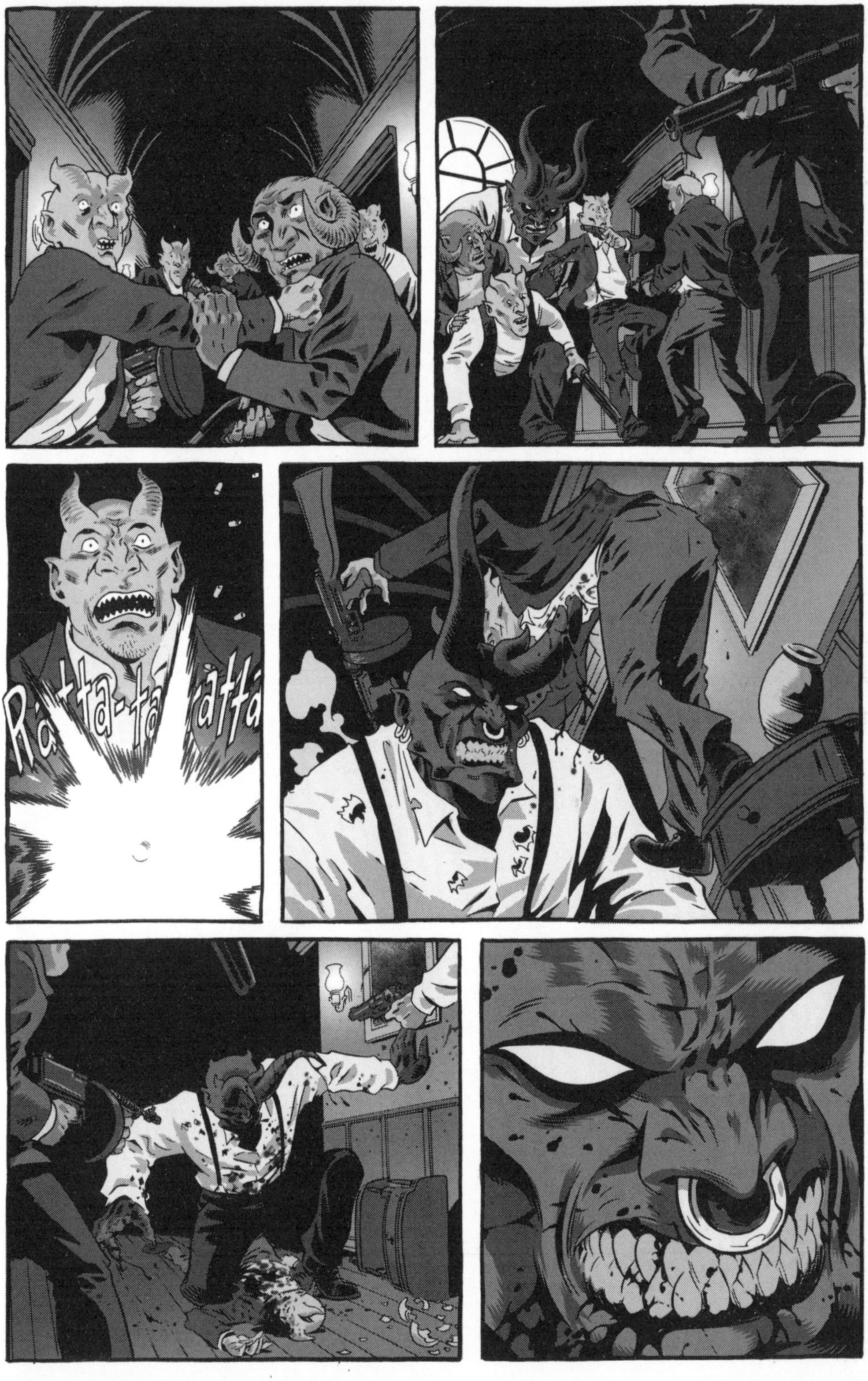
Rátta-tá ráttá

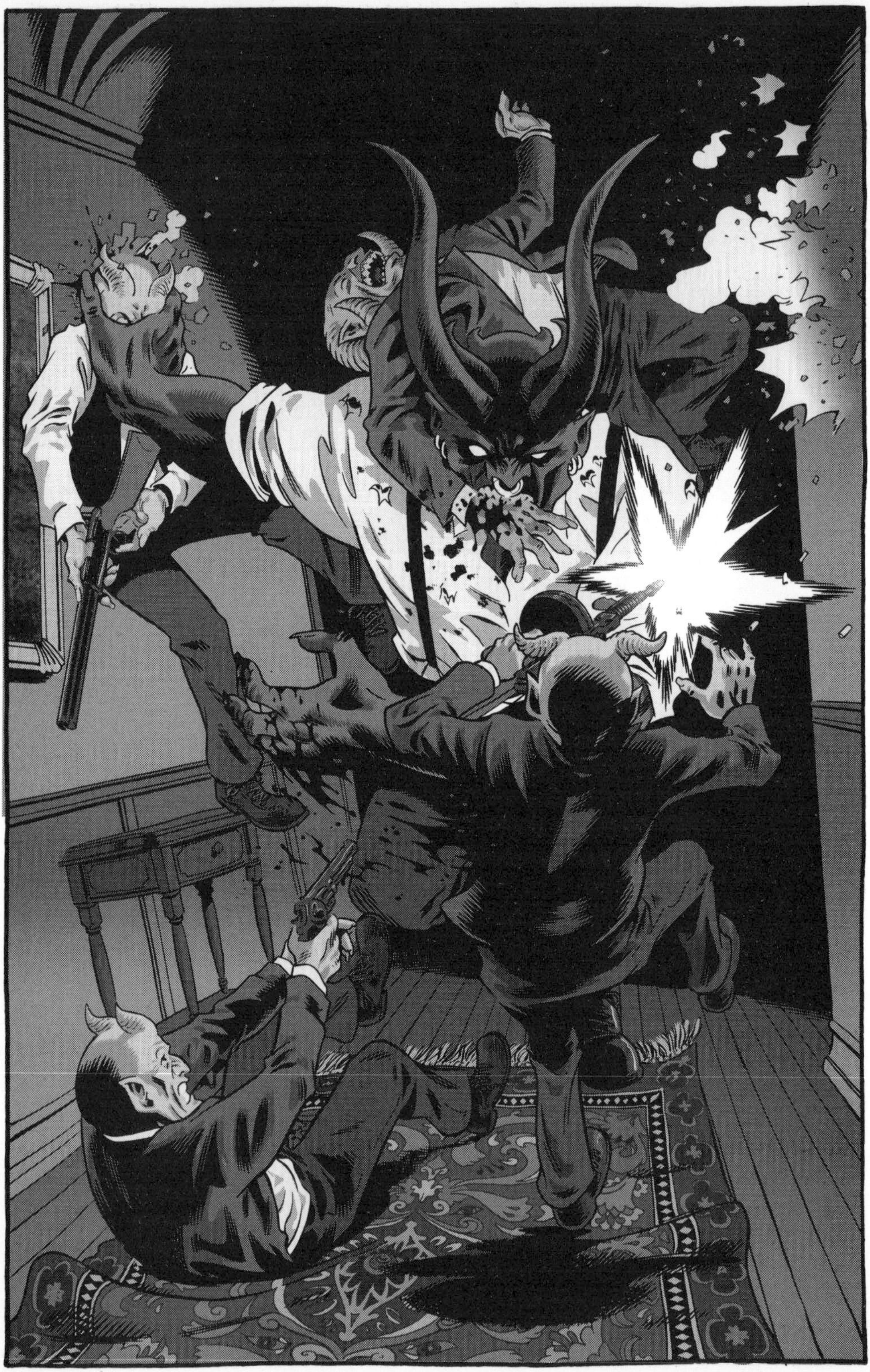

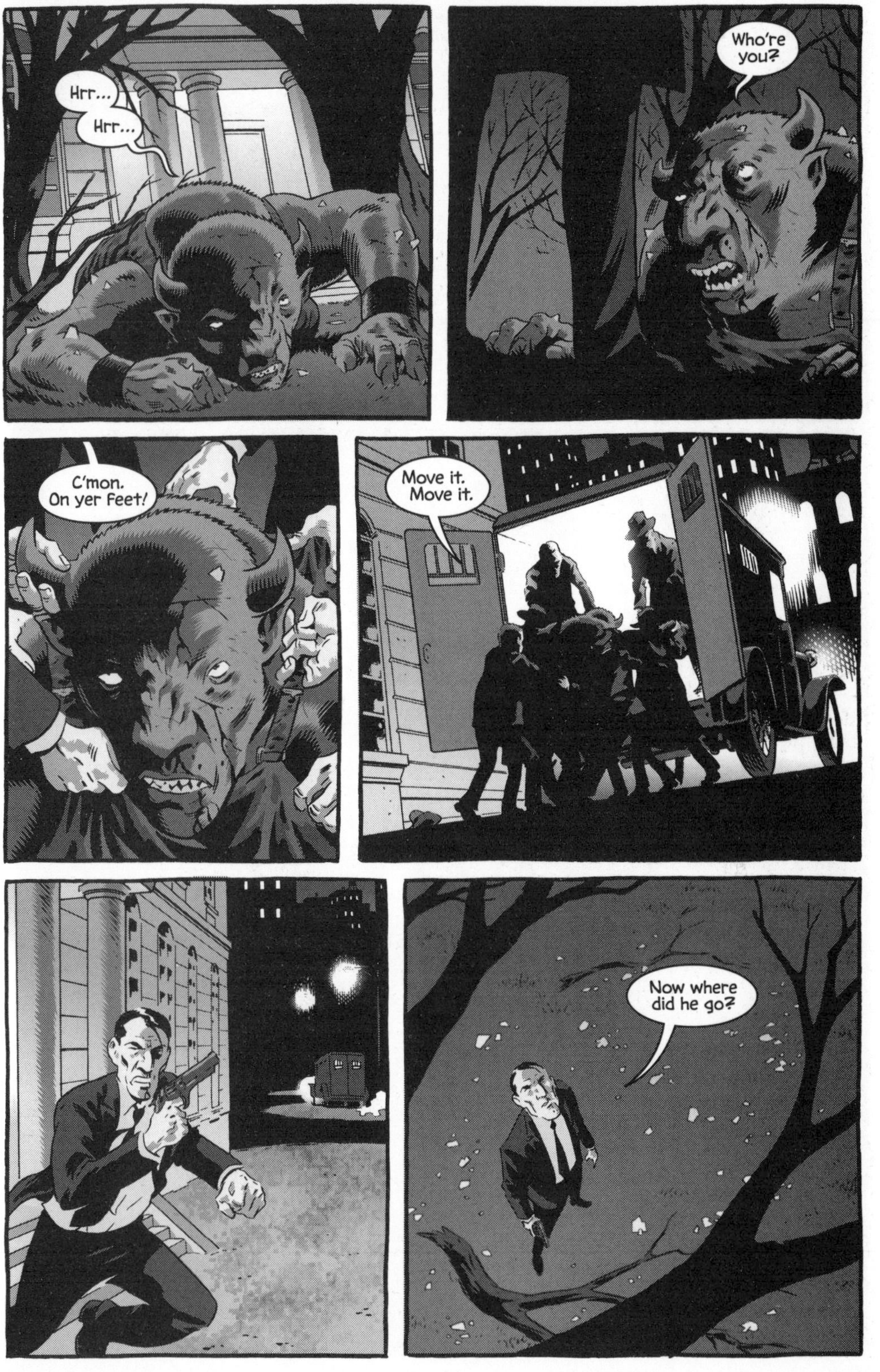
Hrr...
Hrr...
Who're you?
C'mon. On yer feet!
Move it. Move it.
Now where did he go?

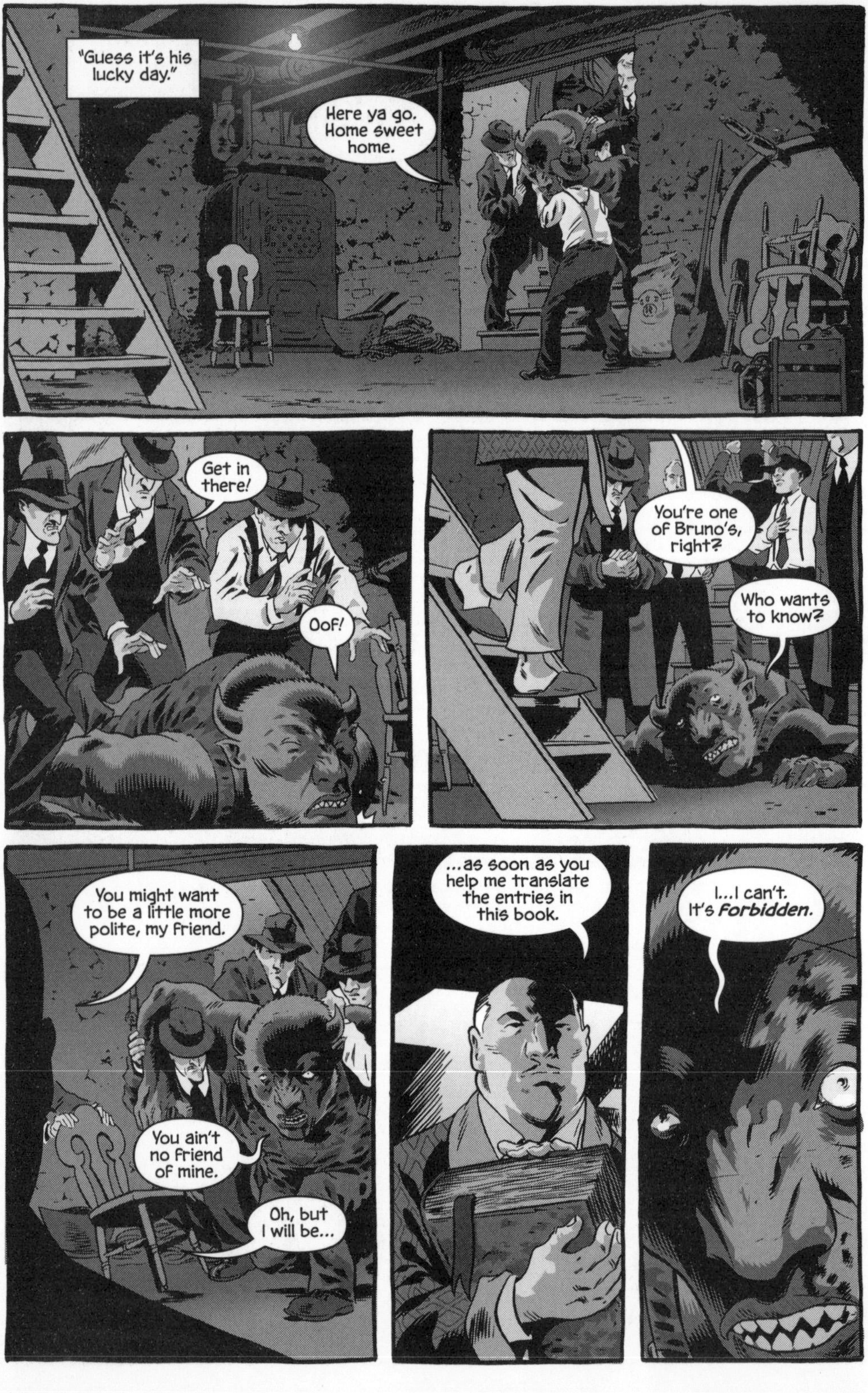
"Guess it's his lucky day."
Here ya go. Home sweet home.
Get in there!
Oof!
You're one of Bruno's, right?
Who wants to know?
You might want to be a little more polite, my friend.
You ain't no friend of mine.
Oh, but I will be...
...as soon as you help me translate the entries in this book.
I...I can't. It's *forbidden*.

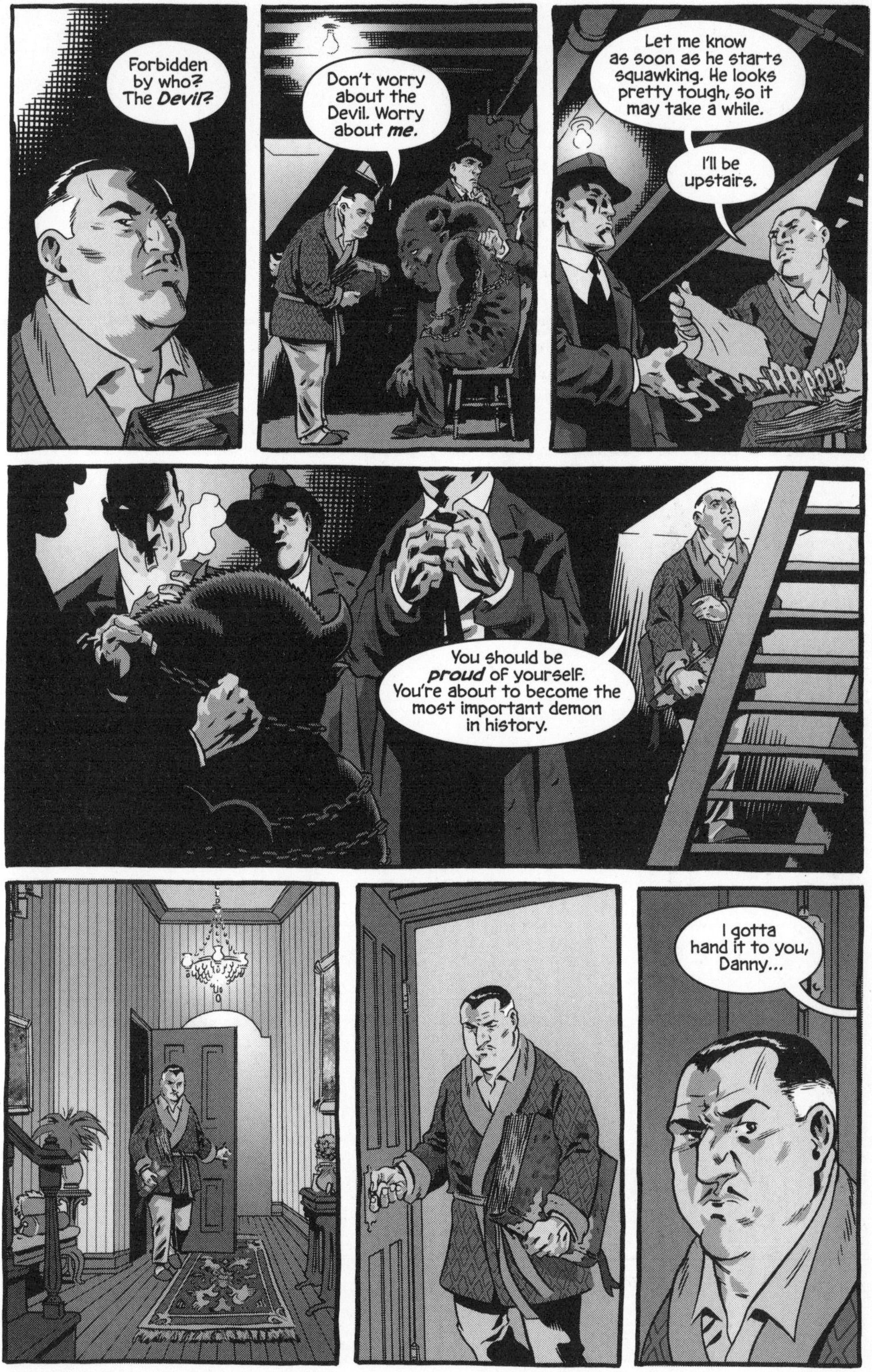
Forbidden by who? The *Devil*?
Don't worry about the Devil. Worry about *me.*
Let me know as soon as he starts squawking. He looks pretty tough, so it may take a while.
I'll be upstairs.
You should be *proud* of yourself. You're about to become the most important demon in history.
I gotta hand it to you, Danny...

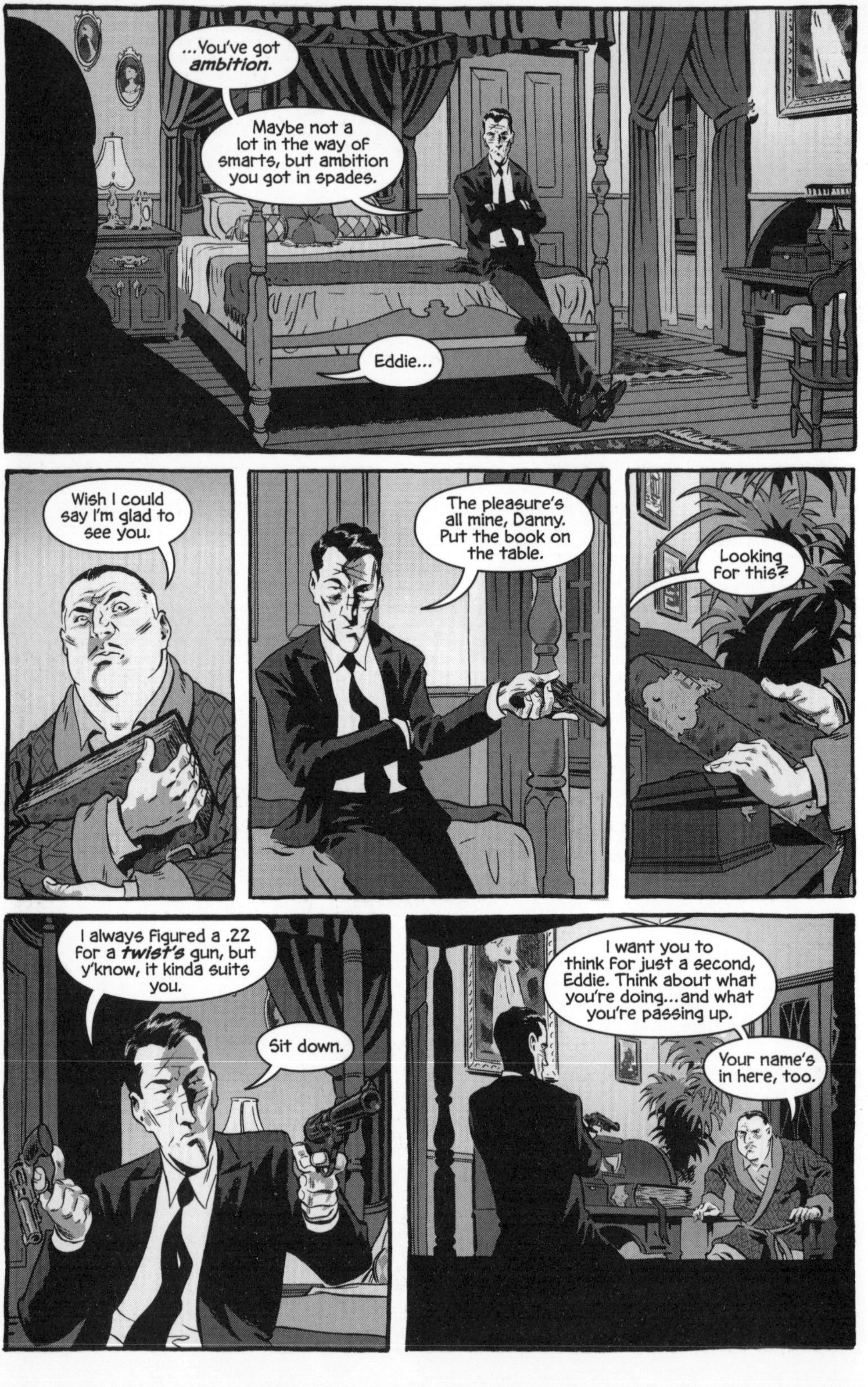
...You've got *ambition.*
Maybe not a lot in the way of smarts, but ambition you got in spades.
Eddie...
Wish I could say I'm glad to see you.
The pleasure's all mine, Danny. Put the book on the table.
Looking for this?
I always figured a .22 for a *twist's* gun, but y'know, it kinda suits you.
Sit down.
I want you to think for just a second, Eddie. Think about what you're doing...and what you're passing up.
Your name's in here, too.

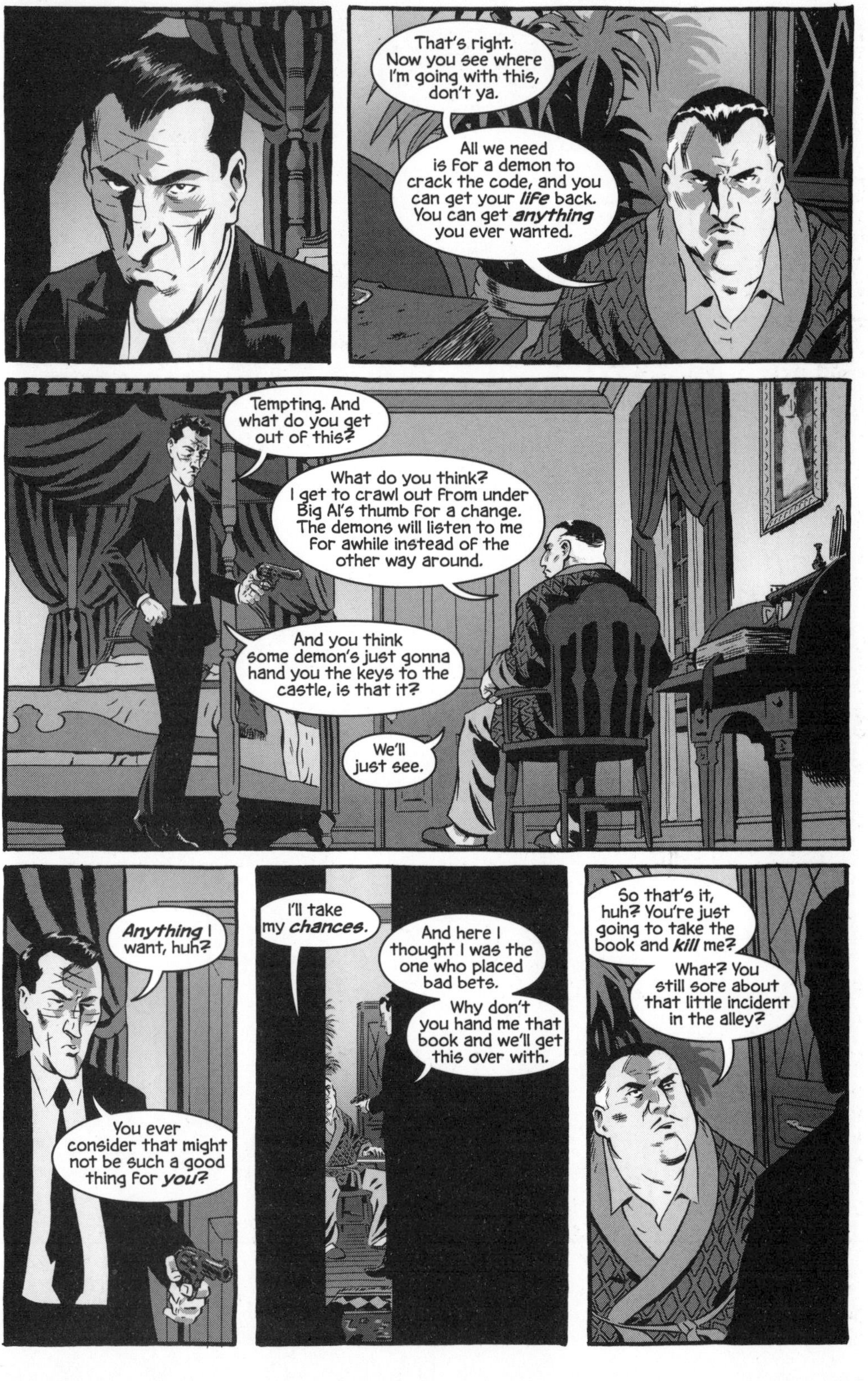
That's right. Now you see where I'm going with this, don't ya.
All we need is for a demon to crack the code, and you can get your *life* back. You can get ***anything*** you ever wanted.
Tempting. And what do you get out of this?
What do you think? I get to crawl out from under Big Al's thumb for a change. The demons will listen to me for awhile instead of the other way around.
And you think some demon's just gonna hand you the keys to the castle, is that it?
We'll just see.
Anything I want, huh?
You ever consider that might not be such a good thing for ***you***?
I'll take my ***chances***.
And here I thought I was the one who placed bad bets.
Why don't you hand me that book and we'll get this over with.
So that's it, huh? You're just going to take the book and ***kill*** me?
What? You still sore about that little incident in the alley?

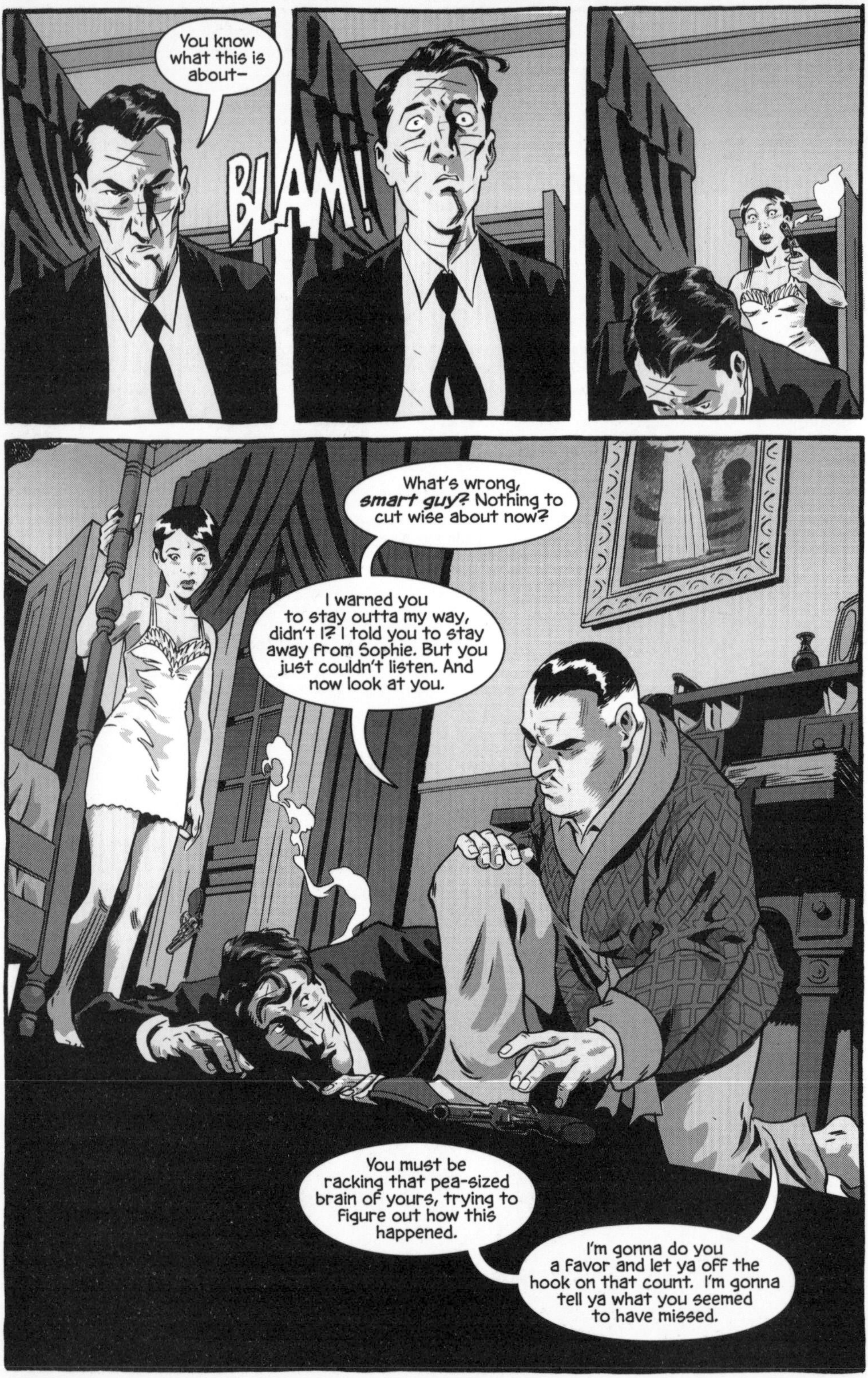
You know what this is about–
BLAM!
What's wrong, smart guy? Nothing to cut wise about now?
I warned you to stay outta my way, didn't I? I told you to stay away from Sophie. But you just couldn't listen. And now look at you.
You must be racking that pea-sized brain of yours, trying to figure out how this happened.
I'm gonna do you a favor and let ya off the hook on that count. I'm gonna tell ya what you seemed to have missed.

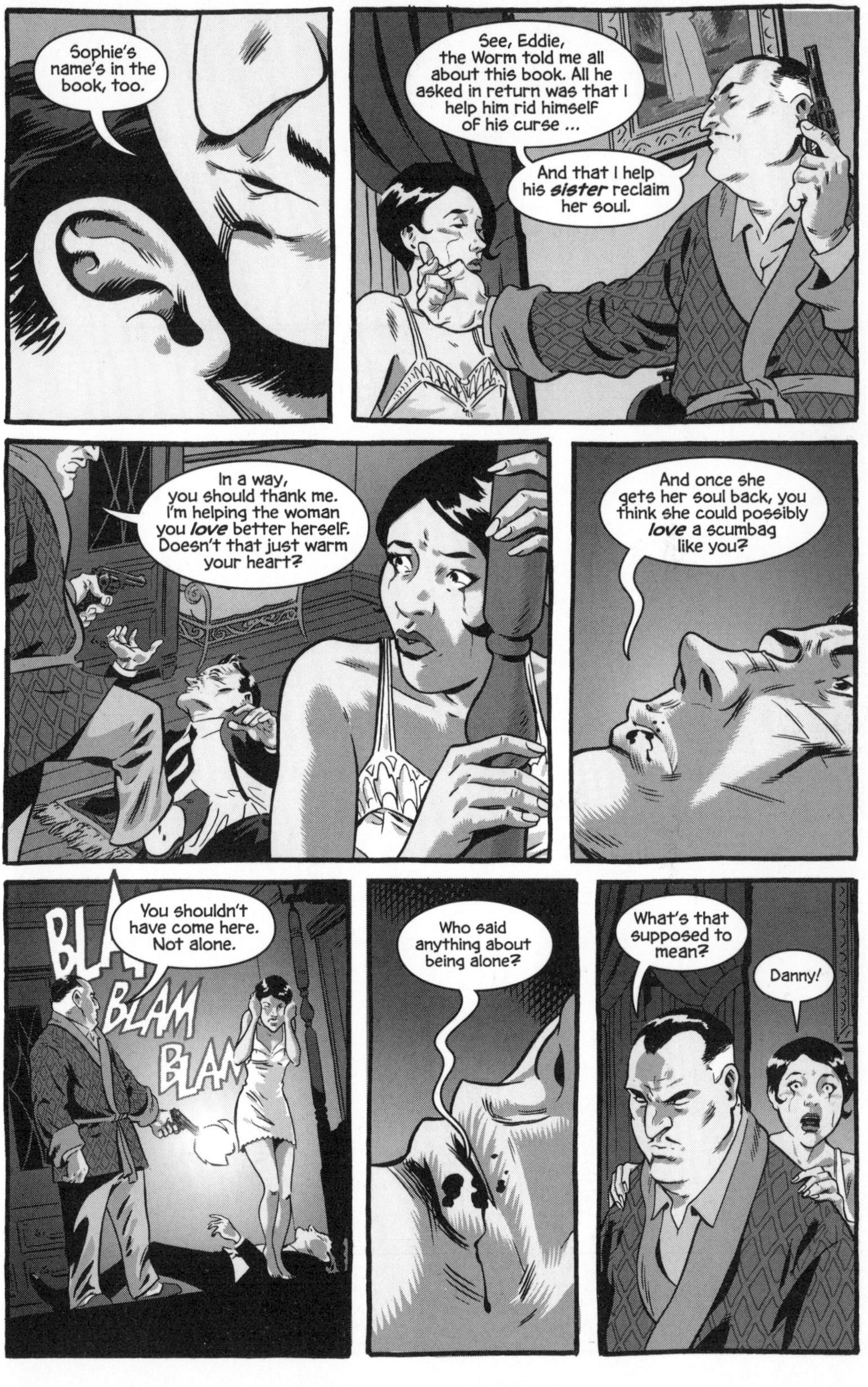
Sophie's name's in the book, too.
See, Eddie, the Worm told me all about this book. All he asked in return was that I help him rid himself of his curse ...
And that I help his *sister* reclaim her soul.
In a way, you should thank me. I'm helping the woman you *love* better herself. Doesn't that just warm your heart?
And once she gets her soul back, you think she could possibly *love* a scumbag like you?
You shouldn't have come here. Not alone.
BLAM
BLAM
BLAM
Who said anything about being alone?
What's that supposed to mean?
Danny!

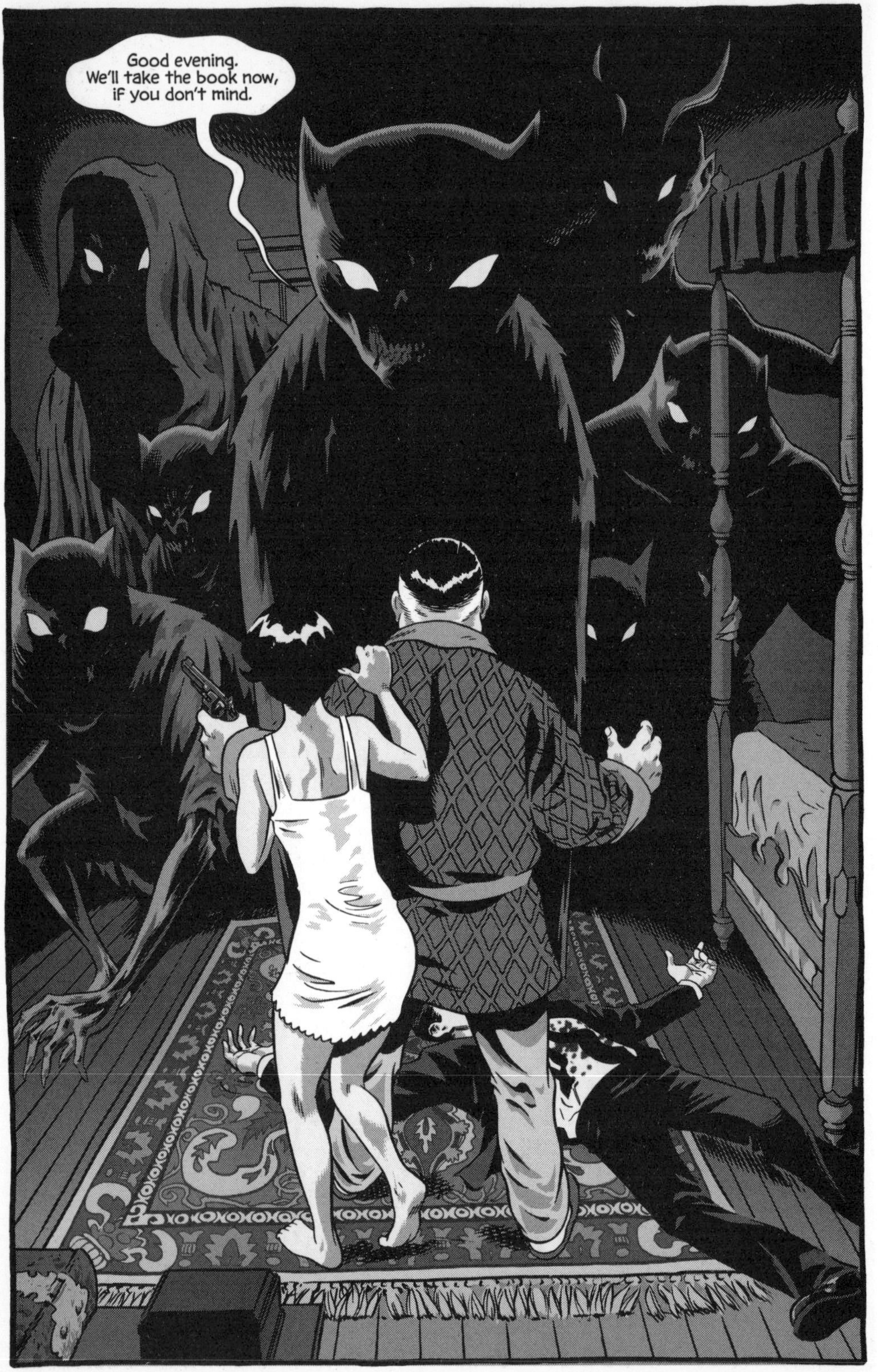
Good evening. We'll take the book now, if you don't mind.

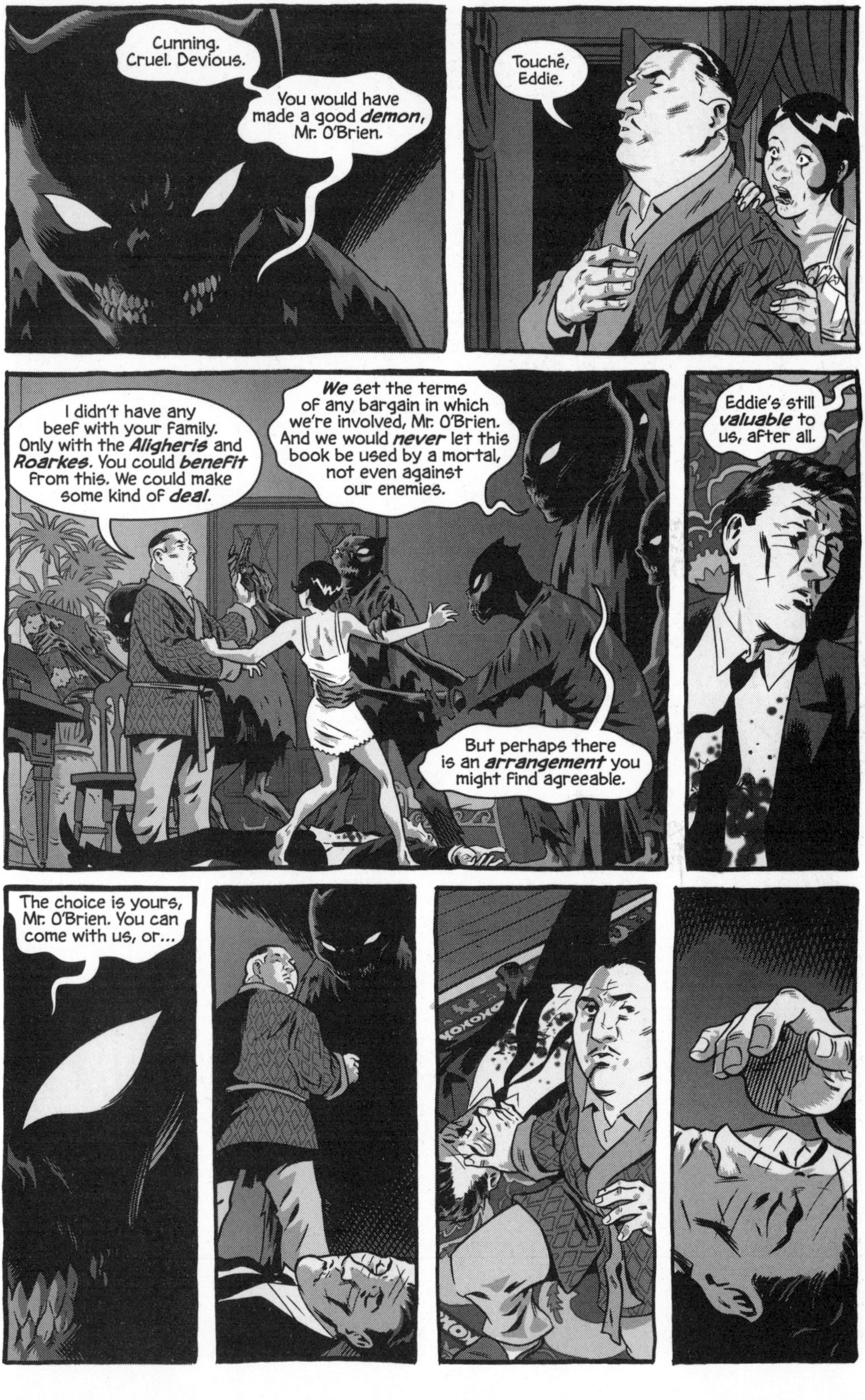
Cunning. Cruel. Devious.
You would have made a good *demon*, Mr. O'Brien.
Touché, Eddie.
I didn't have any beef with your family. Only with the *Aligheris* and *Roarkes*. You could *benefit* from this. We could make some kind of *deal*.
We set the terms of any bargain in which we're involved, Mr. O'Brien. And we would *never* let this book be used by a mortal, not even against our enemies.
But perhaps there is an *arrangement* you might find agreeable.
Eddie's still *valuable* to us, after all.
The choice is yours, Mr. O'Brien. You can come with us, or...

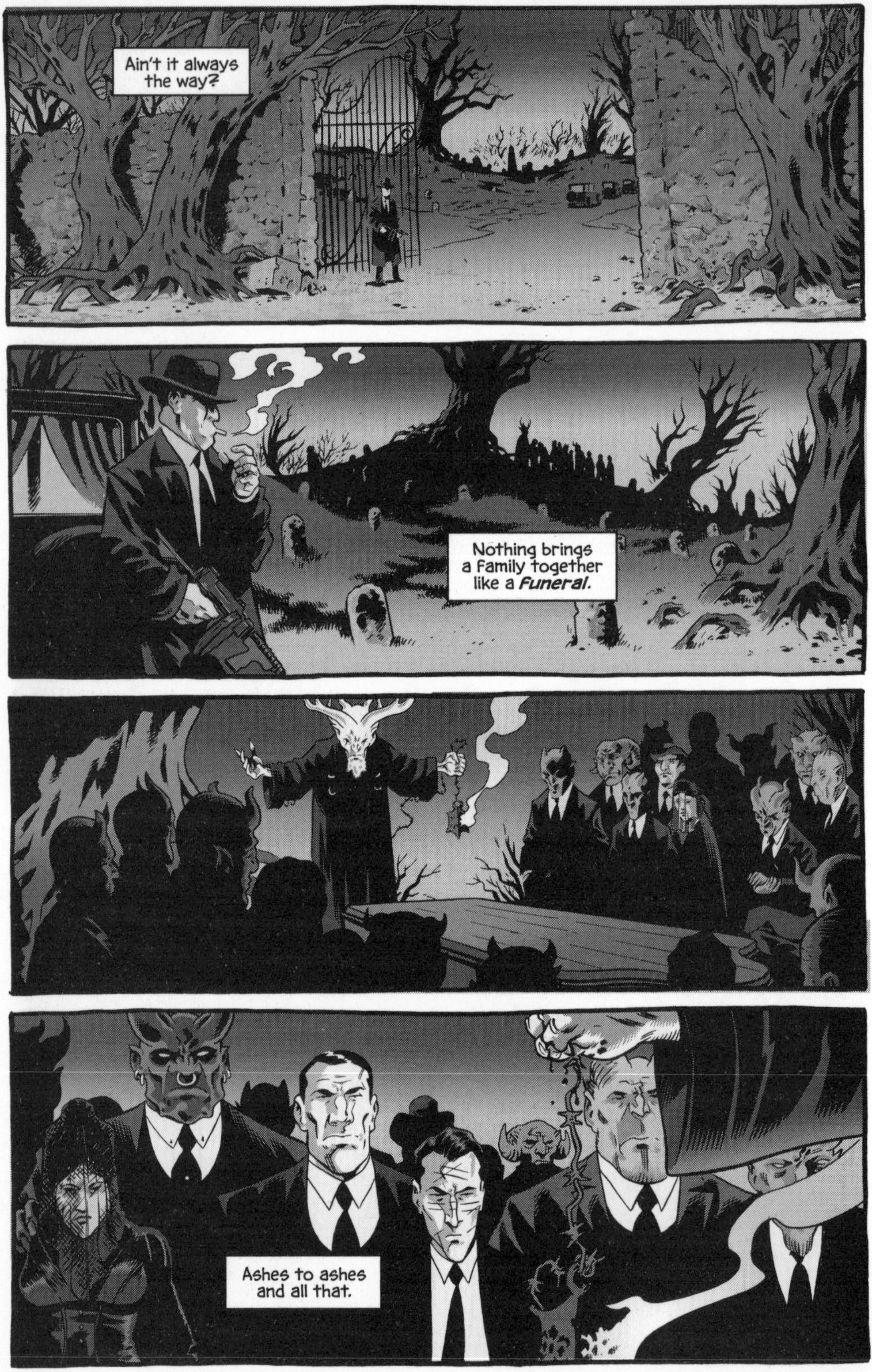
Ain't it always the way?
Nothing brings a family together like a *funeral*.
Ashes to ashes and all that.

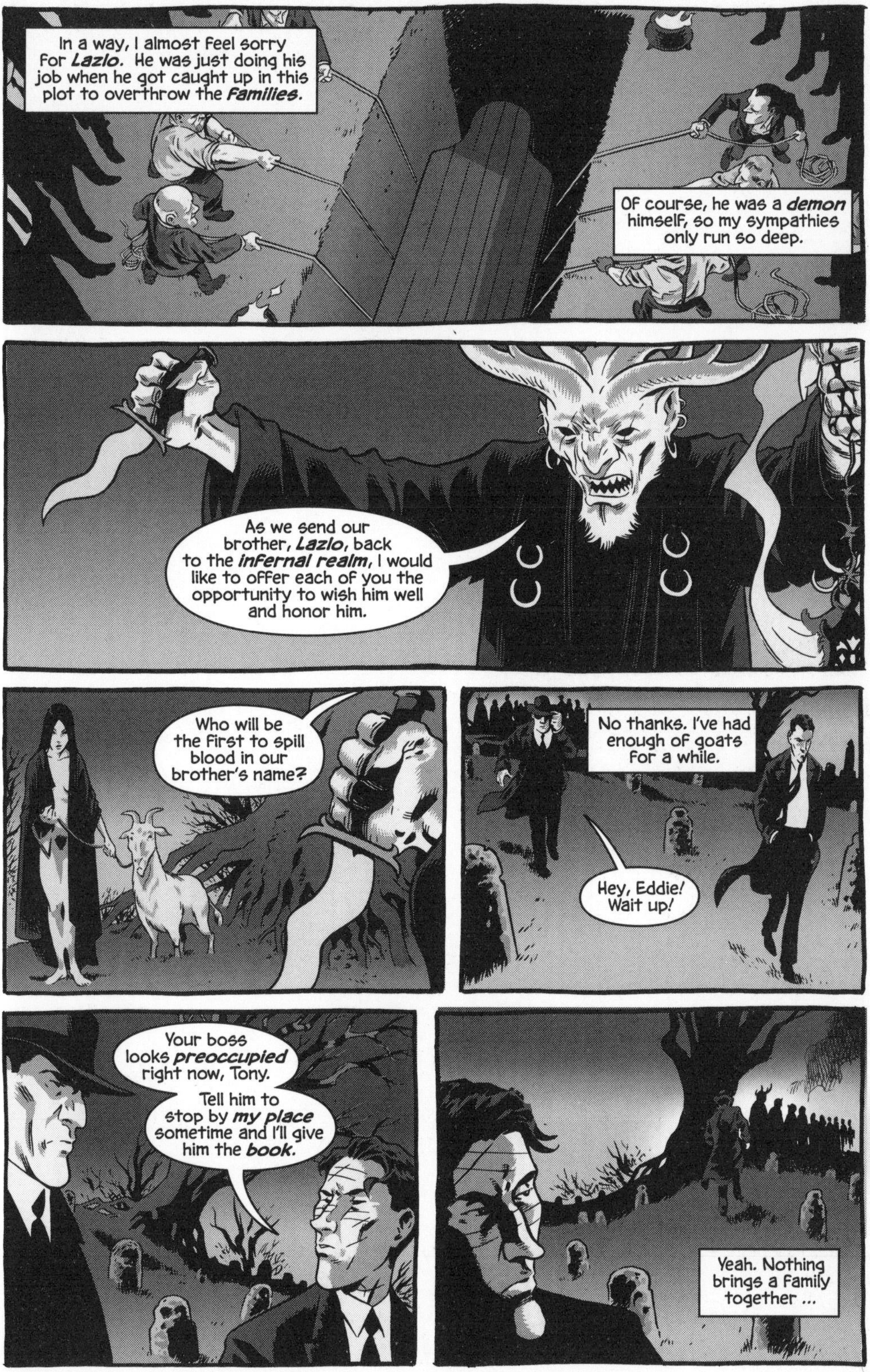
In a way, I almost feel sorry for Lazlo. He was just doing his job when he got caught up in this plot to overthrow the Families.
Of course, he was a demon himself, so my sympathies only run so deep.
As we send our brother, Lazlo, back to the infernal realm, I would like to offer each of you the opportunity to wish him well and honor him.
Who will be the first to spill blood in our brother's name?
No thanks. I've had enough of goats for a while.
Hey, Eddie! Wait up!
Your boss looks preoccupied right now, Tony.
Tell him to stop by my place sometime and I'll give him the book.
Yeah. Nothing brings a Family together ...

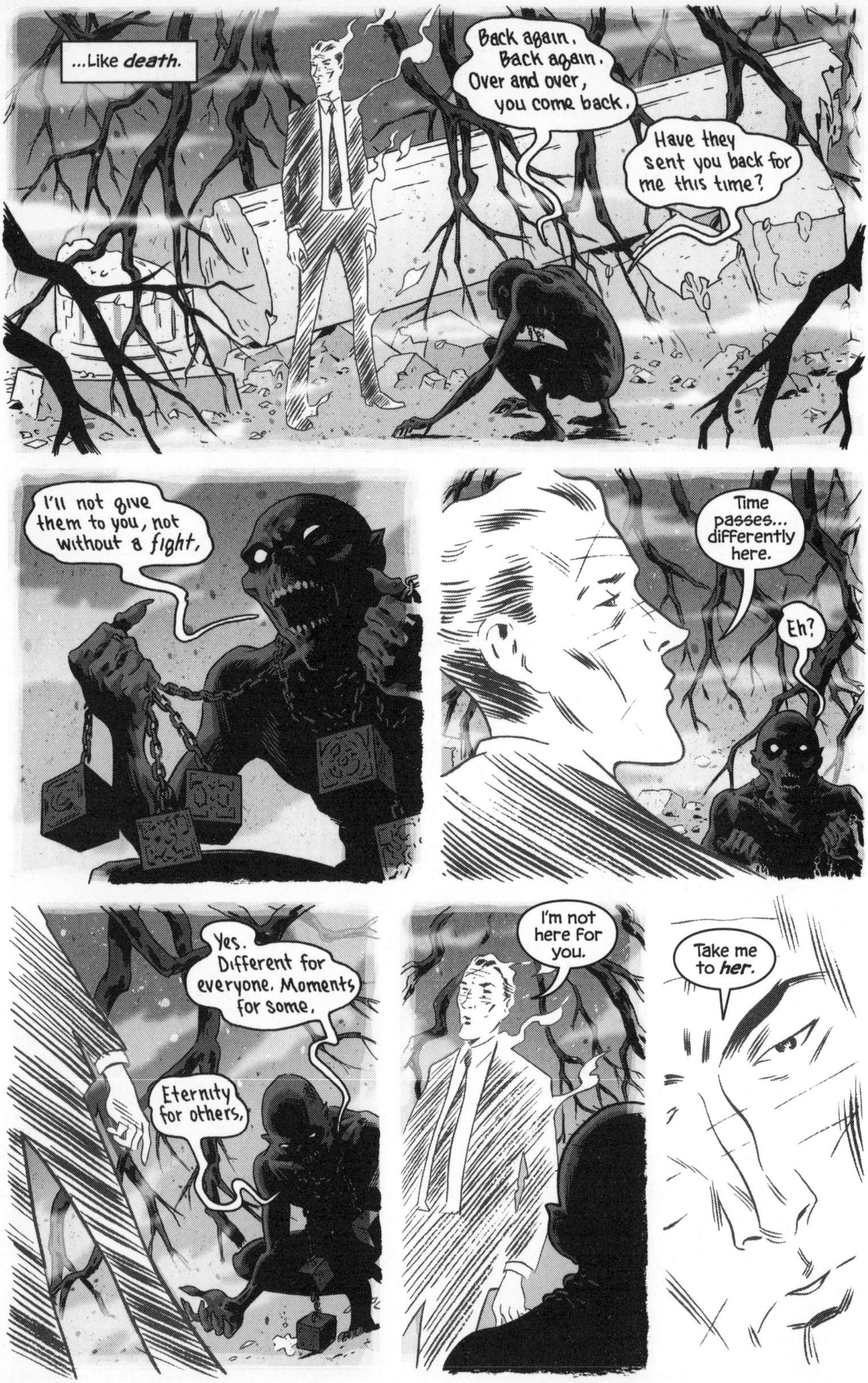
...Like *death*.
Back again. Back again. Over and over, you come back.
Have they sent you back for me this time?
I'll not give them to you, not without a *fight*.
Time passes... differently here.
Eh?
Yes. Different for everyone. Moments for some.
Eternity for others.
I'm not here for you.
Take me to ***her***.

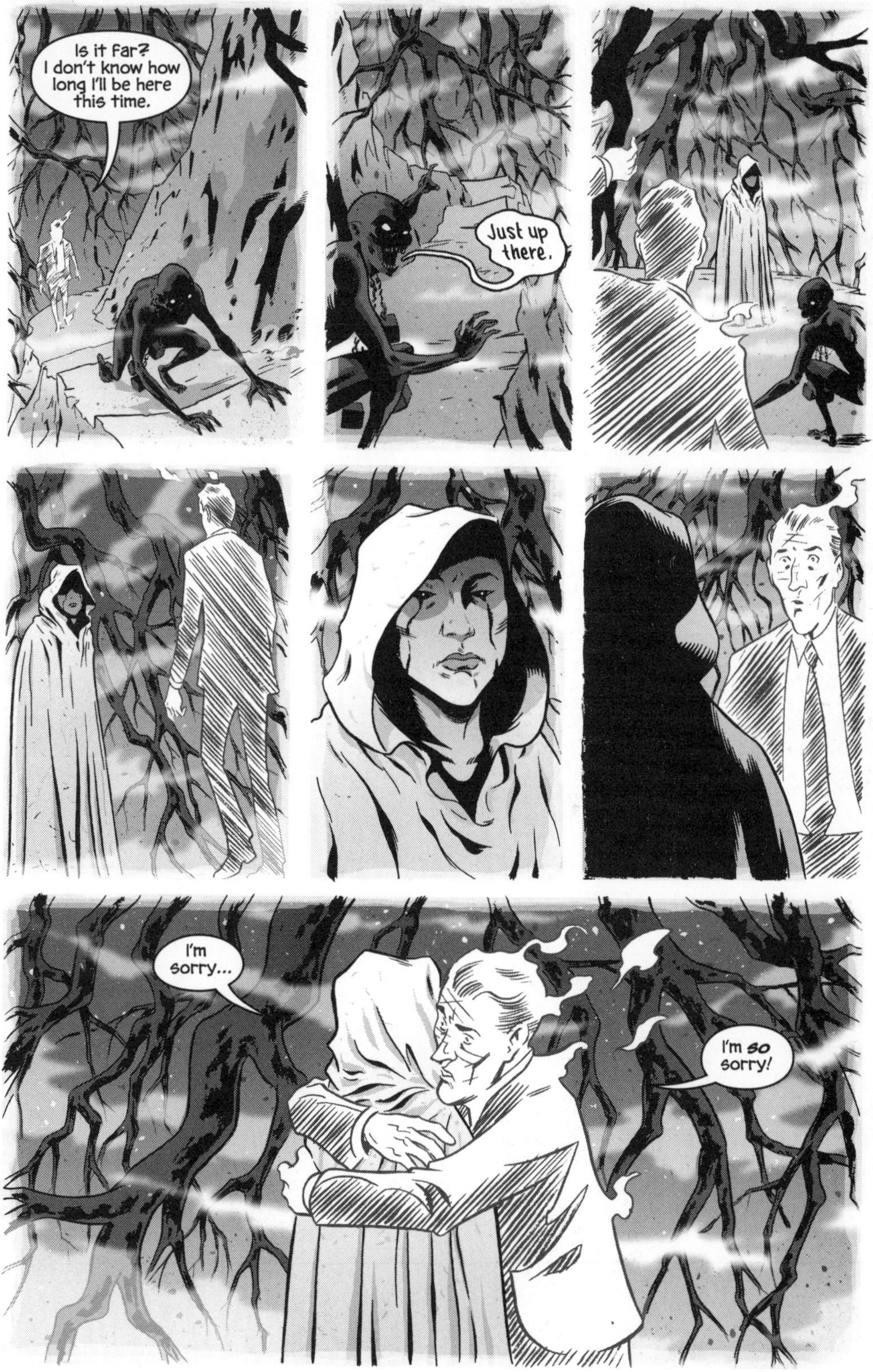

Is it far? I don't know how long I'll be here this time.
Just up there.
I'm sorry...
I'm *so* sorry!

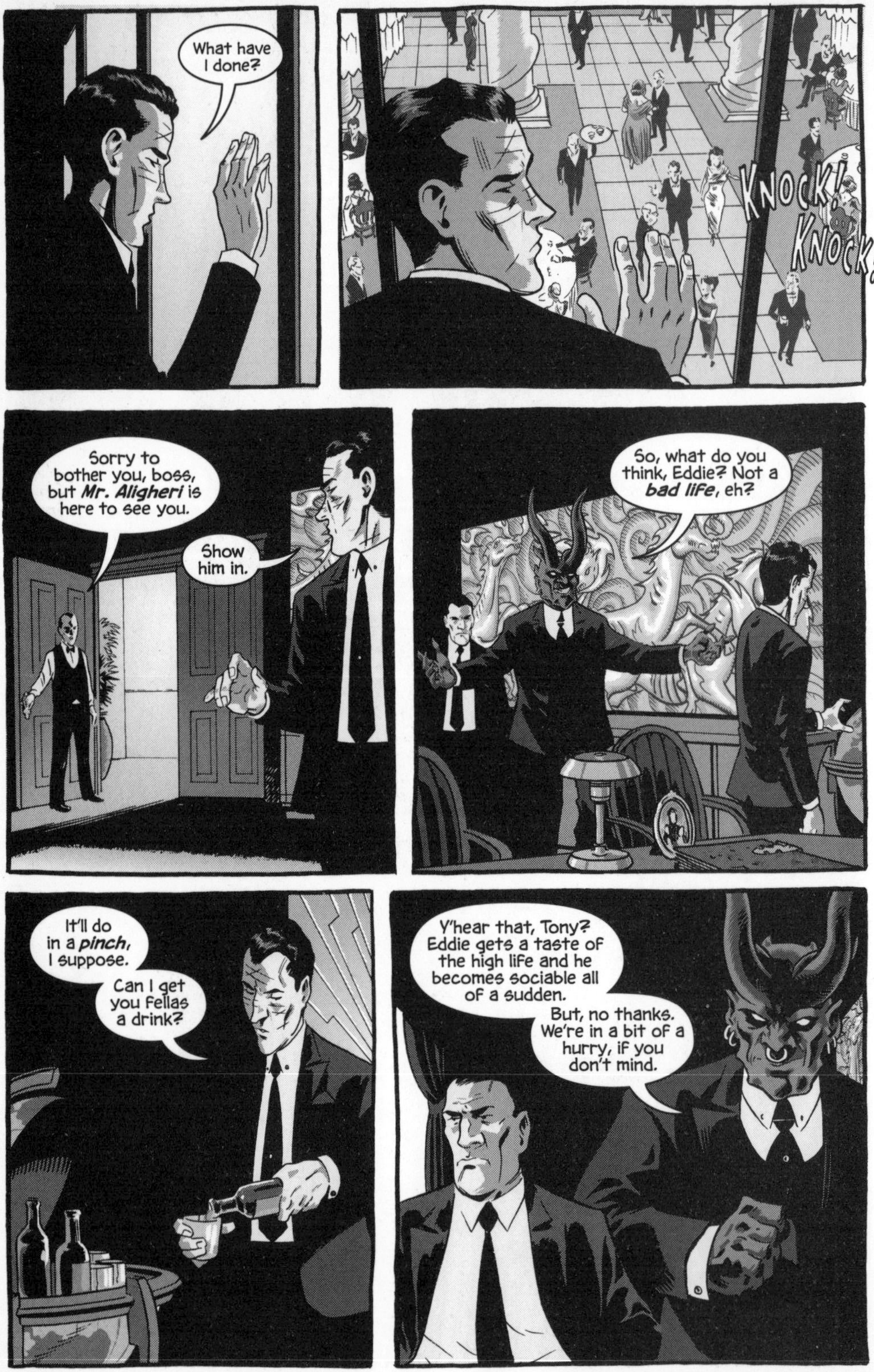
What have I done?
KNOCK! KNOCK!
Sorry to bother you, boss, but Mr. Aligheri is here to see you.
Show him in.
So, what do you think, Eddie? Not a bad life, eh?
It'll do in a pinch, I suppose.
Can I get you fellas a drink?
Y'hear that, Tony? Eddie gets a taste of the high life and he becomes sociable all of a sudden.
But, no thanks. We're in a bit of a hurry, if you don't mind.

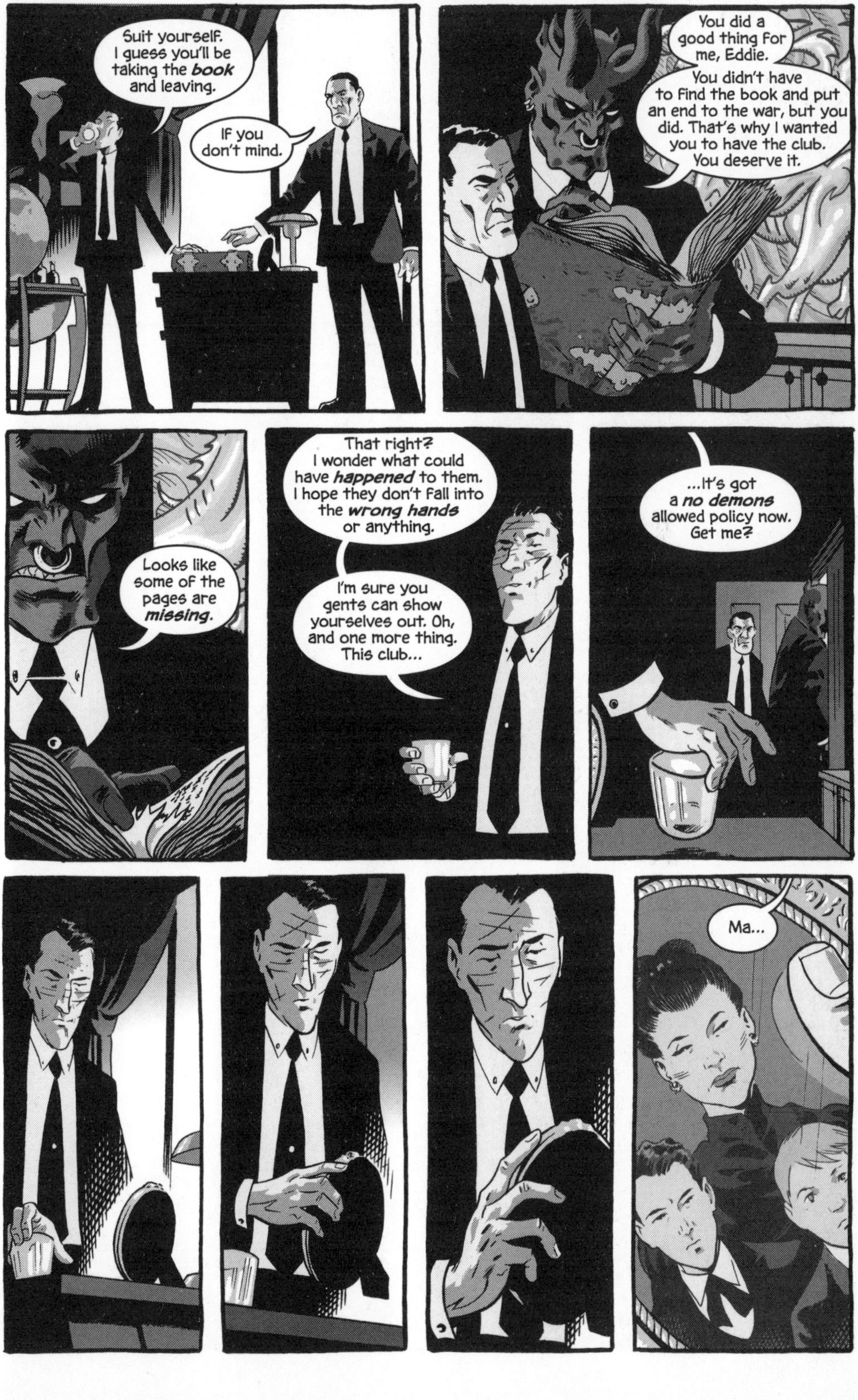
Suit yourself. I guess you'll be taking the *book* and leaving.
If you don't mind.
You did a good thing for me, Eddie.
You didn't have to find the book and put an end to the war, but you did. That's why I wanted you to have the club. You deserve it.
Looks like some of the pages are *missing*.
That right? I wonder what could have *happened* to them. I hope they don't fall into the *wrong hands* or anything.
I'm sure you gents can show yourselves out. Oh, and one more thing. This club...
...It's got a *no demons* allowed policy now. Get me?
Ma...

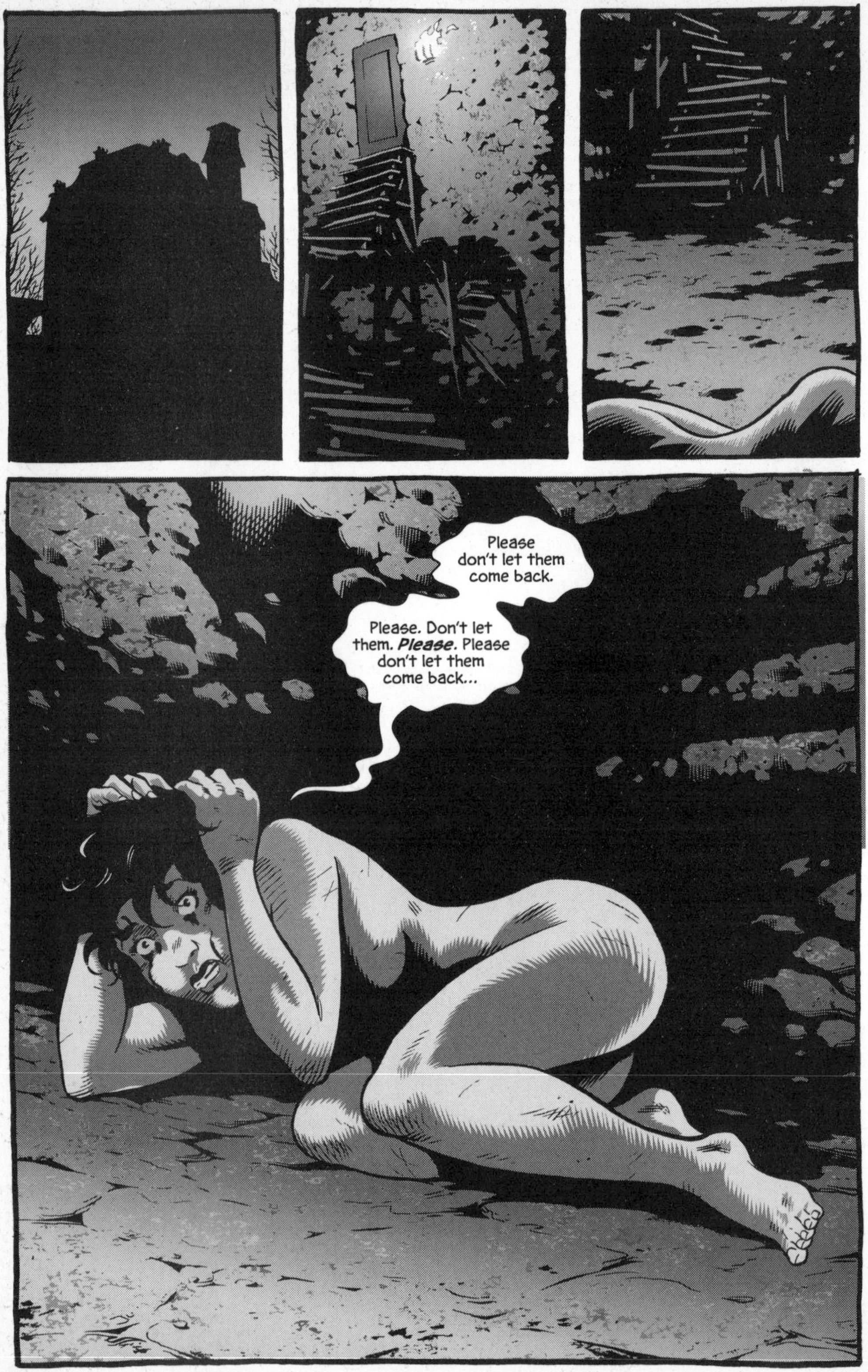
Please don't let them come back.
Please. Don't let them. *Please.* Please don't let them come back...

What follows is a special six-page preview that ran in the back of several Oni Press comics and was posted online for promotional purposes.

The events in this short story take place three days before the start of this graphic novel.

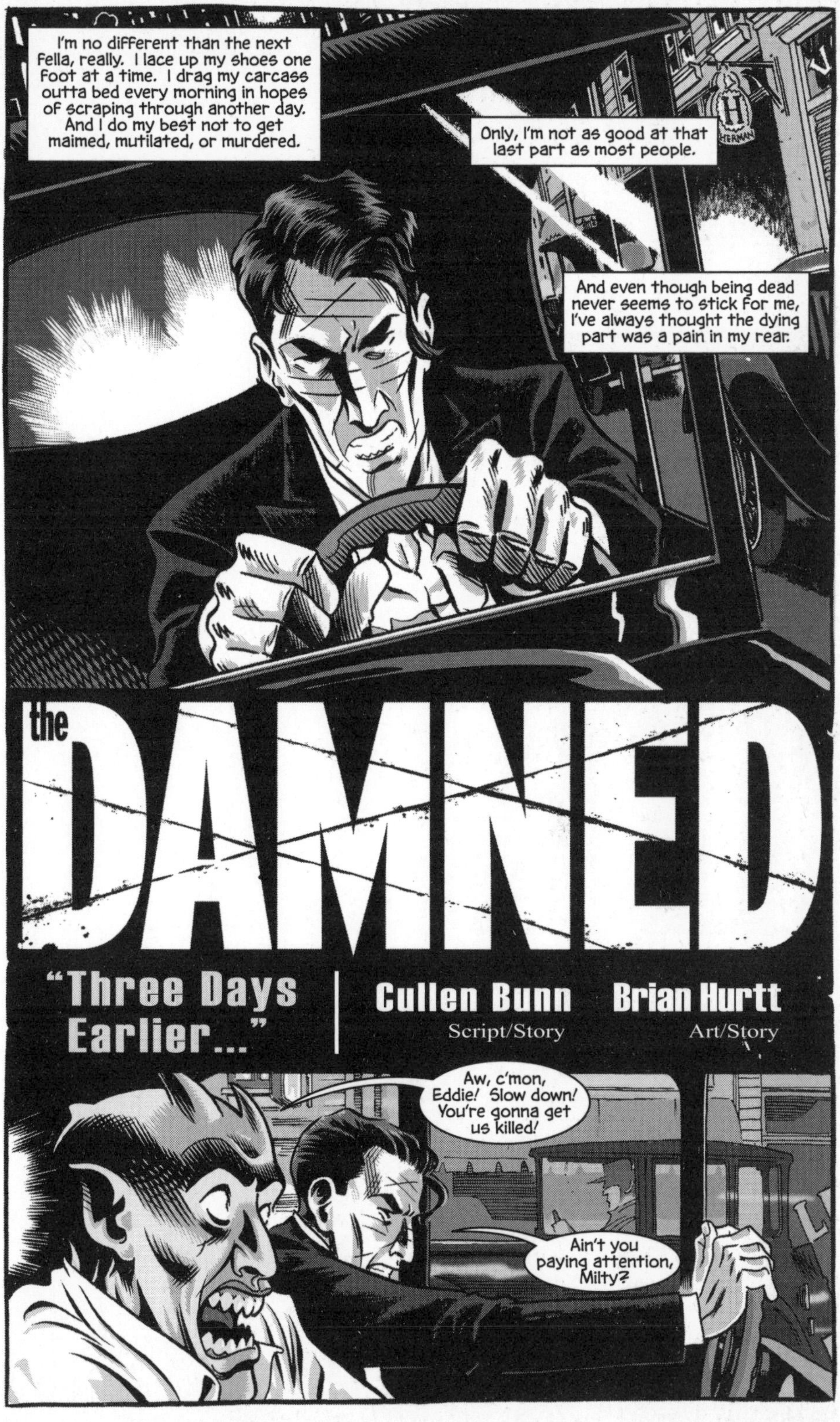
I'm no different than the next fella, really. I lace up my shoes one foot at a time. I drag my carcass outta bed every morning in hopes of scraping through another day. And I do my best not to get maimed, mutilated, or murdered.
Only, I'm not as good at that last part as most people.
And even though being dead never seems to stick for me, I've always thought the dying part was a pain in my rear.
the DAMNED
"Three Days Earlier..."
Cullen Bunn
Script/Story
Brian Hurtt
Art/Story
Aw, c'mon, Eddie! Slow down! You're gonna get us killed!
Ain't you paying attention, Milty?

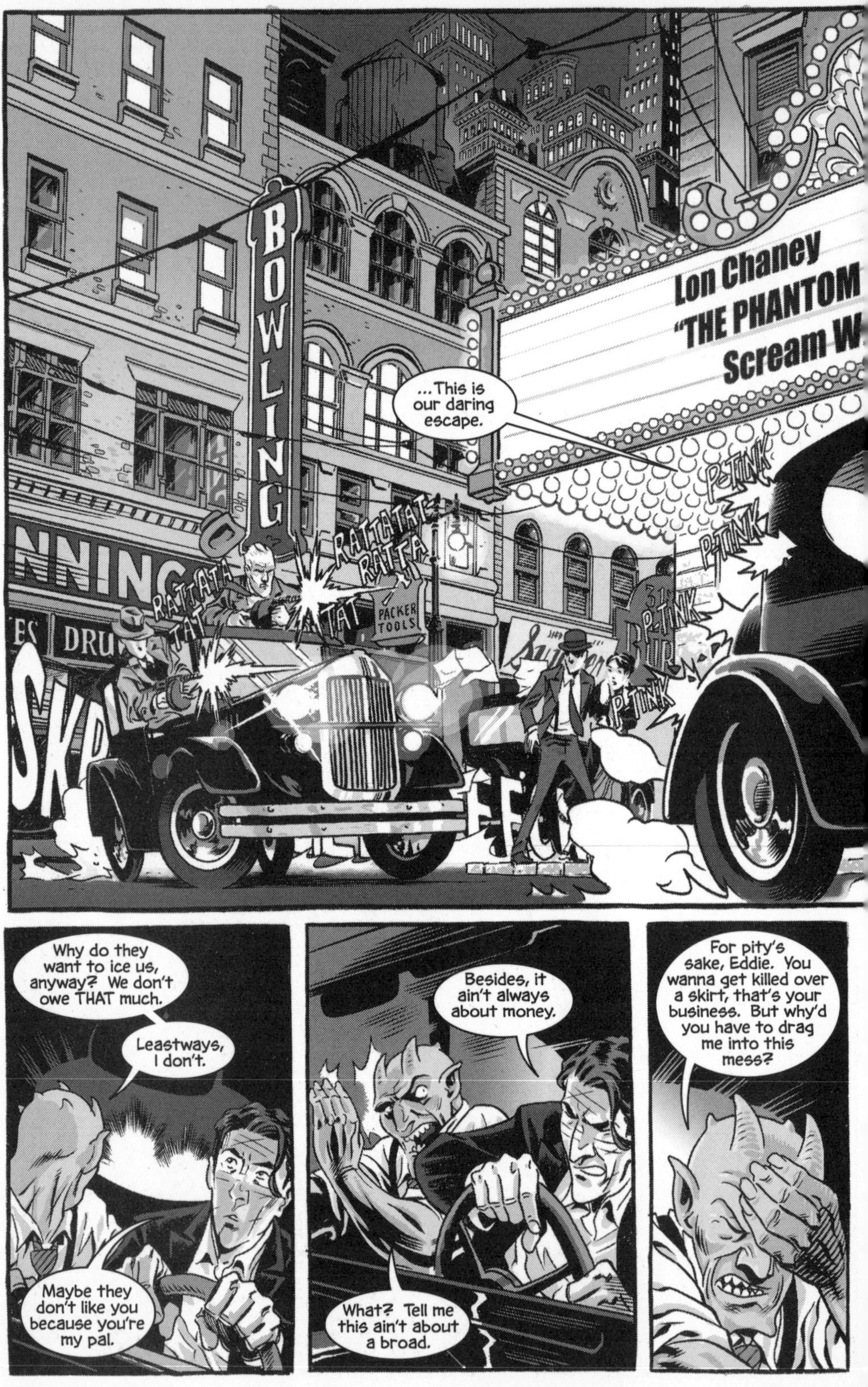
BOWLING
Lon Chaney
"THE PHANTOM
Scream W
NNING
DRU
PACKER TOOLS
...This is our daring escape.
RATTATATA TAT
RATTATAT RATTA
TAT
P-TINK
P-TINK
P-TINK
P-TINK
Why do they want to ice us, anyway? We don't owe THAT much.
Leastways, I don't.
Maybe they don't like you because you're my pal.
Besides, it ain't always about money.
What? Tell me this ain't about a broad.
For pity's sake, Eddie. You wanna get killed over a skirt, that's your business. But why'd you have to drag me into this mess?

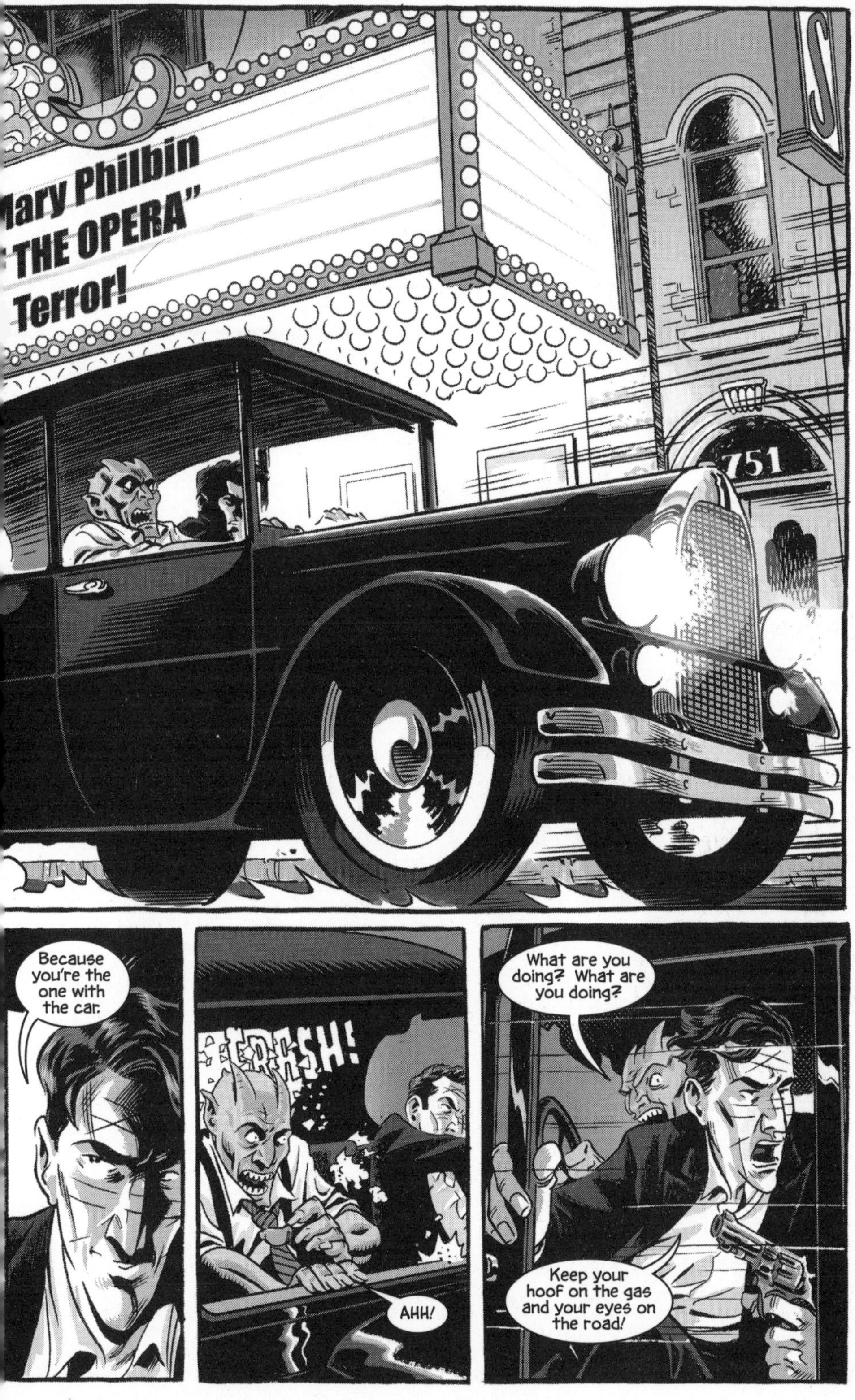
ary Philbin
THE OPERA"
Terror!
751
Because you're the one with the car.
CRASH!
AHH!
What are you doing? What are you doing?
Keep your hoof on the gas and your eyes on the road!

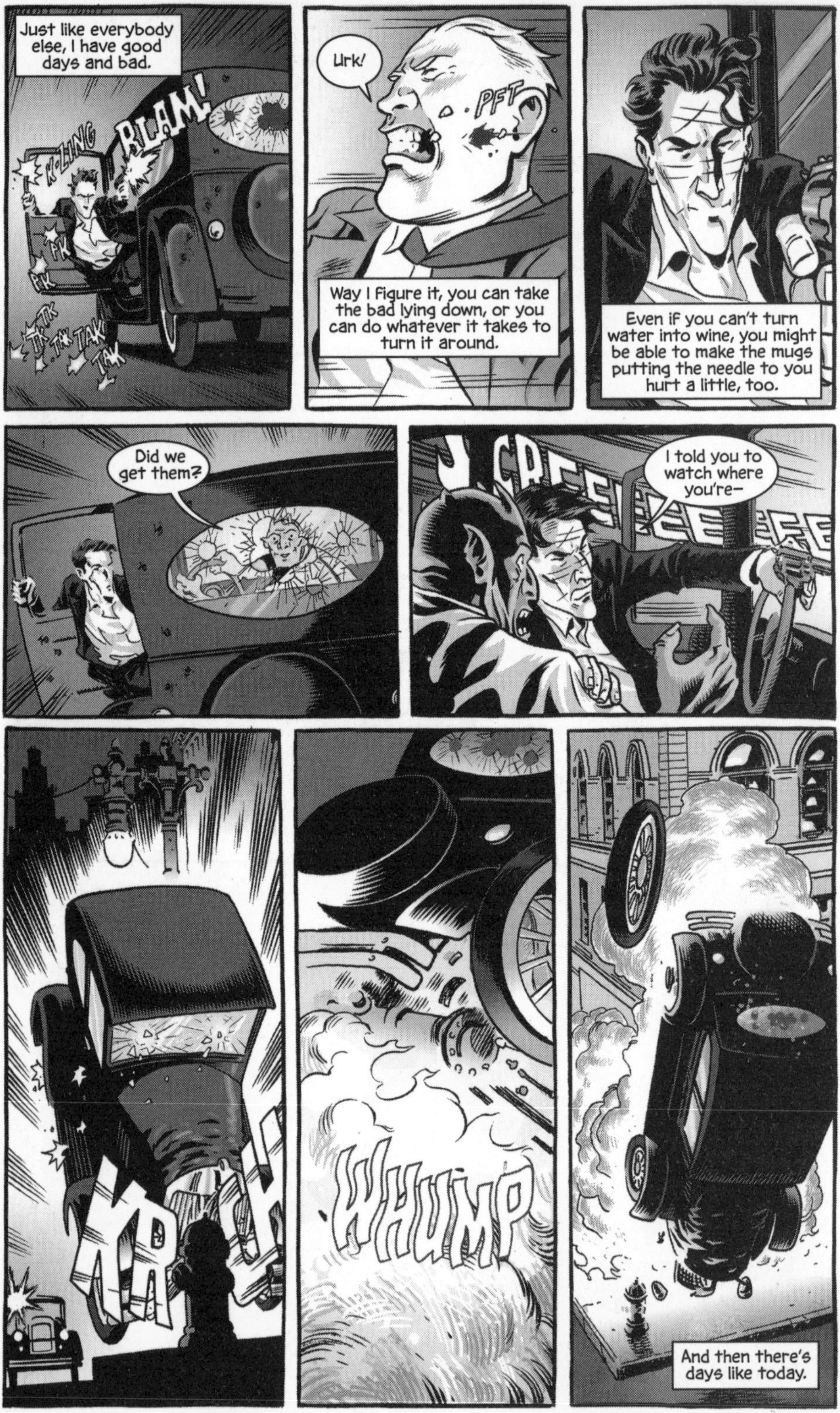

Just like everybody else, I have good days and bad.
K-ZING
BLAM!
PK
PK
TAK TAK TAK TAK TAK
Urk!
PFT
Way I figure it, you can take the bad lying down, or you can do whatever it takes to turn it around.
Even if you can't turn water into wine, you might be able to make the mugs putting the needle to you hurt a little, too.
Did we get them?
I told you to watch where you're—
WHUMP
And then there's days like today.

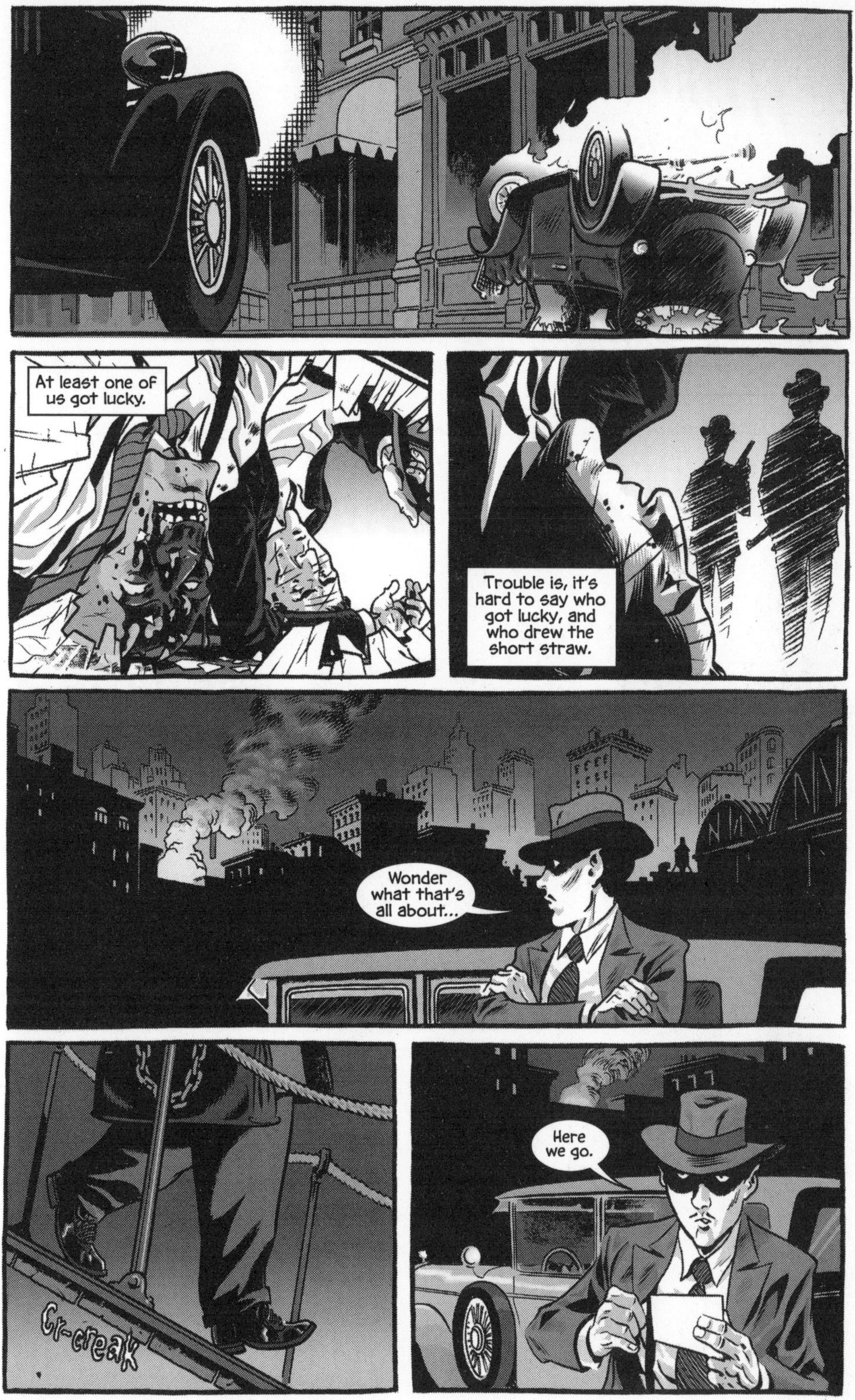
At least one of us got lucky.
Trouble is, it's hard to say who got lucky, and who drew the short straw.
Wonder what that's all about...
Cr-creak
Here we go.

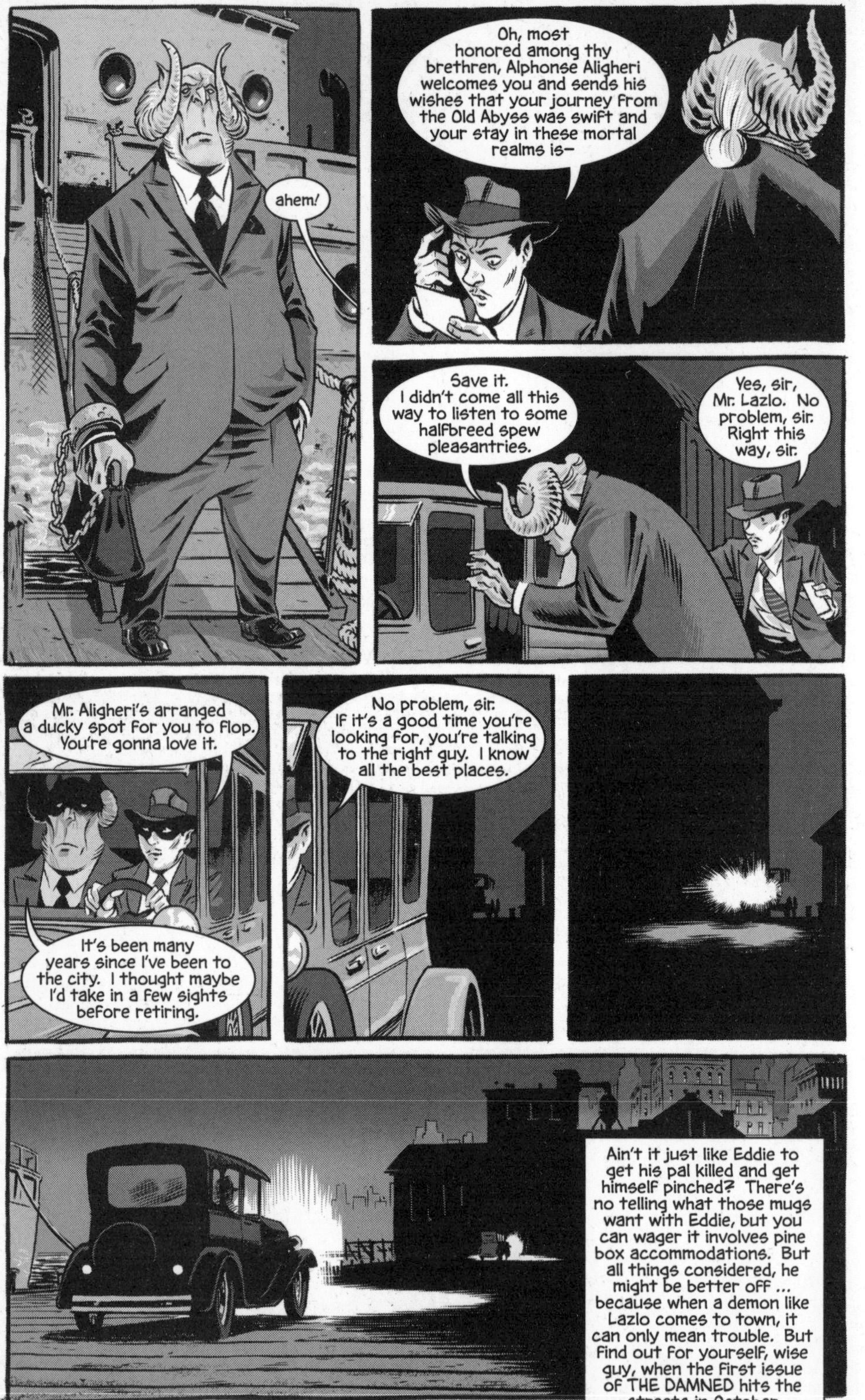
ahem!
Oh, most honored among thy brethren, Alphonse Aligheri welcomes you and sends his wishes that your journey from the Old Abyss was swift and your stay in these mortal realms is—
Save it. I didn't come all this way to listen to some halfbreed spew pleasantries.
Yes, sir, Mr. Lazlo. No problem, sir. Right this way, sir.
Mr. Aligheri's arranged a ducky spot for you to flop. You're gonna love it.
It's been many years since I've been to the city. I thought maybe I'd take in a few sights before retiring.
No problem, sir. If it's a good time you're looking for, you're talking to the right guy. I know all the best places.
Ain't it just like Eddie to get his pal killed and get himself pinched? There's no telling what those mugs want with Eddie, but you can wager it involves pine box accommodations. But all things considered, he might be better off ... because when a demon like Lazlo comes to town, it can only mean trouble. But find out for yourself, wise guy, when the first issue of THE DAMNED hits the streets in October.

CULLEN BUNN

Cullen Bunn was born in the bleachers of Newton Grove High School during an all so crucial Russian Chain match between Chief Wahoo McDaniel and Ivan Koloff, the Russian Nightmare. Just as Ivan was about to put "The Claw" on Wahoo, Cullen's mother screamed out, "Take this Ruskkie!" and hurled the infant at the ring, striking Ivan's bald head, then whipping the baby back by the umbilical cord. Stunned, Ivan was unable to recover before the count of three. The cheers of the crowd form Cullen's earliest memory.

All right. Maybe not. But it is a lovely dream ...

Cullen grew up in (relatively) rural North Carolina, but now lives in the St. Louis area. His fiction and non-fiction have appeared in a number of magazines and anthologies. Somewhere along the way, he founded Undaunted Press and edited the small press horror magazine, *Whispers from the Shattered Forum.* He also managed to win the infamous World Horror Convention Gross-Out Contest four times, an honor for which he is proud, appreciative, and—at least a little—ashamed. Along with several other horror authors, he contributes a serialized horror story, "Countless Haints," to the online shared world, *Ominous Landing.*

He's always looking for a re-match with Ivan, should the opportunity arrive. Bring it, Russkie!

Visit Cullen's website:
www.cullenbunn.com

BRIAN HURTT

Brian Hurtt burst onto the comic scene with the second arc in Greg Rucka's critically acclaimed series *Queen & Country*. He's not put his pencil down since, lending his illustration skills to the *Queen & Country* spin-off *Declassified*, *Skinwalker*, DC's critically acclaimed *Gotham Central*, as well as the DC series *Hard Time*. In 2006 he launched a new creator-owned series with writer Cullen Bunn. Titled *The Damned*, the series saw Brian pencil, ink, tone, and letter a book for the first time ever. He resides just outside of St. Louis in a room covered in black ink.

Visit Brian's website:
thehurttlocker.blogspot.com

OTHER BOOKS FROM BRIAN HURTT & ONI PRESS...

QUEEN & COUNTRY
DECLASSIFIED

QUEEN & COUNTRY: DECLASSIFIED, VOL. 1™

By Greg Rucka,
Brian Hurtt
& Scott Morse
96 pages
black & white interiors
$8.95
ISBN 978-1-929998-58-6

QUEEN & COUNTRY

QUEEN & COUNTRY: VOL. 2: OPERATION: MORNINGSTAR™

By Greg Rucka,
Brian Hurtt,
Christine Norrie
& Bryan Lee O'Malley
88 pages
black & white interiors
$8.95
ISBN 978-1-929998-35-7

SKINWALKER

SKINWALKER™

By Nunzio DeFilippis,
Christina Weir,
Brian Hurtt
& Arthur de la Cruz
120 pages,
black & white interiors
$11.95
ISBN 978-1-929998-45-6

THREE STRIKES

THREE STRIKES™

By Nunzio DeFilippis,
Christina Weir
& Brian Hurtt
144 pages
black & white interiors
$14.95
ISBN 978-1-929998-82-1

OTHER BOOKS FROM ONI PRESS...

THE AWAKENING

AWAKENING™

By Neal Shaffer,
Luca Genovese
104 pages
digest
black &white interiors
$9.95
ISBN 978-1-932664-00-3

THE MARQUIS

MARQUIS, VOL. 1: DANSE MACABRE™

By Guy Davis
176 pages
black & white interiors
$18.95
ISBN 978-1-929998-15-9

PAST LIES

PAST LIES™

By Nunzio DeFilippis
Christina Weir
& Christopher Mitten
168 pages
black & white interiors
$14.95
ISBN 978-1-932664-34-8

THE
TOMB

THE TOMB™

By Nunzio DeFilippis
Christina Weir
& Christopher Mitten
160 pages
digest
black & white interiors
$14.95
ISBN 978-1-929998-95-1

Available at finer comics shops everywhere. For a comics store near you, call 1-888-COMIC-BOOK or visit www.the-master-list.com.

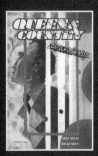

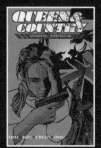

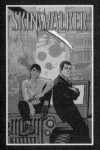

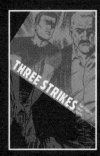

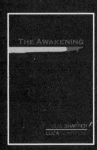

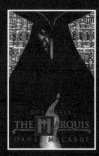

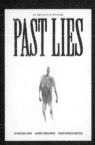

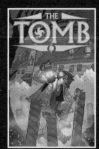